The Resilient Professional

By

Andrew D. Pope

Published by
Llyfrau Cambria Books, Wales, United Kingdom.
Cambria Books is a division of
The Cambria Publishing Co-operative Ltd

A no-nonsense, straightforward and practical guide
to help you develop a more confident personality and more
emotional resilience in today's increasingly stressful
working world.

Dedication:

To my beautiful wife Julie who is
my best friend and most trusted advisor.

CONTENTS

Foreword

Dr Paul T.Thomas
Co-Director/Founder DNA Definitive
Visiting Research & Leadership Fellow, Plymouth University
Founder DNA Wales/UK
BBC Wales Business Doctor

We are already in a 24/7 multi-connected, some would argue over-connected world, in which we find the pressure of work all pervasive. The promise in the 1990's for a work-life balance has never really materialised for the majority of us. In an increasingly uncertain, competitive and fast moving world, companies must rely more and more on individuals to come up with new ideas, to develop creative responses and push for changes before opportunities disappear or minor issues turn into catastrophes. Change, whether in products, market strategies, culture, management, technological processes or work practices, are designed not by machines but by people. We are only now starting to understand that people make great organisations; not processes or policies or for that matter management. It's the human that makes the difference.

The turmoil of the global financial crisis is far-reaching, well beyond purely economic significance. The escalating instability the recession is creating in the workplace in both public and private sectors and the knock-on effect this is having on staff ability to respond and respond sustainably in a positive way is the focus of many in the business world. The relentless speed of change, threat of failure, redundancy, and worries about meeting financial commitments, let alone the normal drive for higher performance at work with diminishing resources are all contributing to higher stress levels.

The goal of this book is to provide theoretically-driven elucidation and practical strategies that will assist us to respond to the

1

chaos of the 21st century organisation and help makes us stronger and better able to not only survive but succeed in these challenging times. In an article some time ago, the Philosopher Luhman points out that society does not communicate with its environment, it communicates about its environment with itself (1985). In his view, all human understanding is shaped in the interaction between the outside world that we observe and our perceptual and cognitive apparatus.

As a result, environmental problems are to a large extent socially defined. Luhman shows how, as a result, the definitions of such problems differ between disciplines. Evidence is mounting that most, if not all, of the environmental problems we encounter are exacerbated by the battle in our minds. In the vain to separate ourselves from what we consider to be nature in the 1950's, we have tended to favour the mechanistic view of people management, and whilst this has changed over the past decade we now have the dilemma of treating people (workers) as individual humans. This fast and growing awareness has triggered a shift in the debate on management matters in the scientific arena, to the issues of health and well-being in the workplace as we have a growing evidence that by doing so makes us more productive and therefore sustainable. It is even getting to the point where it is difficult to argue against this point as the the general tenor of the shift in perspective can be summarised by pointing out that the role of human beings has gone from re-active, via pro-active, to inter-active. The concept of resilience in humans originally comes from physics, where it is defined as a value that characterises a materials resistance to shock. Subsequently it was adopted by ecologists, initially in the same sense as in physics. Thus, applied to humans and organisations, resilience defines their capacity to resist a perturbation or to return to equilibrium after having been subjected to a shock (change). In 2009, I proposed in a BBC documentary a 'new' significance for the term basing it in from the basis of leadership and ground-up staff engagement, moving the traditional approach to what I termed then (wrongly I suspect) a revolution, because it removed the power of management to control and empower frontline, but what was missing was the resilience to endure change itself regardless even when they, the staff owned the change.

Traditionally, human societies have searched for means to reduce uncertainties and risks by increasing control of the physical environment in particular. For example, we generally choose to protect ourselves from secular events (for example by constructing dikes against flooding), and we justify this with reference to medium-term risks, while we prefer to consider the occurrence of millenary events as uncertainties, which are too difficult to take into account. Those responsible for the most part have preferred to ignore such uncertainties, because they are incalculable, and to turn their attention instead to the risks that can be estimated, in particular to those that occur frequently. Whatever the theoretical tool or position we may be inclined to use, there seems to be an underlying reality to identity and act of being in control, which is hard to escape from. That is, as managers, we are forever engaged in some form of social or psychological exchange which is bounded by social conventions and expectations. This exchange appears to be a constant in so much as it exists both as a form of social interaction with others and with social organisations. Importantly, we can be seen to present an individual and their relationship with the self, as highly demanding, with conditions, consequences and circumstances of this relationship pivotal to level of stress and their ability to be resilient.

But from the point of view of certainty and acting as if we are in control for identity's sake, argued here, the rare occurrences and the uncertainties they imply are considered impossible to ignore or control in any human exchange or organisation. It is necessary to take them into account, more so in the fast moving 21st Century, as an integral part of this 'system', while of course at the same time attempting to reduce their negative effects. Thus there are two closely related aspects of resilience, which I feel we must consider. The first concerns the behaviour of the organisation and how we think about it, due to the structure of its attributes and the interactions between people (or should I say individuals), due to notion and act of management and the simple inherent characteristics of the human. The other aspect concerns the perception of perturbations and change, and notably of unexpected or even unforeseeable future events which including the negative 'austerity' measure that seem to be all prevailing at the moment that may or may not be true.

The management act, more so of yesterday than today, now actively encourages risk aversion, it's what we have been teaching for a number of years in our MBA classes and management training. It also demands, through unintentional consequences, conformity. Both these issues eliminate diversity, criticality and creativity, in other words the human and the individual. Additionally, the more formal acts of management you have, the slower the company is to react to customer needs and the more dissatisfaction there is amongst frontline employees and therefore greater the stress levels. Employees feel dis-empowered and high levels of sickness and absenteeism typically result. You only have to glance at some of the global research into 'staff engagement' surveys to note the high levels of dissatisfaction in workers and their organisations and it seems 'Management' cannot cope with people who answer back or innovate around 'rules' to achieve greater outputs. I always remember one employee described themselves as the 'Duracell Bunny' as seen on TV adverts in the UK and added "when I started I was qualified, passionate and driven to delight customers. I quickly realised that my enthusiasm was not what was required. All management wanted was for me to conform to the rules, and procedures - stand on point x, until they tell you its okay to move etc. My energy quickly left me. Now I just turn-up and wait to be told what to do."

This is an excellent example of why we have to change. Andy's work in this is ground-breaking as it examines the utility of resilience, training towards developing a mental toughness and resilience to manage ourselves with practical advice. The resilience book is not like any other though, so don't be put off by its lack of academic speak, or constant reference to other's research. It doesn't do this. It is grounded in all of the above, but it's a refreshingly direct, honest, no-holds-barred and helpful guide to becoming more resilient, self-confident and honest about work and life.

These uncertain times require people to think differently; a paradigm shift from "when this is over..." to "strategies *through* this" to ensure we cannot only 'just survive' but thrive through this pressure. This book engages in confirmatory research via exploration of the link between resilience and mental toughness and its importance in staving off the negative effects of stress in the workplace and all from the practice of one of the best practitioners and change agents in the world. The need for work such as this helps provide the understanding of the internal turmoil people experience in response to external pressures.

Take the first step to regain your control and read this wonderful book.

Dr.P.Thomas is the author of **Reinventing Leadership** published by Cambria Books.
ISBN:**978-0-9932299-4-7**

Introduction

Who is this guide for?

Two people in the same department get told the same piece of bad news. The project they have both been working non-stop on for eight months has been cancelled. Just like that. No discussions or even a put on hold for review. Cancelled!

One of these people appears to take it in their stride and simply gets on with the next project. The other gets frustrated and annoyed and struggles to get re-motivated about anything. So, how would you feel? How would you react to such news? Could you take such a hit then take a quick time out and bounce right back better than ever, ready for your next challenge? If you are like most people your answer may well be "it would be one long monumental struggle" or more likely a straight "no". You might in fact feel nobody real would react in such a positive and useful way.

See if any of these scenarios are familiar to you.

Have you ever felt the onset of being overwhelmed at work? You know, the feeling where things are starting to get right on top of you and you have no real idea how you came to reach this point. Maybe you have taken on too big a project and you are struggling to make headway. Maybe someone said something unpleasant to you, big changes are rumoured, your results are down, a pet project was cancelled, a family member has recently passed, you are having relationship issues or the kids are playing up. Something has happened and you just cannot deal with it anymore. You have had a guts full. You are angry with people and even getting a bit paranoid. Nothing you do seems good enough anymore. Nothing anyone else does seems good enough either. Just one more thing could tip you over the edge. You would almost welcome the opportunity to have a go at someone just to release the pressure.

I know those feelings exactly. I have been there many times and I am sure most other people have at some point or another.

If this is how you feel right now then be aware, going over the edge at work and having a serious sense of humour failure is not a realistic or sustainable option for you. Often times there is no easy road back from an ill-timed or uncontrolled outburst. It could even cost you your job. A manic outburst may give some mental and physical relief and even appear to reduce the immediate symptoms of the stress but it generally leads to many more difficult problems later on. We therefore tend to put a lid on things, bottle things up, grit our teeth and get on with it. We rationalise and tell ourselves we are being silly. Everyone is in the same boat, right? Well, bottling things up is a short-term fix at best. In the longer-term, if we let this stress build up, it could lead to more serious health problems; physical and mental.

So what can you do about it? Can you really develop your ability to avoid these stresses? Can you learn to bounce back from negative situations? Who could you turn to for help and what would you ask them to help you with?

This is for you if you work for a living and you want to learn how to avoid or overcome the overwhelm examples I described above, and many similar scenarios, which can affect you every day. The principles covered here are aimed at helping working professionals but they will be just as helpful when applied to your private life as well. It is sometimes hard to separate these two aspects of our lives nowadays. Both can have an effect on the other; good or bad.

Now it might just surprise you to learn there really are people who do not allow this stress to build up to the sort of levels where they might snap. There are "super-together" people who can keep it on the level when others cannot. People who know how to roll with life's punches and bounce back better than ever. These individuals have the characteristic known as emotional resilience. They are resilient to emotional upsets and seem to be able to get mentally and emotionally stronger after each setback. It certainly surprised me when I found out.

Maybe you have encountered people like this before. What did you think about them? Did you think they must be lucky and have an inborn easy going outlook and emotionally bulletproof character? Maybe you thought they must just drift through life in blissful ignorance and denial, not having a clue what is going on? Did you ever stop and wonder how much more enjoyable your working life might if you could adopt their attitudes and thought processes and use them beneficially in your professional environment?

This is for you if you if you answered yes to the last question.

This is for you if you need to improve your emotional resilience.

This is definitely for you if you are keen to learn new methods and adopt new mindsets.

This is for you if you if you are prepared take full responsibility for your future growth.

This is for you if you if you have tried "pulling your socks up," "growing a set," "manning up" or simply "smiling and getting on with it" and found these ideas not only unhelpful but actually harmful.

This is definitely for you if you manage or lead people and want to become better at it. Your new understanding can be used to help and guide others in your working or personal environment.

Yes, you have read correctly. Emotional resilience is something which can be increased and if you are not scared of hard work and effort and you want some solid practical guidance about where to direct your effort, then this is definitely for you.

Did I just mention hard work and effort? To be fully up front and honest about it there will be hard work and effort. Nothing in life is worth anything if it has not been earned. The cost of anything worthwhile and lasting is always hard work and effort.

This guide will not be for you if you are looking for short cuts to an easy life. If you want low effort "guru" inspired solutions which you can simply buy off the shelf then check out the mighty Interweb; there you will find numerous books, training programmes and self-help guides each promising more results for less effort whenever you splash the cash. If this is what you want then this guide is definitely not for you so let us part as friends and I wish you well on your journey.

If you are still reading this then you are my kind of person. I welcome you as a friend and fellow seeker of knowledge. While we are together I hope I can help you on your journey.

Who am I and what is my angle?

This is the point where you might expect me to recount all the heart rending yet uplifting stories of how I overcame massive adversity and ultimately triumphed in life. The part where, after describing how I battled heroically through all of the many extraordinary issues life has thrown at me, I reveal I now have a secret formula for easily creating resilience. Furthermore, given my now infinitely generous spirit, I am willing to share this knowledge with you mere mortals so you too may be able to gain some small percentage of the infinite happiness which I now possess.

Yeah, right! What a crock!

I am not being disingenuous here. The fact is I am just an average individual, well an average Andy to be more precise. I am the same as pretty much everyone else. I have strong traits and weak traits. I have skills and frailties like everyone else. Certainly, some negative things have happened in my life from time to time but it is really much the same for everyone else. I have just turned 50 years old at the time of writing this and I am happy to report many more good things have happened to me than bad. I am doing well, I am still keen to learn more and I am happy. There is no special heart rending tale and no triumphant secret discovery; there is just life.

There was a temptation for me to introduce the word modern into the mix at this point but after much thought I have elected to stick with the term life. It is really all about context. People in the past had negative emotional and physical events happen to them as well; often more frequently and more seriously depending on when and where they lived. They were no less affected by the events beyond their control or even within their control than we would be. We are no different to them. There is one caveat here. Nowadays many of us do face one huge and potentially damaging new ingredient in the mix; the effect of mass media propaganda and advertising which is primarily driven by television, large corporations and the Interweb. Note, I refer to the Interweb as a catch all phrase for both the Internet and World Wide Web. I am old school and do not want to upset anyone by using the wrong term so Interweb will suffice.

The social pressure to be successful and happy in life has been present in nearly all societies over the centuries but I contend today, in many places and certainly in my social environment, there is far more mass media and social pressure to be both financially successful, physically perfect, emotionally balanced and visibly happy and fulfilled than ever before. Anything less than perfection in all things superficial is seen as failure. We are bombarded morning, noon and night by images and language which highlight just how far below the required standards we actually are. Our size, our shape, our teeth, our hair and even our eyelashes. There is not a part of our body which does not appear to have an unreachable standard of acceptability. Our cars are wrong, our houses are not big enough, our careers are a mess and our relationships are in tatters. We are too old, too young, too thin, too fat, too this too that and just too the other. People like you and I are being conned into believing we have to strive to meet these arbitrary standards in order to achieve real happiness. We feel compelled to try to achieve them and then feel miserable when we are deemed to have failed in the attempt. These artificial media driven bars are set way too high. Even if we do manage to achieve some small success the victory feels hollow. Why do we even try? This state of affairs cannot be right can it? I do not think so. Do you?

When you have this much pressure to perform, especially in your working environment, any negative events, real or perceived, which impact on you can be a real source of mental anguish. Even small negative events, which on a good day you would not even notice or acknowledge, can build up one after another and finally upset your emotional balance.

Am I immune to all this? Have I discovered the secret to successfully avoiding this pressure trap?

No, and did I not mention this already?

I suffer right along with everyone else but I have made improvements and learnt a lot about reducing the impact of modern life on my psyche. What I have learnt from my studies and work with my coaching clients over recent years is enabling me to deal with things which happen in a much more useful way. I can more readily absorb negative emotional and physical impacts, consider them, learn from them and then move on, generally stronger than before. Not in any ostentatious or showy display of emotional mastery or zen-like inscrutability you understand. I just get on with it quietly and calmly and cherish each of the small victories over my inner demons. It does not work all the time but as you will discover later, a properly understood failure can actually be your best friend moving forward. The little victories add up faster than you might think too.

As a professional coach, I have also worked with many clients who were suffering emotional anguish and work related misery out of all proportion to the size and frequency of the actual setbacks. They felt there was no way to shore up the walls of their psyche, get things back into perspective and carry on as before. Together we worked through their issues and they left me armed with a number of practical techniques, mindsets and ideas which could be used time and again to begin to strengthen their emotional resources. They became and are becoming more emotionally and professionally resilient.

My work with such clients, coupled with the knowledge I have gained when examining my own life and emotional strategies, has led me to some understanding of what generally works and what generally does not work. Have I invented anything new? Probably not but I believe the precise mixture of simple ideas, practical tips, illustrative case studies and good old-fashioned common sense will make a refreshing change for many people.

I have always had a strong desire to be of help to others whilst I try to help myself and I wrote this guide in pursuit of this desire to help. I have also thought long and hard about the style and tone which I might use to greatest effect. I have eventually decided a straight-talking and direct approach will work best. Minimal fluff, no new age woo-woo and no touchy-feely stuff other than when absolutely necessary. You can do all of the new age things if you want to but I am not going to encourage them if you do not. If I have made you laugh or smile at any point in this tome then I will state, here and now for the record, I definitely intended to include humour. If you have not laughed or smiled at all then the story I am sticking to is I fully intended to write a serious and sombre guide to professional resilience. We will look at reframing later when I will revisit those last two comments.

Please note, resilience is not about learning how to put up with more and more pressure in order to scrape by a bit longer or hiding your feelings and pretending everything is alright until either the situation resolves itself or you mentally explode. Doing so is a dreadful strategy and a battle no-one can win. It is also not about wishing and hoping or trying to tune in to some cosmic attraction law or secret success formula. Do not even get me started on the last one. No, not a bit of it, this is all about learning practical ways of acknowledging pressure exists in the first place, understanding it and then dealing with it in a positive and useful manner whilst taking full and unequivocal responsibility for yourself whilst doing it. It is also about avoiding as much pressure as possible before it even becomes an issue. An ounce of prevention is better than a pound of cure.

Please also note, this is not an attempt to capture everything about resilience. Far from it. There are many excellent texts on the subject and I would always recommend you to read widely in order to gain greater understanding and insights. No one volume can satisfy all readers. You may find I have left out a great many things which could have fitted nicely. Some of this was by choice on my part and no doubt some of this was by ignorance. I have already mentioned, I am no self-appointed guru. What I have tried to do is deliver on the strapline promise: A no-nonsense, straightforward and practical guide to help you develop a more confident personality and more emotional resilience in today's increasingly stressful working world.

There are no hypothetical concepts or grand airy-fairy theories here; just practical and battle-tested strategies and techniques which I and my clients have all used to good effect over the years.

From a practical perspective then, look upon this guide as a collection of thoughts, ideas, techniques, frameworks and processes which each represent a tool or mindset for becoming more resilient. When you build up your toolkit with more and more individual tools, you will end up with a range of available options to call upon and develop whenever you need more emotional resilience in your life and work. Emotional DIY if you like.

I hope as you read on you will gain a lot of ideas to help yourself and others achieve this objective; it will make me a very happy man. In fact if just one solitary thing herein helps you grow more emotionally resilient, I will still be a very happy man.

Fundamentals

Before you begin to build anything of real value and substance you need a solid foundation. Let us put one in place.

What do I mean by emotional resilience?

In any form of discussion, it is always good to have a working definition of the thing to be discussed. In our case it is the subject of emotional resilience.

As the title implies we will mainly talk about building and maintaining resilience at work but all the points and ideas raised will apply equally well in your personal life too. Please note, I will almost certainly lead you off the main track, as the mood or topic takes me, fully into the woods of personal resilience, but always with a view to illustrating a useful topic or idea. I will then lead you safely back through the trees and undergrowth to the original pathway with new knowledge and techniques which you can take forward and use.

As stated, the resilience we are going to discuss is emotional resilience. I will initially split the discussion and examine emotion and resilience separately then combine things at the end into our working definition of emotional resilience.

Let us start with emotion.

Emotion is often seen as the elephant in the room so let us cut right to the chase. You have emotions and you cannot avoid them. I do not care who you are; you have emotions. No matter how logical you believe or like to think you are, you are a creature driven by your emotions. You might often seem to have no control at all over these emotions. Your logical side often kicks in after the event in an effort to justify actions you took primarily based on your emotions. The emotions lead and logic follows.

So what are emotions?

Let us first consider the scientific aspects.

Much has been discovered over the years by psychologists and psychological researchers on the topic of emotions. A vast number of books, articles and papers have been written on the subject. The good news for you is this is not a deep treatise on psychology and I am not going to bore you with too much jargon or science.

It will, however, be useful to take a simplistic look at three key elements order to help understand what emotions are and how they affect us: The subjective experience, the physiological reaction and the behavioural response.

The Subjective Experience

Modern languages have many words for emotions and, although there is a broad universally shared experience regarding things such as anger, fear, love and sadness for example, we cannot assume it is the same for all people in all situations. The thing to remember is your unique experience of any emotion is far more multi-dimensional and complex. I mentioned anger so ask yourself, is your anger really the same as someone else's anger? Your experience of anger, in any specific context, might range from mild annoyance to screaming rage.

Add in mixed emotions and the waters muddy even more. Ever had a new job? Ever gone out on a date for the first time? Ever got married? Lots of mixed emotions going on in these example scenarios.

You will analyse everything you read herein in a wholly subjective manner. How can it be otherwise? You are a unique individual and you will have a unique take and insight on all the ideas and material discussed. Some situations may resonate with you and some may not and that, my friend, is life. I will also introduce you to the ideas of empathy and emotional intelligence in order to help you explore the concept of subjective experience and gain some useful insights into how others may be thinking and feeling about situations.

The Physiological Reaction

No matter how clever you think you are, no matter how much planning you do before an event, no matter how calm and collected you think you are, your body will have a big say in proceedings. It will definitely have a say where emotions are concerned. In fact, because we are highly emotional creatures, our bodies play a major part in how we feel and interact with the people and world around us.

We are complicated creatures but luckily for us our bodies generally function well on internal automated processes. The human race would not last long if we had to consciously remember when to breathe for example. I will keep it very simple but a little bit of jargon is required here. The human autonomic nervous system has two parts, the sympathetic and parasympathetic nervous systems. Involuntary internal activities like breathing, digestion and circulation are controlled by the parasympathetic system. The sympathetic system largely controls the body's reaction to outside threats and generally tries to keep us safe from external harm.

You may have heard of the fight or flight response. This is the built in response which enables us to react quickly to outside threats. When we are overwhelmed and in a panic situation our automatic systems do our thinking for us. We either prepare to flee or we get ready to meet the danger and fight.

In addition to the sympathetic nervous system activity there are many other systems activated when a potential threat is identified. For example, the endocrine system releases stress hormones, such as adrenaline and cortisol, throughout the body and these powerful chemicals can flood our bodies to assist in the response to any perceived danger. Our automatic systems have to do all this because, when we are in the grip of strong emotions, blood and other vital fluids are drawn away from our higher functioning brain areas in the neocortex and we are left with just our limbic/reptile brain to run the show. We end up with around about the same effective thinking power as let us say a rhesus monkey. Think about the last time you lost the plot. How logical and effective was your thinking?

There are many more systems and sub-systems involved but hopefully you get the picture by now. The unidentified rustle in the bushes on a dark street late at night, the stranger's verbal attack, the important meeting, the first date or the conference presentation cause our bodies to automatically act to protect us from perceived harm.

These generally helpful and well-intentioned automated processes sometimes produce highly undesirable physiological results for us. Whilst we like to believe we live in safe and enlightened times there are still stress creating situations impacting us all the time. They may not be wild animals or club wielding enemy tribesmen but our bodies react the way they always have since modern humans evolved. If you have ever felt your stomach doing aerobics from anxiety, had rapid breathing and sweaty palms or had your heart pounding with fear then you have got a fully working sympathetic nervous system. Our emotions can trigger strong physiological reactions.

Continual stress can cause long-term physical and mental problems so stress management and stress reduction techniques will be a major part of creating a more resilient persona.

The Behavioural Response

This element is concerned with how we actually understand and express emotion. Most humans spend a significant amount of time trying to interpret the emotional states and expressions of other people. Our ability to accurately translate these signals is a large part of what psychologists call Emotional Intelligence (EI). Our overall facial expressions and body language are how we communicate non-verbally. As an aside, if you want to become an effective communicator I recommend you become a keen student of human nature. Understanding of yourself is a good start but it is only half the battle. You must also seek to understand others and your relationships with and to them.

Much of this guide will focus on identifying, and adapting where necessary, our behavioural response to emotion. Changing old non-useful habitual responses into useful responses is the core of improved resilience work. The good news is it can be achieved by anyone prepared to put the hard work and effort in. If you have read this far then you are already well on your way.

Now let us consider how emotions can impact our lives.

Your response to emotions can direct or motivate you to take certain actions or to make certain decisions. Your understanding of the emotions of others can lead you to greater and more useful understanding of other people.

Like it or not, your emotions colour your judgement. Emotional events can be brief or long-lasting; a short row which is easily forgotten or the long-term grief over the death of a close relation.

Emotions can impact on how we make decisions and they can impact what actions we take.

Let us look at a common scenario. Most of us have had to face an important academic exam at some time in our lives. Maybe you have one coming up soon. It is never fun but we know the more studying we do beforehand, the better we are likely to do in the exam.

This is obvious right? Why then do we often put off the studying for something more enjoyable? I have done it often. My mates have phoned and the pub beckoned. I reasoned logically it would do me good to go out as I could always catch up with the missed revision. I would be more relaxed and therefore better able to cope with the pressure and many more reasons just like those. Off I went to the pub. I may well have had a good time but I generally never caught up with the missed study and the pressure inevitably increased due to dwindling time and mounting workload.

The bottom line was, in reality and right then and there, I valued fun far more than studying. Sure, I may have conned myself into thinking I had made a rational and logical decision to go out but it was a wholly emotional one. Having fun by going out was far more attractive than staying in and studying. An emotional decision.

Nearer the exam date I might have responded differently. At this stage the huge emotional concern over failing the exam would likely be far more powerful than the short-term fun of going out. I would have told my friends all sorts of reasons for being unable to go out but the emotional reason came first and it was fear of failure. The emotions involved were not limited just to fear of exam failure. There would also be parental disapproval, peer pressure and embarrassment, examination re-sit pressure and failure to achieve the more distant but still important overall course success. I had failed exams before and did not like the feeling one little bit.

We tend to make emotional decisions in order to maximise positive outcomes and to minimise negative outcomes in a given context. When my exam felt a long way off, I maximised my pleasure and went out. With my exam imminent I maximised my chances of success and minimised my chances of failure. I also had previous negative emotions to reinforce this and they were more powerful the closer I got to exam day. Emotion decided the matter first and I tried to logically justify my decision second.

Strong emotions can hinder us as well as help us.

A good friend of mine avoids exams at all costs. He has sat plenty of them in the past and has done well but now the negative emotions created by sitting and studying for exams far outweigh any positive emotions gained by passing them. He gives all sorts of logical reasons for not wanting or needing to take the exams but the emotional decision based on exam fear trumps all of these.

As I write this, a current coaching client of mine is working on issues around moving on in her career. She has passed up several promotion offers which she desperately wanted and she has seen other less capable people move ahead of her. She has a million logical excuses for why she has not taken the leap. She has even claimed to be a perfectionist. Deep down she knows it is the emotional fear of change and potential failure which is making her decisions for her. Admitting this and working on it will yield real progress for my client. Emotions are powerful drivers for us all.

Take a few minutes to think back on some of your past decisions. Big or small, how did you actually make your decisions? Did you feel compelled to justify your decisions to yourself or to others? How did you justify them? How much influence did emotion really have?

Emotions can allow us to better understand and interact more meaningfully with others.

Humans cannot not communicate. You might want to reread the last short sentence. We leak information all the time whether we are aware of it or not. Even if we are not talking, our silence, our facial expressions and our body language are sending out vast amounts of information to those around us. We can hopefully extract the same information from others based on how we read them. I say hopefully because many people are poor observers of emotional expression. It is a great skill to acquire and I would urge you to begin honing your abilities in this area as soon as possible.

My wife and I love people watching and I would suggest you become a keen student of people's behaviour as well. You can learn a lot about people from their non-verbal communication and interactions. Without being too obvious, spend some time watching people in restaurants, queues, business events, meetings or any other similar situation and see what you can learn from their non-verbal behaviour. It will also help you become more aware of signals you may unknowingly be sending out to others. I give you fair warning though, it can become quite addictive so please do not become a full-blown stalker or voyeur as this could get you into a lot of trouble.

Becoming more emotionally honest with yourself and others can be daunting at first but it will ultimately be incredibly liberating. I will have a lot more to say later on about this.

In case all this talk of emotion has got any of you worried about how you might be spending a lot of time crying and hugging strangers while you pour our heart out, I would just like to mention this absolutely will not be the case. You can do it if you are that way inclined but I will be taking a prosaic and practical approach throughout. Anyone who knows me knows I am not a touchy-feely, woo-woo or huggy kind of person. However, being more aware of your emotions and what they mean to you and others is a key component of resilience so get used to the idea.

To summarise, emotions can serve or hinder us in a wide variety of situations. Emotions can be brief or persistent, simple or complex. Emotions can hold us back or lift us soaring to the heavens. They can motivate us to act and decide and they can give us the wherewithal to interact meaningfully with others. By working on developing our EI we can also increase our emotional resilience.

Now we come to resilience itself and how I define resilience for our purposes.

What is resilience?

In practical terms emotional resilience is regarded as a quality in certain people which allows them to be knocked by certain events and situations in their life yet bounce back stronger than they were previously. They do not let any knocks or failures overwhelm them or drain their resolve; they find a way to rise above it. Psychologists have taken a keen interest in the topic of emotional resilience and have identified a few of the factors which can make someone more resilient. Amongst others, these factors include high self-esteem, a positive attitude, healthy optimism, emotional intelligence and the ability to reframe failure into useful feedback. Even after seemingly major misfortunes, emotionally resilient people are able to take stock, change course and move forward.

Emotional resilience is a quality which almost everyone needs at some stage of life. We will all experience difficulties and even highly traumatic events which can create an upheaval. Resilience is the process by which people can successfully adapt to change. It is the process which allows them to deal with major crises like the death of a loved one, a family tragedy, relationship issues, a job loss or major financial problems.

The good news is, emotional resilience is not a predetermined and unchangeable character trait; it can actually be learnt and enhanced by anyone. However, and this is the part most people do not want to hear about, learning it does require a commitment in time and effort.

This guide is intended to help you become more emotionally resilient primarily at work and, by extension, in your private life. It will include introducing you to the idea of creating support systems, making plans and following through on them, improving your communication and interpersonal problem-solving skills, creating a more positive view of yourself and your skills as well as improving your emotional intelligence. Building emotional resilience is a different process for everyone, and what works for one person may not work for you. You need to try things out, determine what works effectively for you and do more of it. Reading this will of course give you lots of options but it is up to you if you make use of all or any of them.

So finally, we come to my overall working definition of emotional resilience.

Emotional resilience is the ability to experience negative emotional impacts yet bounce back stronger than ever.

Or, to put it another way...

If you could imagine adopting the traits and characteristics of a resilient substance and applying them to your own emotional strategies, what sort of benefits or problems might be the result? It will in fact become a good metaphor for emotional resilience. Metaphors can be powerful. What I do want to do is show the whole spectrum of emotional resilience and emotionally resilient behaviour from a common foundation and I believe using such a metaphorical device will help to illustrate and underpin the many concepts we will discuss. This common foundation will give us a useful platform on which to build the narrative as a whole and also make the ideas and techniques hang together in the most effective way for you. Remember you are the reason I am writing this in the first place.

We need to start with a suitable metaphorical substance so here is an easy question for you.

What do you think is the most resilient substance on earth?

Take some time to think about it. I have had and continue to get many interesting answers to this seemingly easy question and in their own way they are all correct (except the daft or incorrect ones of course). Everyone has their own view of resilience after all. I am not here to tell anyone what is right or wrong. As I have already stated, this is a guru-free zone.

Most people associate resilience with the ability to withstand shock or impact and return to an original state. Over the years I have been asking this of people and given this common association, by far the most common answers to the above question have been diamond and rubber.

The first common answer of diamond is logical in so far as

diamond is commonly taken to be the hardest material on earth. On the plus side it can reduce other substances to dust, it is highly resistance to chemical attack, it can transmit light and it is potentially of great use in the electronics field. On the minus side it can be ground down or abraded by polishing with the dust of other diamonds and it can be split or fractured with relative ease along fault lines or cracks. Diamond dust cannot easily be reformed into a diamond. A broken diamond does not tend to become whole again once the jeweller's chisel has passed through it or the grinding wheel has worn it down.

So, whilst a diamond is hard and durable, adopting its characteristics and applying them to our emotional toolkit would cause more problems than it would solve. Having the events in life, good and bad, simply bounce off our diamond hard emotional exterior with no effect at all puts an emotional wall around us. It would leave us distant and dissociated from others and ourselves. It might protect us but, much like a real diamond, our emotional life would be hard and cold. If a large enough emotionally negative upset occurred, our emotional diamond shell might finally shatter with potentially devastating results and no going back. As an emotionally resilient metaphor diamond is simply not up to the job according to the working definition given in the preceding section.

The second common answer of rubber would appear, at first glance, to be a closer match to the "bounce-back-ability" concept of resilience. I will use the general term rubber here to cover both natural and synthetic varieties. On the plus side rubber can definitely take a hit and return to its former status relatively easily and it does in fact bounce back if it hits something hard. It is useful for damping down and smoothing out vibrations and noise. It is quite resistant chemically and thermally and can be adapted for myriad useful purposes. Our lives would be markedly different without its positive benefits. On the minus side it cannot easily make an impact on its surroundings and often when it does bounce back there is no control or predictability involved. If it is damaged mechanically or chemically it cannot easily reform. It cannot change its state in order to adapt to or accommodate changing conditions.

Why do I not see it as a suitable metaphorical candidate? Whilst, it is resilient in the dictionary sense of the word, the irony is it is simply too inflexible in too many other ways to be a good metaphor for emotional resilience.

Whatever you picked as the most resilient substance, take some time to run through a quick thought experiment and analyse your choice much as I have above. Does it metaphorically meet the standards laid out in our working definition?

As a short aside, I will be encouraging you to run many such exercises and thought experiments as we move along. I like to think of these as focused daydreams. Pose yourself a question or a hypothetical scenario and run through the many different options or possible outcomes like a movie in your mind. Albert Einstein loved thought experiments and if they were useful for him they will definitely be of use to us.

"What is your answer then Mr Big Time Author?" I hear you cry.

Well, after much thought and many thought experiments over the years I have this to offer. In my opinion the one substance which metaphorically fulfils all the requirements of the working definition for emotional resilience is water. Plain, simple and so often taken for granted H_2O.

Allow me to present my thoughts.

Water is so essential, and such a part of our everyday existence, we often forget about it. Many of us unthinkingly turn on our taps and expect nothing less than clean clear drinking water with no thought about how it came to be there. Many of us notice it only when it rains too much and in some places many have huge problems when it does not.

Life on Earth as we understand it could not exist without water. We humans are made up of around sixty percent water. Think about that. We are essentially animated bags of water wandering around the planet. Our bodies are relatively soft and susceptible to attack from the elements, predatory species as well as numerous diseases and pathogens. Thanks to major advances in science, engineering and society we are now more physically resilient as a species and live successfully in almost every environment known to us yet without simple water all this would be impossible. From a scientific point of view, water itself, simple as it appears to be, is not fully understood yet. It is still the subject of much study and interest.

Along with the heat of the sun and the Earth's rotation, water drives our weather. Water cycles round the world as it evaporates, forms rain, flows in rivers and returns to the oceans. We travel on rivers, lakes and oceans and extract food from them too. Water generates fear, fun, reverence and life.

It physically exists as liquid, solid and vapour and it can move relatively smoothly between each state. As liquid water it can fill an ocean and support myriad lifeforms, can grind a coastal cliff into sand or form huge canyons, under pressure it can cut through steel, can quench our thirst or drown us and can transport vital nutrients around our bodies. As solid ice it can form continent flattening glaciers, can reduce mountains to dust, can produce delicate snowflakes, can be used for shelter (igloos) and can be fun for children and adults alike. As a gas or vapour it can blind us as fog, become rain to water the land, run machinery for us as steam and simply amaze us with ethereal beauty.

The list could go on and on so take a minute to think deeply about the impact water has on your life and some of the issues you might have if even a little of the water was taken away.

Now a handful of the many quite interesting physical properties of water. Solid ice is slightly less dense than liquid water which allows ice cubes and icebergs to float. The ice in icebergs is largely made of fresh water which assists buoyancy in the salty oceans. Solid ice also takes up slightly more volume than liquid water and this allows it to burst out of frozen drink containers and also fragment mighty mountains one small piece at a time. Liquid water takes the shape of whatever container it is in. Liquid water finds its own level. Pure water is a poor conductor of electricity due to lack of ionic impurities. Water readily changes state depending on temperature and pressure. It is an effective heating and cooling medium for industrial applications. It is known as the universal solvent because it dissolves more substances than any other. Water vapour (steam) at high pressures has huge energy which can be beneficially utilised by many industries. So far, all snowflakes are thought to be unique in shape.

Water is even difficult to completely destroy. It can be physically and chemically split into hydrogen and oxygen and each of these can become part of other substances but note, if you burn hydrogen in air it gives up a lot of energy and reforms into water again because hydrogen and oxygen readily combine to become water. This is good news for us and the rest of the planet.

Around seventy percent of the Earth's surface is covered in water. The oceans hold over ninety five percent of all the Earth's water. Bear in mind, water also exists in the air as water vapour, it fills rivers and lakes, it forms icecaps and glaciers, it exists in the ground as soil moisture and in the rocks of the earth as aquifers and in all the lifeforms on the planet – all in all there is a lot of water and most of it is salty.

As a metaphor for emotional resilience water ticks all the boxes for me.

Water is a tangible substance with which almost all of us are familiar. We cannot live without it. It is relatively easy to mentally relate the metaphorical attributes of water to the characteristics and attributes of resilient people. For example, water is relentless and patient, it finds the easiest path round obstacles, it forms complex systems and changes readily to the most appropriate state for the prevailing conditions and, whilst it is generally a neutral substance, it can be seen as useful or non-useful depending on its state and context.

It is decided then. One of the perks of being the author is, I get to choose the contents and this includes the metaphors.

I will be using water as the most metaphorically resilient substance on earth from this point onward. I will endeavour to use a different metaphorical view of water and its properties to accompany and enhance the conceptual tone of each main section.

Change is the only constant

In a famously droll quote by Benjamin Franklin, in a letter to Jean-Baptiste Leroy in 1789, he states "Our new Constitution is now established, and has an appearance that promises permanency; but in this world nothing can be said to be certain, except death and taxes."

Much as I enjoy the wit of Mr Franklin, I would argue against his conclusion. Taxes can be avoided, and frequently are if the news reports are to be believed, so they are far from being a certainty. I will admit, currently death is always certain but many people are working diligently on ways to avoid it; whether by scientific, medical or other means.

So, death aside, there is only one other constant we need concern ourselves with for the purposes of developing more effective emotional resilience.

Change.

Change happens. Change happens all the time. We sometimes consciously create changes in our own lives and environment but most of the time change is something which happens outside of our direct control.

Our own bodies are changing automatically every second of every day. Luckily for us usually we do not notice or have to manage this process. We do notice certain changes over time and some people seek to combat these physically, medically and cosmetically; ultimately they have no lasting success.

Directly or indirectly, many events big and small can affect us. Sometimes we are affected by a major change or upheaval. Sometimes it takes a number of small and seemingly insignificant changes over time to have a noticeable impact. For examples of change consider the various actions of other people, note the failure or malfunction of systems, materials and equipment, picture the many natural and growing number of human created environmental changes, even our own bodies can be affected by disease, ailments and the relentless passage of time. All these change types and more can occur every second of every day and they can all affect us to a greater or lesser extent. We will revisit change in a later section on our relationship to systems.

We often try to make changes ourselves; both mentally and physically. Some of us exercise and diet to change our body shape. We participate in activities to alter our moods and feelings. Many of us try to learn new information and skills. We generally try to take actions which impact positively on ourselves and our immediate environment. These types of self-directed change are seen as challenges and therefore positive.

Problems can occur for us when the change is forced upon us by external events or other people. For example perhaps someone said something nasty to you for no reason, worldwide demands for the widgets you make is right down, the new roadworks are making traffic a nightmare, big work changes and a new computer system are being introduced, your sales results are now down because your boss set ridiculous new targets, the personally important project you have been working on is about to be cancelled or a close family member has recently become ill or even died.

The Swiss-born psychiatrist, Elisabeth Kübler-Ross, M.D. (1926 – 2004), and author of "On Death and Dying" (1969), first discussed what is now known as the Kübler-Ross model. In her book she introduced her now famous five stages of grief experienced during the bereavement process. In general, individuals commonly experience denial, anger, bargaining, depression and acceptance though, as Kübler-Ross herself noted in later life, not necessarily in that precise sequence and not necessarily in their entirety.

Many other people have taken this model, adapted it slightly and applied it to the study of change. It matches well because, if you stop and think about it, change is a form of bereavement. The death of an old pattern or situation and its replacement with another. If we have a lot of emotional investment in the old pattern it can hurt to have it taken away. Ask someone who has lost a long-time job or a much loved house and they may well feel the same way about it as if someone close to them has died.

The change model often has seven elements or stages included: shock, denial, frustration, depression, experiment, decision and integration. The change model is often represented by a curved line graph drawn on two axes: morale and competence plotted against time. There is a pdf available with just such a graphical representation of this change curve in the virtual appendix; see the section near the end for details.

Unsurprisingly, when the event occurs and normality is disrupted the first reaction is a degree of shock. This is followed by denial and a refusal to believe something has happened at all. Sometimes evidence is sought to disprove the event. Next comes frustration and anger because there is no avoiding the issue. Things are different and they will have to be dealt with or overcome in some way. Next can come depression. The problems and situation feel insurmountable with no end in sight. Energy levels are low and negative emotions and language predominate. After depression comes experimentation or the toe-dipping phase and with it a willingness to engage more deeply with the new situation. This leads to a decision being made and a positive desire to work with or in the new situation coming to the fore. Finally there is integration and the new situation is accepted and fully taken on board. There is now a new normal.

If a new skill or a better way of achieving a task is the new normal outcome it stands to reason competence will have improved but this is not always the case with morale; not everyone will bounce back better than ever. Resilient people do tend to end up better than ever and, if you adopt some or all of the practical tools, techniques and mindsets contained herein, you can start to learn to do the same.

Not everyone is affected by change in exactly the same way. People pass through the stages of change at different rates and experience different levels of emotional stress at each stage. For some people the journey may be swift and uneventful. For others it may be protracted and painful. Some may never emerge. They may stay rooted in the denial stage or sink into a deep depression from which they may struggle to recover.

Resilient people are no different in terms of stages or sequence. When impacted by an emotionally negative experience or event they have to pass through the stages the same as everyone else. What makes a resilient person different is their ability to spend just the right amount of time in a stage then move on. Sometimes this skill is consciously applied and sometimes it just happens because of their general personality and mental attitudes when dealing with the world.

Prolonged periods of unsought and significant change, with no breathing space to reflect and fully integrate, can lead to severe stress on an individual. This can reduce emotional resilience or even destroy it. You have to be your own leader and learn to recognise the signs and symptoms of stress and I will cover some of these in the next section.

Effects of negative stress

As I mentioned earlier, stress seems almost endemic in the modern world. Rightly or wrongly, we almost take it for granted we will have significant negative stress as a part of our everyday lives, especially our professional lives. We will define stress here as your body's reaction to any internal or external change which requires a corrective adjustment or response. The body reacts to these changes with a variety of physical, mental and emotional responses.

Stress is indeed a normal feature of life due to the myriad events which happen to you and around you. The things you do and the things other people do put stress on your mind and body. You can experience stress from the environments you find yourself in.

So when does stress become significant enough to affect your mental and physical well-being?

As humans we are actually well able to deal with stress and react appropriately to it. We can actually thrive on stress. No stress at all would be bad for us. We would not be able to develop our coping skills or character attributes which we do when overcoming challenges and problems or achieving goals. Stress can work in our favour, keeping us alert and ready to avoid problems and danger. Issues can arise and develop when stress becomes too negative or too sustained. When you face constant and continuous challenges without relief or relaxation between events you can become exhausted or overworked and this is when stress related tension can build up.

The more technical term for negative stress which continues unabated is distress; a negative stress reaction. Distress can lead to various physical symptoms including headaches, stomach upsets, raised blood pressure, chest pain and sleeping problems. Stress lowers your physical and mental defences so has the potential bring on or worsen certain symptoms or diseases. Sustained bouts of negative stress can lead to anxiety and depression. Not a good thing.

We naturally tend to try and reduce the symptoms of stress but we can often exacerbate the situation when we self-medicate in a harmful manner. Even though it might feel better in the short-term things can get worse long-term when people turn to alcohol, tobacco or drugs in an attempt to relieve their stress. Unfortunately, instead of relieving the stress and returning the body to a relaxed state, these substances tend to keep the body in a highly stressed state and actually cause more problems further down the line. Without careful control, even some healthy ways to reduce stress, dieting and exercise for example, can become unhealthy obsessions with their own long-term negative impacts. Consider how many millions of working days are lost each year due to negative stress, depression or anxiety.

As we have discussed, negative stress can affect all aspects of your life, including your emotions, behaviour, cognitive ability and physical well-being. We are all unique and the causes and symptoms of stress will be different for all of us. No part of our bodies is immune and, because people handle stress differently, the actual way the symptoms of stress manifest themselves can vary markedly between individuals. They do however fall into broadly similar categories so we do have something to work with. Rather unhelpfully, the symptoms of negative stress can often be vague and they may appear to be identical to those caused by medical conditions. It is important to discuss any noticeable symptoms with your doctor. It is worth following-up if you are experiencing any or all of the following stress symptoms.

Some emotional symptoms of sustained negative stress can include: Becoming easily agitated, frustrated and moody and often with no obvious cause. Feeling completely overwhelmed, losing control or feeling the need to take control when previously you did not care. Having difficulty relaxing and calming your thoughts. Having extremely low self-esteem, feeling lonely, worthless and depressed and you may well start to avoid other people. Others around you may be noticing these symptoms too but ironically, the same symptoms which cause others to take notice also make approaching you and offering assistance difficult if not impossible. It is a vicious cycle from which it is hard to break free.

Some common physical symptoms of sustained negative stress can include: Low energy or lethargy, headaches and stomach upsets including gastric irregularities and nausea, aches, pains, tense muscles, chest pains and even an increased heart rate. You might suffer from an inability to sleep well, known as insomnia. You might get frequent coughs, colds and infections. You might find you lose your sexual appetite and possible even your sexual ability. You may appear more nervous than usual and your hands and feet may sweat excessively coupled with a drier than normal mouth. You may even start to grind your teeth or develop some other nervous and uncontrollable tic.

There are also cognitive and behavioural symptoms of sustained negative stress and these can include: Constant and often unnecessary worrying, racing and disjointed thoughts with an inability to focus, increased forgetfulness and general feeling of disorganisation coupled with poor judgement, a highly pessimistic outlook and a tendency to see the bad side in everything. Your appetite may change and you might start to become unreliable and evade your responsibilities. You may drink more alcohol, smoke more cigarettes or even turn to drugs in an effort to self-medicate and you may well appear more nervous to others by developing tics or fidgeting excessively.

Whilst we are on this point, sustained negative stress can have a big and often damaging impact on one of our greatest assets in the modern world; our personal and professional relationships. We rely more and more on our relationships nowadays. They can take years to grow and flourish. Unfortunately, when we are negatively stressed and the behavioural symptoms are expressing themselves, we often become someone who is particularly unlikable or hard to deal with. Professional relationships are often based on the attributes which our stress symptoms undermine such as our reliability and approachability. Professional relationships are vital in smoothing our way through the world of work but when unwanted stress-related behaviours surface these relationships are likely to suffer first and be the hardest to re-establish afterwards. If you let things go for too long you could even affect your personal relationships. Sustained negative stress can change the way you interact with everyone and it is especially hard for those close to you as they see the biggest changes of all. Unfortunately, many of the behavioural and physical symptoms involve pushing such people away even though they are the people most able to assist you in breaking the cycle. No one said life was fair.

So what have we learnt here? A little negative stress every now and then is not something to be unduly concerned about. Ongoing or sustained negative stress can cause or exacerbate many more serious health problems. If you are really concerned about your stress levels and health I recommend visiting your doctor and having a chat with them as soon as possible.

Stress is a part of life but how you handle it is what matters most. The second best thing you can do to prevent stress overload and the health consequences which come with it is to know your stress symptoms and address the issues early.

The best thing to do is to minimise the causes of negative stress before they happen; which is a big part of why I wrote this guide.

Developing a high level of personal and professional resilience will serve you well in nipping stress in the bud before it has a chance to fully develop.

The buck stops here

To make real progress in any undertaking there is one vitally important thing you have to both understand and accept.

The concept of personal responsibility; you have to embrace and take full responsibility for your own life.

It is a really fundamental and basic idea yet one which appears to be misunderstood or ignored by many people. I have met many apparently highly intelligent and highly motivated people who have failed to achieve what they wanted to achieve because they failed to grasp this essential concept of taking personal responsibility for their own lives.

Let me illustrate the idea with a brief story.

Whilst visiting a certain industry conference at a large multi-conference venue I was having a quiet coffee and relaxing with my thoughts when a fellow delegate, I will call him Dave, joined me at my table. I was in a mellow mood so when he started chatting I was happy to go along with it.

We did the introductions and it turned out he was an independent insurance salesman. I asked Dave why he was at this particular conference and he replied he was there for the cutting edge marketing and sales strategies. He immediately followed this by saying whilst it was an interesting conference and had provided some great ideas there was probably no chance of any improvement in his profits as the insurance industry had been hammered by recent global events and was unlikely to recover any time soon. It was a heck of an introductory statement. This particular view of the insurance industry surprised me as I believed there was always a need for good insurance products. I also believe with the right tools and some focused effort there are clients out there for every professional and in every market. I was now keen to hear more from this guy.

"So business isn't going well then?" I asked.

He replied, "No, not really. The glory days are long gone of course. All the terrorists and foreign wars are destroying my business. Add in the global recession and excessive government interference and it's a wonder I can sell anything at all. I do get lots of appointments but nobody is buying insurance from me anymore."

"Do you do a lot of specialist insurance work abroad then? Is that why the terrorists and foreign wars are a problem?" I asked.

He looked quite surprised by the question. "No, I sell general insurance products to householders in the south of England. The wars and terrorists are making people think twice about my products though. They're also trying to save money because of the recession."

The conversation went on in broadly the same vein for a short while before we finished our coffees and went our separate ways. I was initially staggered by his colossally negative attitude but the story is also particularly relevant here regarding where he lays the blame for his situation.

There are two distinct ways of interacting with the world. You can be passive and simply react to random events and situations as they happen to you or you can be active and seek to control specific events and situations in order to have an impact on their outcome. One way has you drifting along with little purpose and trying to deal with whatever comes your way and the other has you moving and responding with purpose by actively engaging and applying some control on the world and the events unfolding around you.

Which stance do you think Dave was adopting?

The irony for Dave was even though he was getting lots of appointments with people who were very likely interested in his products, his belief system was actively discouraging them from buying. With his belief system, language and physiology, Dave was sending his potential clients a clear signal not to buy his product. When they did not buy he used the result to justify his faith in blaming everyone and everything else for his sales problems. Dave had turned himself into a victim and was keeping himself in the role very effectively.

If you are in any way passive and letting the vagaries of life affect you as they will then you are nurturing a victim mentality. I would like to recommend you adopt a much more active and self-determining stance as soon as you possibly can. Helping you do this is what much of this guide is about.

It all comes down to accepting responsibility for yourself, your actions and your responses to situations and events. There is only one person on this planet who can take full responsibility for your life and your responses to occurrences within it and that person is you. Nobody else. You. The buck really does stop here.

"The buck stops here" is a phrase which was made popular by former U.S. President Harry S Truman. Harry S kept a sign with the phrase on his White House desk. It refers to the fact he, as the President, had to make the decisions and accept the ultimate responsibility for those decisions. We would all do well to follow his example and accept full responsibility for our lives and actions. By the way, the S in Harry S Truman name did not stand for anything, it was pretentiously there to make him appear more statesman-like. The middle D in my name does stand for something; Douglas. This is a pretention-free zone.

How would Dave's scenario look if he fully embraced the active stance and took responsibility for his responses to it? For starters he might pay more attention to the sales and marketing strategies he was learning at the conference. Then he might see the people at his appointments were willing to become clients if he simply helped them buy a quality product which was right for them and at a good value price. He might acknowledge poor sales actually had nothing to do with terrorists. Even the new government legislation he was moaning about might actually do him a favour because potential clients would welcome good advice about it from an experienced and trusted adviser like Dave.

We will look more closely at helpful new ways to look at situations later on but for now just be aware; until you make the decision to take full responsibility for your own life, and your response to the events affecting it, you will just be adrift on the waters of random chance.

As you will also discover soon, once you make this decision and accept full responsibility for your response to situations and events, your available options will increase dramatically and your emotional resilience will begin to build.

Choice & direction

As I mentioned in the previous section, good things happen once we take full responsibility for our own lives. What we are really taking responsibility for is choice.

Life is a continual series of choices. It really is.

Luckily for us many important internal things are chosen and acted upon for us automatically. Take your breathing for example. This is an important factor in your continued existence as a viable entity and you would be in trouble if you had to keep making the choice and then breathing as a conscious activity. I do not know about you but I get side-tracked very easily so it would be a real issue for me. Our bodies make millions of useful and essential choices for us every second of every day which we are simply not aware of.

Situations and events, good, bad and neutral, happen to us in life all the time. They occur either by random chance or by the actions of some external agency. This often feels like any choice has been taken away from us. There are, however, still many choices available to us. It is the choice about how we respond to the various events and situations which has such a huge bearing on the outcome and how we relate to the outcome.

Nobody else in the world can control your feelings or emotions. Your feelings and emotions are responses to events and situations. Other people can change the situations and events but they cannot control what you feel about those situations and events. You can choose to respond in a certain way and have certain emotions and feelings. You can also choose to stop responding in ways which are not useful to you or others. For example, picture a scenario in which you are driving in traffic and someone cuts sharply into your lane right in front of you; this seems to happen more and more nowadays. Most of us would get an initial fright closely followed by righteous indignation then anger. Tooting of the horn and wild gesticulations often occur plus language is used which would make a street gang member blush. If the other person immediately apologises for the error we might calm down quickly but what usually happens is they appear not to even notice our ranting or worse they laugh at us and drive off. Now what do we do? Do we calm down and go about our day as if nothing happened? Not in my experience; it is a fight or flight scenario now and we often choose fight because we feel safe and powerful in our little metal bubbles. We hold onto our rage, we nurture it as it festers and it can grow as a result. You might think, "How dare they do that to me. I'll show them I'm not to be messed with. I'll give them a taste of their own medicine." You might even chase after them and try to do who knows what. Failing this you punish other innocent road users instead. It is the gift which keeps on giving. There have been murders committed during episodes of this road rage phenomenon. Do I have the moral high ground here? Hardly. I find myself responding in exactly the same way on occasions. My point is I am choosing to keep the rage going. I cannot blame my fight or flight system at this point because after the initial automatic reaction has subsided I am now back in control. I am choosing to stay mad and sustain my anger. I can also choose not to be mad. I can choose to calm down and drive more safely. What non-useful activities or mind states are you choosing to prolong?

Then there are the general choices we make just because we can. We are creatures of free will and when the opportunity presents itself we are often willing and able to make choices. These can be choices ranging from minimal potential life impact to potentially life changing or life threatening impact. For example, consider this question, "Do I have a vanilla ice cream and sit down to enjoy the view, do I go for the guided valley nature walk or do I go bungee jumping with the dodgy looking adventure sports company located in the rundown old shed at the top of the cliff?" My actual choice will have a range of outcomes and impacts, up to and including death, but it could also lead to some life enhancing excitement.

Consciously examining some of our good and bad habits may reveal, even though we do the same things again and again by subconsciously making the same choices again and again, we could actually make different choices at any stage if we choose to. It is how we break a habit. We choose and commit to begin to consciously break out of the repetitive cycle and follow a different path.

If you find yourself making choices on autopilot try asking yourself why you are choosing a particular option. Ask yourself what other options are available and analyse them. You may already be making the best available choice but it is always worth checking.

Ultimately, whether we make the right choices or the wrong choices is not really the issue in this section. It is your unique life and who is to actually say whether a choice is right or wrong? It is the actual act of making a choice which is important here. One thing you cannot do in life is not to make any choices at all. In fact logically speaking if you make a firm decision not to make any choices this represents an actual choice. When you try to make no choices at all you cast your lot to the fickle whims of fate. You take no control whatsoever. At best, this results in sub-optimal outcomes; at worst it means your out of control life will probably suck.

People are all different so the process you take to choose between options may be completely different to mine. I am not about to advise you or anyone else how to choose effectively between options. There are, in fact, many excellent resources available out there in print and Interweb land to help you do this better if you feel you need some additional help.

The real point here is we need to analyse the options in the way which suits us best, and at the appropriate level for the potential risks involved, then make a choice. Once we have chosen we fully commit to the choice and take full responsibility for and ownership of it. It is as simple as that.

Does this mean once we choose something we are stuck with it? No, the ownership part of the above statement means you maintain control of the whole process.

General George S Patton once said, "A good plan violently executed now is better than a perfect plan executed next week." I am not advocating you start violently executing anything but his point is well made. Doing something good straight away is better than trying to make it perfect and never getting started. The demon of perfectionism and why you need to avoid it is looked at later on and we will also examine the merits of flexibility and point of view. The point here is you can always change direction once you are in motion. As long as you are pointing roughly where you want to go you can make numerous adjustments to your course in order to reach your destination.

Let me illustrate this idea with a thought experiment. Nowadays, most people believe, and take for granted, electronic navigation and satellite technology can guide us unerringly to our intended destinations. Take a moment to consider just how it is achieved in practice. An aircraft flight for example has a desired destination and when the well-maintained, correctly fuelled and expertly piloted plane takes off, we have high confidence it will get there as planned. A flight plan is calculated and generated which the plane and pilot will follow through the air to the destination in ideal conditions. All well and good so far. Now consider some of the many variables which can affect this. There is weather which can affect the plane's ability to hold a perfect course. There are inherent and sometimes random errors in the accuracy of the instruments and controls because no mechanical or electronic system can be perfect. There can also be human inconsistency or error involved because, and let us be brutally honest here, none of us are perfect. The pilot and the systems on board are constantly checking the actual position against the desired target. There will almost always be an error or discrepancy as a result of this comparison. The pilot or autopilot system then adjusts the direction of the plane to guide it back to the desired flight path. Because nothing is ever perfect the next check will reveal another discrepancy and another adjustment will be made. This occurs throughout the flight. For the technically minded reader this process of comparing a desired position to an actual position then adjusting to correct it is known as a negative feedback system and it forms the basis of many modern control systems.

My point is the aircraft is essentially off-course for almost its entire journey. A boat on the water faces many similar variables affecting its ability to steer a perfect course. Continual adjustments are made until the desired port is reached. Even when following your satellite navigation in the car you can find yourself moved away from the ideal journey plan by any number of unplanned variables.

Think of some of your own examples too. You use negative feedback constantly every day. With this new information in mind, try a little thought experiment and imagine how some of the everyday and largely automatic activities and tasks, which you often take for granted, would be next to impossible without negative feedback to guide you.

The thing is the systems generally work for us. We almost always get where we need to be. We start off with a reasonable idea of what we want to achieve or where we want to be and we set off, confident we can make enough compensating adjustments to achieve the outcome we desired.

If an airline tried to plan every last detail of a flight in advance they would never fly anywhere. Likewise if you decided to think about, and consider how to avoid or deal specifically with, every single potential issue in one of your plans or projects you would never get it going. You would be buried in possibilities yet never take any action for fear of missing something important.

What if you make a very poor choice? What if you get it wrong with catastrophic results?

Poor choices in high risk situations can indeed have huge repercussions. Nobody can predict all the outcomes in all scenarios. As I said earlier, life is a series of choices. You will make poor choices from time to time, as we all do in our lives. However, the higher the stakes then the more effort you need to put into analysing your options before choosing. No decision or choice can be perfect but it is up to you to weigh up the options appropriately according to your preferred method. You can in fact choose how much analysis you apply to your choices. Deliberate or random negative events, breakdowns and even unexpected environmental changes can also throw us off-course, both metaphorically and physically. We then have to re-evaluate our decision and potentially choose a fresh direction. The point is the choice points are almost always there.

So, choosing a good direction to aim at and moving intentionally towards it means any small errors or deviations will not affect you too much and, if detected, can be corrected to put you back on track. Having a direction and confidently getting started on the path increases your capacity to act with purpose.

Developing the habit of consciously analysing as many of your choices as possible will yield better or more useful outcomes more of the time. For you this will also mean enhanced emotional resilience.

Blame & personal power

There is one last fundamental concept which I want to introduce you to. Blame and its effect on your personal power.

The idea and definition of personal power which I will use is this:

Personal power is your level of ability to successfully change individual areas of your life or even the entire direction of your life. An example of demonstrating personal power would be changing a habit such as smoking or poor diet or by learning to control an emotional reaction to a repeated negative emotional impact. One way to measure someone's personal power is by how quickly and effectively they can introduce or achieve behavioural or cognitive pattern changes.

Hopefully you will notice the mention of controlling emotional reactions to negative emotional fits nicely within the scope of our definition of emotional resilience.

If all the techniques, mind sets, attitudes and strategies of emotional resilience form your toolkit for bouncing back from negative emotional impacts, personal power could be thought of as your current ability to apply and use these tools in order to be more resilient.

You have already been introduced to the idea of choices and their importance as well as accepting full ownership and responsibility for those choices. Your personal power plays an important role in your ability to be resilient so anything which reduces your personal power is a bad thing. Fatigue, illness, poor environment, overwhelm and constant change are examples of impacts which can all serve to reduce your personal power and, by extension, your resilience. This guide will help you develop your resilience and personal power in order to combat the various things which life throws at us and also the many obstacles we put in our own way.

Sometimes the self-imposed obstacles, limits and barriers are the most detrimental to our well-being. Let us look at a major self-imposed roadblock many people create without so much as a second thought. It is super-harmful in terms of personal power yet it is easily avoided with a little bit of focus on the way we think and the language we use.

This powerful source of self-generated negative behaviour is called blame.

Blame. A very simple word for a very powerful agent of personal power reduction.

The instant you blame someone else or something else for any event or situation in your life you hand them or it all your personal power in relation to the event or situation. Think about it for a minute. Compare these two responses to the same problem: "Business is down because the global financial crisis has forced people to save their money and stop buying our product." "Business is down for some reason, how can we start to generate more prospects and clients in order to raise our sales level?" The first one is a statement which lays blame squarely at the door of the global financial crisis. It is in effect saying the global financial crisis has caused the loss of business. The second statement apportions no blame, it simply acknowledges there has been a change in the sales level and goes on to look for ways to go about remedying the situation.

Where does the personal power reside based on each of the two responses? By laying blame externally, the first one gives away all the situational personal power. The second one increases personal power by taking full responsibility for and ownership of the situation as it currently is, rather than looking for a way to blame something or someone else. The first response also instantly results in a passive stance, i.e. sales will only pick up when the global crisis ends. The second response instantly promotes an active stance, i.e. asking a question about proactively improving the situation.

Remember Dave the insurance guy? Did blaming the foreign wars and terrorists along with government interference help him improve his situation? Of course not. Laying the blame wholly on external influences destroyed his ability to take responsibility and make better choices. His personal power was all but annihilated in this situation. Dave's language is the language of negativity and blame. Dave has turned himself into a victim.

I would just like to reinforce and clarify what is meant by responsibility. When I mention responsibility it is not used in the sense of Dave taking responsibility for the drop in sales. The drop in sales could have numerous causal factors including some created by Dave himself. Here it is used in the sense in which Dave takes full responsibility for his response to the situation and the choices he subsequently makes. There is a huge difference in emphasis.

If Dave had taken responsibility he would have retained all of his personal power to make choices and own the problem solution himself. His choices would likely be better for it and his self-esteem, self-image and emotional resilience would all be increased as well.

Now give some serious thought to the following questions:

Are you using the language of blame and negativity in the same way as insurance man Dave?

Do you find yourself laying blame externally and becoming passive rather than taking full responsibility for your situational response and taking the active stance?

Do you feel other people and events seem to dictate and control the large majority of situations and events which affect your life?

Would you like more control over your response to situations and events than you currently have?

If the answer to any of these questions is yes then maybe it is time you started regaining your personal power by taking more responsibility and reducing blame to a minimum.

As an author's note; from this point on I will not specifically refer to personal power again. The catch-all term of emotional resilience, or simply the word resilience, will be perfectly suited for our purposes of getting the message across successfully.

Our route and your journey

From this point on the various parts are written to be self-contained and stand-alone but they are also designed to link and form a complete whole which is greater than the sum of the parts.

I recommend reading right through first to get the big picture then dipping back in to the various parts and sections whenever it best suits you. When combined and used together these tools form a very powerful toolkit. I like to think of it as an inoculation against negative stress; an emotional resilience vaccine if you will. Each section develops the subject content from the ground up and offers accessible and highly practical tools, techniques and strategies for you to use yourself, or to help others, in order to build your emotional resilience.

I love the writing journey with its ups and downs and twists and turns; I laugh and cry and learn and grow. This is part of my journey as a writer.

This guide now forms part of your journey and only you can make this journey. You will discover you can get help and help others along the way but only you can commit to making real and lasting changes in your life. This tome will provide you with a lot of ideas, tools and techniques but you will have to try them, assess them, adopt them and apply them in order to grow and develop. Nobody else can do this for you. Always be aware; to get the best from anything it is essential to try things out with an open mind. Life is not a spectator sport so get involved.

The overall structure follows an inside-out approach. By this I mean I will start out by encouraging you to look inside of yourself and at tools for working with your own psyche then I will gradually start to encourage you to look outside of yourself and adopt tools and ideas aimed at the wider world and your relationship to it and with other people in it. Whilst there may be some crossover here and there, I believe I have structured things nicely to achieve this aim; the overall logical flow certainly works for me.

Section 1: Friend or foe?

This part encourages you to look deeply inward. It examines how you see yourself and how you motivate yourself. It examines how you gather information and make sense of it. You will also look at ways to modify your emotions whenever you choose. You will also look at how flexible and adaptable you are in your relationships with the wider world.

Section 2: Success and failure

This part shines a light on the twin concepts of success and failure. Is there even a difference? How do you decide which one applies in any given situation? You will look at the beneficial concept of goals and how to design and achieve them then take a look at the very unhelpful trait of perfectionism.

Section 3: Look at it this way

This part focuses on the way you think about the things you do or the things which happen to you. There are inbuilt biases and potential thought traps within all of us which can lead us to draw erroneous conclusions. You will also look at new ways to look at things which happen in your life and how to adopt different perspectives in order to create fresh new options.

Section 4: Action stations

This is where you get stuck into getting unstuck. You will start to look at how you can have an impact on the outer world and also what can stop you having an impact. You will discover how to overcome overwhelm and panic in dynamic situations through prioritising and taking action. You will look at balancing action with positive inaction and your relationship with time and why it is so important to you.

Section 5: Systems within systems

Here you will examine why you cannot avoid systems and why this is no bad thing. It is a look at how you fit into the world and how you can better work with others. You will look next at the topic of positive paranoia and discover it is as easy as ABC. You will then examine emotional intelligence and dive into improving your assertiveness. Finally, you will look at the power of helping others as well as reaching out and seeking help yourself.

I will include a case study narrative at the end of each of these parts to further highlight or illustrate some of the points covered in the text. Some of these are taken from my own experience and others are from the experiences of my many coaching clients; who will always remain completely anonymous of course.

I have also made the decision to provide a virtual appendix only available to you and my other valued readers, on my website for any expanded articles, new case studies, informative diagrams, additional material, bibliographies, responses to reader questions or indeed anything else which might interest you on the topic of emotional resilience. This also means the content will not go out of date any time soon. You will find the details for all this at the end and I will indicate in the text whenever you can access useful additional material.

A final note to define the term "process" given my frequent use of it. A process is a bit like a recipe. If you follow a recipe accurately you will generally get a result close to the one intended by the creator or recorder of the recipe. I also use the term "technique" with the same recipe-like definition.

There is a small caveat here. Because we are dealing throughout with intensely human behaviours and emotions, and given none of us is the same or will respond, think, feel and act in the same way, it is nigh on impossible to provide a process to give a wholly predictable or guaranteed outcome. As a technical point the processes and techniques I supply are therefore known as heuristic processes. These are broad brush recipes which tend to yield the same general type of intended outcome for you and one which is generally sufficient to fulfil your objective. Your outcomes will therefore be specifically different from mine but broadly the same. Technically speaking, any defined process which can yield exactly the same result each time if closely followed, is called an algorithm. There are no algorithms in here; humans and algorithms do not mix well.

Section 1: Friend or Foe?

Resilient water is neither good nor bad, it simply is. Water always adopts the perfect state for the prevailing conditions. Water as a liquid always takes the shape of its container and always remains level. You could benefit greatly in many areas of your life by following water's example.

Introduction to section

It is all in the mind they say.

This section will look at the ways you communicate with yourself.

We all have a conscious and a subconscious mind.

One is huge, deep and infinitely capable of creative, dynamic interaction with the sensory data flowing into your body every second of every day. Amongst many other things it stores and retrieves your memories. It compares any new data with existing data then formulates suitable courses of action for you. It controls your emotions and all your bodily functions and responses. This is your subconscious mind. It is incredibly powerful and flexible. We cannot really access it directly on a conscious level but it can certainly communicate with us when it wants or needs to. Potentially our biggest blind spot, and consequently our most productive area for self-improvement, is our ability to ignore the messages coming from our subconscious mind.

The other mind is your quite limited (sorry but it is true and it applies to all of us) conscious mind which is the one we are actually aware of, most of the time, when we are awake. I like to think of it as an up-to-date executive summary report tool we can use to get an overview of what is going on at any point in time. In reality, we cannot even get a complete overview because our conscious mind really is limited in what it can do or concentrate on at any one time. We have to build up a series of snapshots by focusing on a number of specific areas in order to build up our still incomplete conscious picture of the world. We will look at a few snapshot techniques in this section which may prove very useful to you and help you start to access some of the vast resources we have in our subconscious mind.

We will also look at some of the simple yet damaging things you might be doing or thinking right now which hinder you from reaching your full potential. Do not worry because we will also look at ways to put these right.

It is a fascinating area to investigate and I hope you enjoy part one of the journey.

Self-esteem, self-image & self-belief

What is self-esteem? What is self-image? What is self-belief? What is this apparent holy trinity which we are supposed to have in order to be happy?

I grew up hearing these terms quite often. "The boy lacks self-esteem," they would say. "He has a poor self-image," they would say. "He has no belief in himself." All well and good I suppose but apart from vague instructions like "pull your socks up" or "just get on with it" there was no actual help in improving these apparently gross failings in my mental make-up. I always tried hard to get my head around the concepts of self-image, self-esteem and self-belief yet I never quite grasped them until much later in my life. Over the years I have read a huge number of self-help texts to find out more but I always struggled to find clear and simple working definitions. Now, when working with clients on this aspect of themselves, I tend to use my own rough and ready descriptions and, whilst I may well be accused of over simplifying the situation by some purists, I find they work well and are readily understood. To be completely honest with you, I have never really got on with purists and they have never liked me much either.

One basic way of looking at the situation is by examining the literal meaning of the terms. Esteem means respect or admiration so your level of self-esteem simply refers to your level of self-respect or personal admiration. Likewise, self-image is how you would see yourself if you could see from another's viewpoint. Do you impress yourself or disappoint yourself? Belief, in our context, simply means the confidence you have in a likely outcome occurring so self-belief would be the level of confidence you have in your ability to make certain things happen. These very simple definitions have some merit but there is a far more useful way of looking at the subject.

We humans are a construct of our personal make-up and our personal view of the world. From now on I will refer to our unique view of the world as our worldview. Everything we think, do and feel is linked to our personal make-up and our behavioural patterns as well as everything also being influenced by all our unique experiences throughout our lives.

Let us first take a look at our personal make-up, or personality.

Over the years there have been many different definitions of personality. However, many contemporary psychologists can agree on the following broad definition:

Personality is the pattern of characteristic thoughts, emotions and behaviours which distinguishes one person from another and which persists over time and situation.

Our personalities are formed early in life. They are part biological and part nurture in origin and there is some conjecture as to the proportions of each. You may have heard this called the nature/nurture debate. There are also debates about personality traits versus personality types. In fact there are ongoing debates and new research happening all the time. If this sort of thing interests you there are huge numbers of printed resources and mountains of on-line resources available to you; go ahead and fill your boots.

For example, one person might have a personality which is practical, independent, organised, reserved, suspicious and calm. Another might be more interested in variety, impulsive, helpful, disorganised and insecure. These personality attributes will definitely influence how these people interact with the world around them and also how they process incoming information.

The personality is generally very slow to change and, unless we have an intense episode of psychological trauma or a brain injury of some kind later in life, it can be reasonably said our overall personality is essentially stable over time and circumstance. With work and practice, we can enhance or reduce the effects of the various facets of our personalities over time but in general our personality will be unique to us and we will think, feel and behave in largely predictable ways over our lifetime; mid-life crises notwithstanding.

Our personal view of our individual world on the other hand is a much more dynamic and changeable mental construct. As we progress through life we build up a unique internal representation of the territory, or world, around us and an image of how capable we are of navigating the territory successfully.

We get all our information about the world through our senses. Does the statement sound weird? Think about it for a minute. Where else does our information come from? It is how we process it and give it personal meaning which makes the difference. We all make these unique mental and emotional maps, both consciously and subconsciously, to help us navigate and understand our unique world; let us call them world maps from this point on. Remember, a map can only ever be a description of something, it can never be the something itself. There is a colossal amount of sensory information coming at us all the time. Because we cannot pay attention to everything we have to be selective. Now factor in the notion of our personalities and our world maps acting like selective filters on the information we can pay attention to. Actually, because we are selective we only tend to get around half our useable information directly through our senses and the other half we simply make up, to fill in the blanks as it were, from our existing pool of previously selected and filtered information. Did I mention it can get a bit complicated? It definitely can.

When we are very young we have a very limited world map. We are obviously dependent on others but we adapt quickly. If we cry for example and find we get fed each time we cry, it will appear to be a good thing because we like getting fed. We therefore cry more and more and the behaviour is reinforced. Our worldview map now has "crying equals food" written on it. Sometime later most of us (hopefully) learn crying does not always get us fed so we reluctantly abandon this behaviour and replace it with other behaviours and tactics we know or hope will get us fed regularly. We have rewritten our map of the world.

All our experiences through life can add to or alter this map and many more stable clusters or generalities can form there. We can usefully classify these various stable clusters as being our values, beliefs and knowledge. As new information comes in, after filtering by our personality and our existing worldview, we compare it to our world map and either ignore it or use it to update the map in some way. We often form stereotypes and make many assumptions based on this world map. We rely on our stereotypes and assumptions to make our lives less complicated but in my experience, many such stereotypes and assumptions do not always work out so well.

Finally, we come to self-esteem, self-image and self-belief. Our self-image is what we think about and how we see ourselves or our map of the world at any particular time and context and our self-esteem is how we subjectively feel about the self-image, i.e. our positive or negative evaluation of ourselves. Our self-belief is how we perceive our ability to carry out or fulfil the role our self-image portrays.

For example, self-image, self-esteem and self-belief can be specifically stated at any point as in, "I know I can write well, I believe I am a good writer and I am feeling happy about this belief" or more generally stated at any point as in, "I can do evil things, I believe I am an evil person and I generally feel disgusted with myself."

Here is a little metaphor I like to use to illustrate the relationship between personality, personal worldview, self-image, self-belief and self-esteem. Personality is like having a fixed bag of tools. You might well add or adapt some tools over time but essentially what you have is what you have to work with. Your worldview is what you know about the tools themselves and how the tools can be used by you to work with various materials and in various situations. Your self-image is how you see yourself in that world map and in relation to those tools, your self-belief is what you think about your ability to use those tools effectively in any given situation and your self-esteem is how you feel about those current abilities at any given time.

Does knowing all this affect our goal of building more emotional resilience? My answer is yes, it does affect our goal and in a very good way. We can definitely use the new knowledge to help improve our emotional resilience.

To help you with improvement we first need to look at what kind of engine drives our self-image, self-esteem and self-belief. We have noted personality is relatively stable over time.

Our personal world map can and does change quite often but only after the selected and filtered information is allowed in; we can then choose to accept or reject that selected and filtered information. Making deliberate and considered changes to our world map is obviously one way to alter the way we interact with our surroundings. This is definitely a useful area to work on in terms of improving emotional resilience and we will take a good look at some ideas, tools and mindsets which will help you do this in Part Three.

Right, now let us examine self-image, self-esteem and self-belief which are a dynamic and fast changing part of ourselves. In my experience, they offer you the most value in terms of being leverage points for emotional resilience improvement.

Think of a time when things were going really well, maybe with a task at work or during a sporting event, and someone delivered some unwarranted and harsh criticism about your performance. What happened next? Assuming you did not hit them and get arrested, you probably began internally analysing the feedback. Even if you did not ask for it you will still analyse it. You will compare what was said with what you know and believe about yourself and note any difference. You will also talk to yourself about it using your internal voice.

If you are alone and working on something, the minute there is a hitch, the analysis process begins but at the end of it your internal voice is there to either offer support or criticism. Depending on how this process goes, your self-esteem, self-image and self-belief can get stronger or become diminished.

The self-esteem, self-image and self-belief trinity is essentially driven by a continuous internal narrative you have with yourself.

Essentially everything we will cover is geared toward helping you positively develop your self-image, self-esteem and self-belief. Every time you start to use one of the tools, techniques or thought processes you will be improving this internal trinity. From this point on I will usually refer to self-esteem only but be aware the trinity is a closely linked whole and I am really referring to all three.

For myself, and many of my clients, the single most powerful internal influencer in this self-analysis process is the internal voice we all have. It can really seal the deal for good or ill. In effect your self-esteem, self-image and self-belief are determined by the quality of your continuous internal narrative.

Your inner voice

Have you ever found yourself having an internal debate? Have you ever had a stand-up internal row with yourself about something? Have you ever tried to talk yourself through a task in order to maintain focus? Have you ever criticised yourself or tried to talk yourself out of doing something? Have you ever tried to encourage yourself and get your energy or effort level up? If you are on your own you may even find yourself talking to yourself out loud as you wrestle with an issue or dilemma.

You may well be asking yourself a question right now, "I wonder, have I ever talked to myself?"

I have a plaque on my office wall which reads, "I always talk to myself because I love getting expert advice." It makes me smile but is it actually as superficial and trite as it first appears?

The idea of talking to ourselves may seem strange to some people, so what purpose is served by this seemingly irrational behaviour? Let us dig a little deeper into the pros and cons of internal self-talk.

Most normal people talk to themselves regularly and doing this has many benefits for you as an individual.

At a basic level, there are two kinds or modes of self-talk conversations. The first one is when you are giving yourself feedback or running an internal commentary; you are narrating or talking through something inside your own head. The other is when you are having an actual dialogue or two-way conversation with your internal voice. If you can find the time and space to talk out loud to yourself it is a great way for your conscious brain to communicate with your subconscious. I will now refer only to the internal voice or conversation but the explanations will cover or apply to both modes.

We interact with the world through our senses and talking to ourselves internally adds a new sensory dimension to our thought processes and our ability to learn effectively.

Here are a few of the many benefits positive internal self-talk can bring you:

Gaining improved self-esteem when using positive internal self-talk.

Giving yourself a verbal and emotional pat on the back for a job well done, even if nobody else does, can be a real boost.

Internally debating both sides of a difficult decision can throw up interesting new options for you.

Having your own personal and internal motivational speaker to give you a pep talk whenever you need it.

Having a good mental rant and blowing off some steam creates your own internal pressure relief valve which helps shake off stress and anxiety.

Understanding yourself better by inviting your subconscious into your internal conversations might help you discover new levels of self-awareness.

Rehearsing a difficult conversation or interaction in a safe internal environment can relax you and give you confidence before the event.

Boosting your memory using internal verbal repetition can boost your memory retention.

Talking to yourself internally can improve your performance, improve your attention span and focus your concentration during important or even critical activities and tasks.

Keeping yourself company in times of unwanted solitude.

When have you found talking internally to yourself beneficial?

We have examined the incredibly important quality of having healthy self-esteem and a good self-image in the previous section and noted it is essentially a continuously changing narrative which we play and develop internally. We established an internal model which is effectively our representation of ourselves to ourselves. We can dynamically alter the narrative based on our analysis and framing of reference events which happen to us. We can even alter our personal narrative of past experiences to change them to a more useful version. We compare current events and our response to them with our reference narrative in order to benchmark our intellectual, physical and emotional performance in any given situation. We then rewrite our narrative accordingly. So, with this model in mind, does it not seem clearly obvious that maintaining a positive and supportive inner voice can work wonders on our self-esteem and our self-image.

What if this internal voice is somewhat less than supportive of you? Suppose it is downright negative. Suppose it sees bad in all you do, think, say or feel? What if this inner voice is constantly sabotaging all your plans and performance?

Your self-esteem and self-image will take a bashing. Once or twice maybe and there will likely be no harm done but imagine if this inner voice was relentless in its criticism and negativity. It will not take long before everything appears to be a problem, nothing you do is any good and nothing you attempt will seem likely to succeed. What a dreadful way to live. There are people who do this to themselves all day and every day. It is all too easy to drag yourself down with poor self-talk. Once it gets a hold it spirals down until everything seems bad. I know this from personal experience as you will see when you read the first case study. It can then take a lot of concentrated and focused effort to bring yourself back to a positive frame of mind and a positive self-image. It is a great deal easier to maintain high self-esteem and a good self-image than it is to raise them up again from a low point.

In my experience, resilient people tend to maintain a healthy self-image and a medium to high self-esteem level at all times. One of the main ways they do this is through careful control of their inner voice. Negative things happen to resilient people in the same way they happen to everyone else. The key difference is in how they prevent their internal voice undermining their self-esteem unnecessarily when a negative emotional experience occurs and they also use it to bring themselves quickly back up to the same or better self-esteem levels after the event. It stands to reason therefore, if you want more emotional resilience, you would do well to learn to carefully control your inner voice.

How can you learn simple and practical ways to control or train this inner voice of yours in order to make it more helpful to you?

The trick is to force it to say useful and supportive things. End of story. Turn the voice into your ally and friend.

The first thing to bear in mind, no pun intended, is this simple fact; this is actually you talking to you. No-one else can be or is involved in the interchange. You therefore actually have full control over the conversation.

The second thing is with a bit of assertiveness and an enquiring open attitude you can have a proper chat with your inner voice to find out what it really wants. You do not need to be at the mercy of any of its negative rants, angry tirades or bullying language.

The third thing is deep down there is almost always a positive reason why the voice says the things to you which it does. For example, your inner voice might always highlight the pointlessness of trying anything new due to the high chance of failure. It (you) may be doing this in order to prevent you being disappointed and hurt. Whilst this may be protecting you in one way it is holding you back in so many others. Being more emotionally resilient will let you cope with any such disappointments and let you bounce right back.

This all takes concentration, practice and courage. Courage may sound like a strange word to use but think about it. If you have been the victim of sustained negative self-talk the voice really does seem to have a mind of its own. It seems to have all the power. To mentally and emotionally take on the voice and bend it to your will, to wrest control of your psyche from it, is a truly courageous act. Consider this fact as you make the decision to take control. If this is not a boost for your self-esteem and self-image then I do not know what is.

I recommend using some visualisation techniques and internal role play as your primary tools for getting the upper hand so let us get right to it.

We are going to play about with the image and character of your internal voice. We will have some fun by altering its voice, sex, age, appearance, size, location, attitude and language but you are free to play about as you see fit; it is your internal voice after all.

Find some time and a quiet place to relax and start the process.

Let your inner voice speak to you. It might well be saying what a stupid time wasting idea this visualisation thing is. Good, you are definitely on the right track for trying something new.

Listen to the voice and try to work out where it is coming from. Is it speaking to you from inside your head? Does it appear to be talking from somewhere outside your head? Remember it is not a real voice, it is the voice of your subconscious. It could therefore appear to come from anywhere.

If you could give the voice a shape and a form, what would it look like? Is it large or small? Is it male or female? Is it even human? Does the voice belong to someone else you know like a parent, a sibling or a spouse? Does the image scare you? Is it in colour or black and white? Is it loud or quiet?

Spend some time trying to answer these and any other useful questions to help you form a mental image of your inner voice. It is personal so build a personal relationship with it.

Now comes the fun part. Your inner voice will probably resist this bit the most because it will see it is about to lose its power to control you. You are about to take control of it.

Let us start with the tone of the voice. If it is loud, deep and slow then make it speak very quietly, quickly and high pitched. For example many clients of mine like to turn the voice into a cartoon mouse. Create a version which is non-threatening and which makes you smile.

Try moving the voice so far away so you can hardly hear it any more. What about putting it in your shoe or pocket? How does this change your relationship with the voice?

If the image is large and scary make it small and cute. Try a fluffy kitten with a squeaky voice for example. Can you imagine a cute fluffy kitten with a high squeaky voice telling you what to do and you doing it? No way. Turn it into a non-scary kids cartoon version of itself. Be creative and have fun with the exercise. If your voice represents your spouse then make them tiny. Mentally dress them as a clown. Change the image.

If the voice is in your head try moving it to the palm of your hand. Mentally picture the cute fluffy kitten with the high pitched voice telling you what a failure you are. This image always makes me laugh. If it is your tiny spouse dressed as clown try mentally shining a big spotlight on them. They know you could crush them like a bug if they misbehave or you could just pull their trousers down and really embarrass them. It is your image after all.

It is always surprising to my clients just how polite and supportive their inner voice becomes when they have the ability to send it away, embarrass it or completely squash it.

When my inner voice starts berating me for any reason it is instantly put on the naughty step, like a whining toddler, and it will sit there with a gag in its mouth until it agrees to play nice. This image works well for me. When the voice is ready to talk to me as an adult we talk.

If you want your voice to be more helpful then transform it into something or someone which will help. I like to transform my inner voice into someone I respect and would listen to so I have a representation of famous physicist Albert Einstein. I like to talk to Einstein when I need to work out a problem or a difficulty. We sit at a mental table and discuss the situation like adults - we have flip charts and pens and everything. It is my image and it works for me.
Who or what could you use?

For mentally walking me through a task I have my inner voice take on the persona of blind Master Po, played by Keye Luke, from the TV Series Kung Fu. I am showing my age now but his patient voice in my head walking me through a task forces me to concentrate and smile at the same time. Who could coach you through a sequence of events or tasks?

We will discuss the subject of reframing later and when doing it myself I cannot help but imagine the inimitable Del Boy Trotter (brilliantly played by David Jason) from the UK TV series Only Fools and Horses telling me his particular spin on whatever situation I find myself in. I always develop a different and frequently more useful perspective on things when doing it like this. It is also a lot of fun.

To motivate myself I use an image of a small and irate Mr T sitting on my shoulder (see the GOYA section in part four for more on this) and he bawls and screams in a really loud positive way which makes me both laugh and take the action I need to.

Visualisation is fun and powerful and I use it a lot. This stuff works for me and I also know I am not alone. Many of my clients over the years have had great fun and have seen huge self-esteem improvements by applying and practising these techniques. Despite any reservations you may have, go ahead and give it a go.

You cannot ever get rid of the voice because ultimately it is you. You can, however, take full mental control of how it behaves, what it says and its relationship with you. The negative voice will try and fight back whenever it sees an opportunity. You need to be constantly on guard for this and forcefully put it back in line. Make it build your self-esteem and self-image rather than destroy it. Make it say supportive things and let it be your ally and friend.

Author's note. Of all the many beneficial techniques and practical ideas presented herein, I believe this one is by far the most powerful and effective. Changing your negative self-talk to positive self-talk can change your life. In fact, introducing just this one change can supercharge your self-esteem and self-image. Your emotional resilience will go up and stay up as a result.

Give yourself a break

You will make mistakes. This is a fact. We all make mistakes from time to time. If you ever try anything new you will almost certainly make some mistakes along the new path.

Usually these mistakes will be small ones, you know the kind we know about but no-one else really notices, with no real harm done.

Occasionally we will make real big mistakes. Real show stopping doozies everyone seems to know about. There is nowhere to hide. We hold our hands up, take the heat and secretly hope someone else has an even bigger disaster to take attention away from us. Be honest, we have all been there.

When we make a mistake it is natural to think about it and run an internal dialogue to review it. A post event self-debrief if you like.

I have worked with and coached many clients and, based on their comments about the mistakes they have made, I have noticed something interesting about how their self-debriefing language style changes as a result of the coaching experience.

For example, suppose Jake has been told off by his boss for allowing the photocopier to run out of paper prior to an important meeting. Jake goes over the event in his mind. "It's not fair, my boss always yells at me. He must think I'm a complete idiot. I am always making mistakes and getting caught. I'm destined to be the world's worst admin assistant, assuming I make it to the end of the week of course."

This is an example of what I call pessimistic event analysis. Jake uses universally encompassing words such as "complete" and "always." It is pessimistic and negative language. Phrases like "It's not fair," "He must think" and "I'm destined to" place power and control away from Jake and toward other people. He gloomily predicts his demise by week's end. Do you think this language and analysis will do much for Jake's self-esteem? Have you ever talked to yourself like this? Did it do you any good?

Another example for you. Suppose Jenny was told off for the same thing a week later. When she goes over events in her mind this is how her dialogue runs. "Good grief, the boss was bouncing over the empty paper thing. He must be having a bad day because he rarely yells at me like that. I actually did check the paper this morning but someone must have used a stack of it without telling me. I will send a note to everyone to let me know when paper gets low so hopefully it will not happen again. I will also definitely check if he needs anything copied before the next big meeting - it is down to me after all. Maybe we can come up with a better system in the future."

This is an example of what I call optimistic event analysis. Jenny uses specific behavioural references to analyse the event. She notes the boss's anger is unusual and probably not entirely caused by the paper. She notes her own behaviour and possible reasons the problem occurred. Importantly she takes responsibility for her part in the situation and she identifies actions to prevent it happening again; a learning activity. She even looks for ways to eliminate the problem entirely; a growth activity. Will Jenny bounce back from this event? Almost certainly. I would even predict her performance will improve overall as a result. Do you analyse events like this?

We all sit on a spectrum somewhere between optimism and pessimism and things are often dependent on the context of the event as well. In my experience and in most situations, naturally resilient people tend to be at the optimistic event analysis end of the spectrum. My clients often make this change; thinking more like Jenny than Jake.

The whole idea is simply this; do not beat yourself up about things. Have the internal review, because you are human and it is what we do, but make it an optimistic event analysis where you adopt a supportive and curious style of positive internal conversation. Control your inner voice again and have it work on your behalf.

Treat all negative events as valuable life lessons. Give thanks for the opportunity to learn, examine the options available to make positive improvements, choose the best options you can and move on with a positive attitude. That is what being resilient means.

Positivity versus Negativity

Before I tell you what I believe positivity to be and how you can use it to your advantage, let me mention several things which are commonly mistaken for positivity. These really do not do much of anything for you.

Think back to a time when you have felt down or miserable for some reason. Were you ever given some well-meant but useless advice? "Look on the bright side" or "think positive" for example. This is what many people consider to be positivity. Did it work? Probably not. It never did for me either. This sort of cheerfully vague advice annoys me and generally sends me deeper into my bad mood.

Another popular technique for attempting to generate a positive frame of mind, beloved particularly by the sales industry and espoused in many self-helps products, is the positive affirmation. This is the idea you can forcefully and passionately tell yourself, often whilst looking in the mirror, how good and successful you are. The result is you are supposed to start believing the message and taking on the traits, talents and mindsets mentioned. For example, "I am a fearless salesperson who will shrug off the word no in order to get to the inevitable yes. I will succeed because I am the world's greatest salesperson. I am strong and I am a winner." Sometimes you are urged to make fierce noises and punch the air. Does any of this really work? In my experience it does not really do anything in any long-term or meaningful way. It might help you get out of the house and crack on with your daily grind but will it make you a better salesperson in the long-term? In reality, some top-notch sales training or mentoring from a highly successful salesperson would be much more effective for you. To add balance, affirmations will do you no real harm so if it sounds like your kind of thing then go for it and I wish you well.

Then there is the happy-clappy everything is wonderful school of positivity. The adherents of this belief system contend if you simply smile like your life depended on it, ignore everything bad or problematic, engage only with what is good and lovely then really hope, wish and cross your fingers and toes, everything will work out just fine and dandy. You could even sing happy songs, read up-beat literature or try your positive affirmations (see above). You might have guessed I am not a big fan of this approach either.

Here is where I believe the real power of positivity lies. It is all to do with your outcome mindset and it is controllable using a very straightforward and logical technique. It all comes down to a simple switch of emphasis and focus regarding how you approach a particular task or situation.

In a previous section we looked at how adopting either a pessimistic or optimistic stance when reviewing an event made a huge difference to your feelings about it. We will now look at how important your choice of outcome view prior to engaging with a task or situation can be.

I am a big fan of preparation and mental rehearsal before any event or activity. Top athletes visualise both the process and the successful outcome of events. If they rate it so highly then it is good enough for me. I also recommend making an honest appraisal of any potential pitfalls or hazards which might occur and pre-planning ways to avoid or cope with them. This approach is a solid and well-proven one; forewarned is forearmed. Getting the right balance is key.

When we humans have something on our minds we find ourselves under the influence of something psychologists term a confirmation bias. With this bias active, we tend to see and believe any evidence which confirms our thinking and we tend to miss or ignore any evidence which goes against our thinking. Think about it for a few minutes.

As a small aside, we humans are subject to a host of biases and automatic responses in our day to day thinking. We run a lot of automatic programs and use frequent mental shortcuts to help us keep some sense of order and a feeling of self-control in a very chaotic and noisy world. Generally they help us muddle through successfully but occasionally they also cause thought traps and can lead us in some very odd directions. We will look at some of these later and it is a fascinating area of study should you wish to pursue it in a wider context.

As an example, have you ever bought a car (new or second-hand)? Did you ever notice you began to see many examples of the same model, and even the same colour, of car on the roads? Your new vehicle is a fresh and novel item for you and you will also see and drive it often. Sub-consciously it is right in the front of your mind so you have a bias which allows you to identify, as mentally interesting, similar vehicles to your own. There are not any more out there, it is simply the fact you are noticing them more now because your brain is primed to do so.

Think about the possible effect of two different outcome approaches.

If you approach any task or situation by focusing more on the potential things which could go wrong you will begin to see many more problems; these problems will also appear bigger and potentially more disastrous than normal. Success will be too distant and your way appears blocked with many issues and concerns. If something does go wrong, as you rightly predicted, you will get an internal "I told you so" moment and dwell on the problem almost to the exclusion of everything else. It is only a matter of time before everything else starts to go wrong too; it is disaster all the way down. How can any task or activity approached like this go well? You created a self-fulfilling disaster prophesy and you were inevitably proved right. This then informs your self-esteem narrative you have failed, your self-image takes a hit and your resilience diminishes. What is the point of going on when everything you do is destined to fail. If this sounds a bit too dramatic do not be fooled, it is all too easy to get into this vicious circle or spiral of gloom. You have helped yourself to become a victim. I have been there in the past and many of my clients have been there too. It is a bad place.

In contrast, if you approach any task or situation by focusing on a successful outcome you will see fewer problems and many more possibilities for success. If you do come across a problem, because you pre-planned for it, it can be solved and is actually part of the journey toward success. Your self-esteem narrative has you pegged as a problem solver and not a victim. Your self-image is of someone who can achieve an outcome despite some setbacks. You know setbacks are a part of any meaningful progress and you are confident when tackling them. Every time you do tackle an issue successfully you provide evidence to back up your initial mindset. Everything you do in this activity or situation is helping you get to your desired outcome which you have so strongly focused on. Your emotional resilience is high which means you bounce back more readily from any problems which do occur. You have created what is known as a positive loop or virtuous circle. This is a good place to be and this is real positivity in action.

There is often a very short distance between the two extremes of thought so be on your guard against slipping back into old and non-useful habitual mindsets. You can now use this mental priming technique to shift things to your advantage. Always analyse and pre-prepare for any potential problems which might arise but then approach any task or situation by focusing primarily on achieving the successful outcome you want. Trust to your plan and keep your eyes on the prize.

Adding this simple switch in emphasis to an outcome approach for all your upcoming tasks and situations will prove to be a very useful and powerful tool in your growing resilience toolkit.

The enemy of positivity is of course negativity.

Because your positive mindset is your greatest asset you need to treat and guard it as such.

We have covered identifying and dealing with your inner negativity but there are two classes of external negativity I want to mention: passive negativity and aggressive negativity. Both of these can be equally damaging and we will look at how you can protect yourself from both of them in the next two sections.

Create a negativity neutralising shield

I now want to introduce you to one of my favourite words. Admittedly it is an old-fashioned kind of a word but then I am an old-fashioned kind of guy and I make no apologies for it.

The word is gumption. It is a lovely word you can really get your mouth working on.

Gumption can be defined as shrewd or spirited initiative and resourcefulness. It can be used to mean enterprise, inventiveness and ingenuity. It can also be used to indicate courage and tenacity.

I believe highly resilient people carry large amounts of gumption in their emotional toolkit and make use of it often.

We all have a personal store of gumption. Remember when you dug real deep and managed to finish the vital task; against the odds and with only minutes to spare? Gumption. Remember when you came up with a brilliant problem solution when everyone else had given up? You proved it would work and it did. Gumption. Remember when you flew the alien craft up into the mother ship then uploaded the computer virus which downed the alien defences letting the US Air Force save Earth? Definitely gumption. Okay, I admit I might have seen the last one in a movie but you get the general idea.

We all have gumption to a greater or lesser extent. Imagine it as personal fuel in a tank the same as a car would have. When things go well we tend to have more of it - our tank fills. Having high gumption levels helps us be resilient. Being resilient maintains our gumption levels. It is a nice beneficial or virtuous circle.

A positive, confident, effective and resilient mindset is your most valuable asset. If you do not have it yet then this guide will help you develop it; which is hopefully why you have been reading it. When you do achieve the mindset and attitudes you desire you had better make sure you repel all external attacks upon it.

This section will cover avoiding or dealing with passive types of external negativity by which I mean negative impacts which are not necessarily directed right at you but, if ignored or missed, can still reduce your gumption levels and by extension your emotional resilience.

Passive negativity is everywhere. Negativity is a powerful emotion. Emotions can be every bit as contagious as germs and viruses. Negativity also seems to spread much faster than positivity and even a small amount of it can shred a positive mindset or a happy atmosphere very quickly. There is a high level of passive negativity in the media so choose your viewing, reading or listening material carefully. There are many passively negative environments which can bring you down and there are also passive and aggressively negative people out there. The aggressively negative people are fully able to ruin your tranquillity and balance and will go out of their way to do it. I will talk about them more in the next section.

You need to be aware there is a level of passive negativity all around you and you need to keep up your defences.

I recommend you create and maintain a kind of psychic shield or a virtual negativity repellent. You might well be smiling or laughing at these ideas but read on and try them - negativity is out there and it is stalking you right now.

Here is a nice little visualisation technique which I use, and teach, in order to help detect and ward off negativity and negative people. It can be a lot of fun yet immensely practical and effective. Give it a go.

This is how I do it so feel free to copy it or develop your own visualisation; the important thing is making sure it works for you.

My personal psychic shield visualisation consists of two main elements: A negativity detector and a positivity bubble.

I actually used to picture an old-fashioned world war two radar-like device beaming out detector rays. Any negative language, negative physiology or even negative environmental condition would trigger my detector. Whenever I realised I was in a negative environment or with negative people I used to imagine a virtual warning alarm and flashing lights in my mind. This was the time to apply the defensive positivity bubble. When I first started experimenting with the idea I actually pictured the shield as a kind of glowing electric blue bubble which I imagined to be instantly all around me and extending as far as I needed. Needing to avoid negativity is a serious business. The bubble was my trigger for becoming more positive myself in order to fend off any of the surrounding negativity which tried to attach itself to me. The point of the visualisation for me was also to create a bit of fun and bring a smile to my face when I had most need of it. You could for example imagine the negative person's head has suddenly turned into a party balloon and their voice sounds like a cartoon chipmunk. It would certainly amuse me anyway.

The visualisation of the radar detector kept me attuned and highly aware of my surroundings. The second I heard or sensed any general or specific negativity, either in a situation or in the people around me, I would apply the bubble, check my positivity resources and become more positive myself. This would involve a quick check on my internal voice, my physiology and my current emotional state and mindset. If any of these were not as positive as I needed them to be I would sort it out. We have already looked at our inner voice and as you read on you will find numerous ways to help you enhance your other positivity resources too. When all my attitudes and mental states were as I wanted and at their most effective I could safely assess the situation and identify any specific gumption destroying threats. I might then try and reduce the negativity of the situation around me or even turn it positive. Failing this option I would remove myself to a more conducive situation or environment. I still use this strategy and highly recommend you start to do the same. Personally this virtual shield concept has become such a natural part of my mental make-up over time I do not really need to consciously visualise anything at all anymore.

To summarise, I always recommend to all my clients they adopt the following habits:

Try at all times in your life to surround yourself with positive people and positive experiences. Negative people can be a huge and terrible drain on your spirits and can destroy your carefully constructed mindsets so avoid them at all costs. Examine your relationships with certain people you think may be negative and examine how you feel after interacting with them. Are they helping you or hindering you? How do you think people feel after interacting with you? Are you using negative language or thinking negative thoughts? This type of ongoing analysis is an interesting habit to develop and can be very illuminating and helpful to you and your gumption levels. Try the virtual shield idea and see if it works for you.

Remember, like attracts like so make sure you are as positive as you can be and positive people will naturally gravitate towards you.

Avoid gumption vampires

In this section I want to put you on your guard against one of the most potent destroyers of gumption I know about.

Aggressively negative people. These guys will deliberately drag you right down and keep you there if you let them.

I call them gumption vampires and they will drain all the good energy right out of you just like a blood-sucking movie vampire.

I mentioned your inner voice being a problem, well they are external problem voices. There is an old saying which goes, "misery loves company." Trust me on this and make sure you are not in their company.

It just takes one gumption vampire in a room full of people to start to drag things down. The whole environment can become toxic and you can feel your positive outlook start to wilt. I have seen them sabotage meetings, training sessions, relationships, social events and even things they have arranged for their own enjoyment.

How will you identify these aggressively negative people?

An important thing to note is their negativity is very deliberately directed outward at every opportunity and at any available target. It is an embedded part of their current worldview and their relationship with the world. Those negative people are ready and willing to rain on anyone's parade whenever they can. They do not discriminate. If you are in range they will purposely try and work their perverse magic on you.

They will use the language of negativity as a primary weapon. Everything will be stated as a problem or a potential problem. They will try to steer conversations to areas they wish to be negative about.

For example they might say something along the lines of, "It seems OK at the minute but wait until the European boss gets here, then it will be downhill all the way." Or maybe, "This organisation does not care about us, we are just a number to them." They will say these things with conviction too; they really do believe this stuff. It is their conviction which can drag others into their world and this is what they want. They do not necessarily desire making others as fully negative as themselves but they certainly feel better when someone reinforces their worldview by agreeing or adding their own negative observations. From the skewed perspective of the negative person, this support bolsters their self-image and self-esteem.

They do not even need to speak. Deliberately negative body language and calculated silence can be just as effective as the spoken word; sometimes more effective.

How do I know all this? Unfortunately, I was just such a negative person for many years. I was a gumption vampire. At my negative best I would elevate it to an art form. I was not a good person to be around in a working environment. Luckily for me I wised up and made the changes I needed to. It took a while and it is probably still a work in progress, but maintaining a positive mindset is definitely the way to go; both for myself and the people around me.

What can you do about avoiding aggressively negative people? Hopefully your negativity detector and negativity neutralising shield will stand you in good stead but sometimes a powerful gumption vampire can catch you unawares and blast right through those defences.

Before I tackle this, here is a key thing to be aware of. You cannot change them. You cannot actually change anyone directly. You can only change yourself and your attitudes. Do not waste the tiniest drop of your precious time and energy trying to talk them round or cheer them up. If they want to change and they ask for help then help them. Until then they have chosen to remain negative and you must respect their choice. You do not of course have to engage with them on their terms. You can choose who to engage with and when on your own terms. Realising this simple fact alone has created huge light bulb moments for some of my clients.

"What about normally happy people who are just having a down day?" I hear you cry. "Do we avoid them too?"

I was told this little tale many years ago and it has stuck in my mind ever since. A certain baboon troupe alpha male stubbed his big toe on a rock. It hurt and he was upset. He was in a particularly bad mood that day. Baboon troupes have a very hierarchical structure so to make himself feel better he expressed his negativity in his favourite way; he hit the next level down baboon on the head with a stick. He knew this one would not fight back because he was lower down the social scale. What a result, he now felt a lot better. Unsurprisingly this attack put the second baboon in a bad mood. The members of this troupe tended to copy their leaders. "He is in charge so he must know what he is doing" they all thought. This second baboon hit the next level down one with a rock and immediately felt better. This behaviour repeated on down the social ladder until the smallest and lowliest baboon was hit by a lump of smelly elephant dung. His day was inexplicably ruined and he had no other baboon to take his frustration out on.

This tale was told to me when I was introduced to the idea of karma. I love the essential philosophy of karma. In the Buddhist tradition, karma refers to your intention driven actions leading to balancing future consequences. You might know it more colloquially as, "What goes around, comes around." The idea of karma is, in this example, the alpha male baboon will pay for his negative actions somehow at some unknown time in the future. The smallest baboon is the victim of a karmic dump and he now has a choice to make about how to deal with it moving forward. The concepts of karma and karmic balance, and their relationship with emotional resilience, have always fascinated me.

People who are having a down day are fully entitled to feel bad. We all have the option. They have many choices open to them in terms of dealing with the down situation. If they choose to take out their frustration on others, even if it is out of character, they have chosen to pursue the aggressively negative option. They will be looking for the equivalent of the next level down baboon. It is not your job to be the smaller baboon so if they choose the option then yes, avoid them too.

If you are in a one to one conversational situation with an aggressively negative person I recommend getting away from them as soon as you are able. Do not allow the conversation to go down any route you are not happy with. If you want to give them the benefit of the doubt, try to steer the conversation down more acceptable paths but, if they want to play only by their rules and carry on with their negativity, I recommend you move on quickly. Do not accept their karmic garbage.

In social or business situations where physically moving away and ignoring them is not such an easy thing to do, you still have to avoid the karmic dump. Initially I would recommend you only engage with the positive people there, try to ignore the negative ones and keep to the emotional and moral high ground. If it is a business meeting it is the chairperson's role to control things. If they do not control things you probably have better ways to spend your time so here is a radical option you could try. Simply stand up, offer your apologies and say you need to be somewhere else you had completely forgotten about, thank everyone then leave. Who cares what people think about this, at least you are not there anymore and you left politely. You can obviously do the same at social events as well. It may be annoying but your emotional equilibrium is more valuable than putting up with poor company just to be polite. Life is too short.

This is a guide to both improving and preserving emotional resilience. The key thing to remember is, whilst you could spend time debating with, arguing against, pacifying or even simply listening to aggressively negative people, you will never leave the situation feeling better than you went in. Never. Even if you feel you have succeeded or won the encounter it will be a hollow victory and you will be diminished. The really effective and emotionally resilient technique is the approach where you neutralise and/or physically distance yourself from aggressively negative people.

If you are the chairperson at a business event where any aggressive negativity is taking hold then it is down to you to stop it. These situations are rare but they do happen. In my experience there are several workable and assertive options open to you.

Option one. If there is an individual being problematic, try putting your coaching skills to good use. Assume politely they are being negative but with a positive intention. For example, if they are adamantly and continually saying a project or plan is doomed to failure, it may be they just do not have the verbal skills to elaborate why they think it will fail. They really do want to protect the organisation from a potential problem area but they do not know how to get their point across in a non-negative way. Use questions to get the positive intention from them for everyone's benefit. This guide is not actually about the noble art of coaching others so, if it is an area which interests you, I would encourage you to do some further research and even investigate some training.

Option two. If option one does not work and they appear to be disruptive for their own negative reasons or agenda, I recommend giving them an assertive and robust challenge. Explain the meeting is important and everyone's time is valuable. Ask them to state clearly what their problem is so everyone there can discuss and possibly resolve it. Give them their say, have the discussion and then proceed as appropriate. They may well not say anything at all under these conditions and the meeting can proceed without further interruption. If this does not work, point out this meeting is not the best place to continue with the discussion, tell them you will meet with them privately and ask them to leave. This is assertive behaviour on your part. You will likely win the respect of others at the meeting and you have kept the moral high ground by not entering into a pointless argument and not letting them hijack your meeting with their agenda. Carry on with the meeting and speak to other person or their line manager later on.

Option three. Despite all your attempts to revive it, if there is a general breakdown in the mood, and lack of progress as a result, simply call the meeting to a halt there and then. Explain to them, because everyone's time is valuable, and you do not see the likelihood of any progress being made on this occasion, you will reschedule it for a later date. Note who was causing problems and take it up with them privately or with their line manager if appropriate. I recommend you do not invite them to the next meeting. There may be some protests from people and you will feel pressure to cave in but stick to your guns as you are in control.

At a social event the host or hostess will have the same role and responsibility for control as the chairperson of a meeting but if you are the host or hostess then using diplomacy and tact will be the best options available to you.

Aggressively negative personalities and alcohol generally are not a good combination. You can choose your guests but you cannot always control what they do or say, especially with booze flowing. The aggressively negative person will try to engage with anyone daft enough or unfortunate enough to listen. Deal with things as soon as you see issues developing. Do not get into an argument with them as you will lose out emotionally in the end. If they have a partner, politely ask them to sort things out. Never let the person be among the last to leave. Diplomatically calling the whole event to an end and shepherding everyone out is the option to go for; then cross the problem person off your social list.

All the above scenarios utilise the "neutralise and distance" approach. Another powerful tool in your growing resilience toolkit.

Here is something we have not discussed yet. What if you are the aggressively negative person? Here are two warning signs you may need to be aware of:

In work, you stop getting invited to meetings and everyone avoids you. Big signal.

Your social life becomes non-existent. Big signal.

We naturally gravitate to people who are like us, so if you are currently negative or have a negative internal voice you will find yourself drawn to others just like you. Reading this and acting on as much of it as possible will definitely help. Change your internal voice and your outlook and you will find yourself drawn to better company. Better company will also be drawn to you. Your self-esteem and self-image will improve. Your gumption levels will increase to record highs and you will find yourself feeling much more emotionally resilient.

Mindfulness & state management

Mindfulness is one of the new kids on the block. It has a lot of great press nowadays and it is growing in popularity. It is treated as a complete subject area in its own right and numerous material has been produced in praise of it. Am I about to burst the bubble of mindfulness? Am I about to reveal our new hero has feet of clay? Am I about to debunk the creators and expose them as the charlatans they really are?

No, I am not. I am actually a big fan of mindfulness and practice it daily myself. It is also not a new concept at all. The origins of mindfulness are to be found in the ancient Buddhist traditions.

In the context of everyday life, mindfulness is usefully defined as moment-by-moment awareness of one's thoughts, feelings, physical sensations and immediate environment. It is characterised mainly by a neutral acceptance of incoming sensory information and thoughts, i.e. attention to and study of incoming thoughts and feelings without judging whether they are right or wrong. Often practised as part of a meditation session, mindfulness focuses one's attention onto what is happening in the moment; instead of its normal focus on the past or future.

Is practising mindfulness really a practical goal for a guide like this which promises practical tools? It is obviously not always convenient to drop down into a yoga pose, gaze at your navel for an hour or so and meditate on your mental state. How then can you make best use of mindfulness and still go about your day?

Especially for you and my other wonderful readers, I have adapted and condensed some Neurolinguistic Programming (NLP) and mindfulness techniques into one simple, two-stage technique which is useful and practical enough to help you to monitor and control your mental state, and by extension your ability to remain emotionally resilient, in your everyday life. I am a big fan of NLP and will say more about it in the Goals section of Part 2.

On any given day of your life you will be faced with many different situations. Each of these will require you to utilise a unique set of skills, processes and mental abilities in order to cope adequately and effectively. There is one ingredient in the mix which can have a huge impact on the quality of your performance. This key ingredient is your state of mind. Call it your mood or your attitude if it helps. From this point on I will refer to the term "state" by which I mean your mental and physiological condition at any particular moment.

Think about it. If you have a delicate negotiation to deal with, is it beneficial to you to be in a distracted or vague state of mind? If you are presenting a life time achievement award to a valued member of staff, is it a good idea to exhibit a frustrated or angry attitude. If you have to give bad news to someone, is it any good being in a devilish or high-spirited mood? Not really. Things often change quickly and we can be put into situations by others when we are not in the right frame of mind to deal with them successfully or tactfully. I know I have been there many times in the past.

We cannot just pretend to be in a different mood either. Most people, myself included, are poor actors. Smiling inanely and trying to look happy will not cut it. Our entire physiology gives the game away. Our bodies, facial expressions and tone of voice always tell the real story and people are attuned to reading and interpreting such signs. This ability to transmit such signals ourselves and to read signs and signals in other people is so ingrained in us we have a name for it; we call it body language. Now we might not know exactly what the signals imply but we know full well when they do not match the mood the other person is trying to convey. There is what is known as an incongruence or a mismatch. We notice mismatches.

The practical mindfulness technique we are going to look at is actually in two parts. If time was not important you could do a full mindfulness meditation to achieve your ideal state of mind then move serenely on with your day. If you have this much free time every day you probably would not be sitting here reading this. If on the other hand you are like me and countless others who are constantly working against the clock then you need a technique which removes the guesswork and cuts straight to the chase.

Stage one involves going quickly to a neutral, relaxed or centred state. Stage two involves choosing which state would be most beneficial and getting quickly into it. Here is the really clever bit. If you put some work in up front you can develop a whole collection of useful resource states which you can use again and again whenever you want. How cool is that?

Let us use an example scenario to walk you through the process. Let us assume you are a head teacher at a school. At two o'clock this afternoon you have to meet with some parents to discuss their son's growing bad behaviour in class. This would be best done with tact and diplomacy and in a sincere, compassionate yet authoritative manner. Normally this will not be a problem for a fantastic head teacher like yourself but today is different. Today you have to head up a meeting with your entire teaching staff to tell them they are having their pay and holidays cut by twenty five percent as of next week. This meeting is scheduled to finish by ten to two and it will not be a pleasant encounter for anyone. You will likely emerge in an emotional state far removed from the one which would be most useful to meet the parents with at two. What can you do about it?

Before we work on setting up resources let us get you working on getting into a neutral and centred state of mind. Doing this centring step first allows the transition between states to be readily achieved.

It involves some visualisation and sensory exploration and can actually be very therapeutic. I do this exercise when I am feeling a bit tired and it can feel like a couple of hours solid sleep in terms of getting me re-energised. If it was a drug it would probably be illegal. Find a quiet space where you can stand comfortably and take a few deep breaths. Breathing deeply is important so start the breathing cycle by drawing air in through your nose and expanding your stomach as you do so. This will really fill your lungs as your diaphragm is drawn down. Breathe out slowly for as long as you can manage. Do this cycle several times and focus your thoughts on the activity of breathing. Now let the tension out of your body by starting with your neck and shoulders and relaxing the muscles as much as possible. Keeping the deep breathing cycles going throughout, move down and relax your arms, hands, fingers and on down to your torso and legs. Do not relax to the point where you fall over as that would be silly; just feel yourself standing effortlessly. Now start to pay attention to the pressure created on the soles of your feet and your shoes. Now imagine your shoes have gone and you are starting to put roots down into the ground. Roots from the bottom of your feet are working their way downward. You are fully connected with the earth and drawing energy in from all around you. Keep breathing deeply, focus on feeling your connection with the earth and just enjoy the sensation. I do this for only a few minutes in total and feel renewed every time. Too new-age hippy for you? I used to think like this and so did many of my clients; give it a go. Practice until you get comfortable and used to doing this exercise and you might just amaze yourself.

The short grounding exercise will have got you centred and in a relaxed neutral state so on with stage two.

To be able to switch states quickly and effectively the trick is to plan ahead. You are going to learn how to install the mental and physiological resources which will be most useful to you for a given circumstance. When you do this you will have them available when needed; like a mental and physiological Swiss Army knife.

For your "head teacher going to your difficult meeting with the parents" scenario we determined you would benefit most from a state which provided an ability to be tactful and diplomatic in a sincere and compassionate yet authoritative manner. Try out this exercise right now.

Find a quiet space where you can stand comfortably and take a few deep breaths exactly as you did for the centring exercise. This will again involve visualisation and sensory exploration. Think back to a time when you were embodying the characteristics you need later. Recall a time when you were tactful and diplomatic. Recall a time when you were sincere and compassionate yet still authoritative and fully in control. It may be a time when the same scenario occurred and you were really well prepared mentally and physically and performed at your absolute best when dealing with the situation. If you have no beneficial reference material you could imagine a hero of yours, someone you really respect, who would be perfect in just such a situation. To our brains, there is actually little if any difference placed on real versus imagined imagery; the memory data is stored in the same way and in the same locations and is recalled using the same channels. We can use this to our advantage here.

As you picture yourself, or your hero, recall how you were standing. How did you appear to the outside world? What facial expressions did you have? Hear yourself talking. What tone of voice did you use? What words did you choose? Step inside this past you or step into your hero's body. What emotions were you feeling? How did the world around you appear? How were you feeling physically? Take some time to really explore your mental and physical state when you, or your hero, were performing at the peak of ability in the scenario.

One way to usefully check in and see if you have envisioned all the required resources is to ask yourself, "Am I ready and fully confident to meet the parents, right this second?" If the answer is yes and you feel you cannot get any more useful information now is the time to anchor things.

An anchor is something which holds something in place just as a boat which is anchored properly will stay in one spot. The anchors you will use will instantly remind your body to retrieve and instantly take on the desired resources which you installed at an earlier point. Some people like to use a physical anchor such as pinching a thumb and finger together or touching an earlobe for example. Others prefer to use sound and might mentally sing part of a song or quietly tap a particular rhythm. Other people prefer a visual anchor type and this is actually my own preferred style. Whenever I speak in front of an audience, just before I go on I picture myself surrounded in a column of green light with golden sparkles in it. This column of light, which obviously only I can see by the way, stays with me for the duration of the event and triggers the mindset and physiology which I know makes me the best speaker I can be at the time. I use different colour/sparkle combinations for different useful states and find it works well for me. This is the key here; use whatever feels most useful and is most effective for you. They are your anchors after all.

Back to the exercise. When you are at a point where you have really recreated the desired physiological and mental state which will be most useful to you then simply apply your anchor. Squeeze those fingers or touch your ear, hum or sing the tune or visualise the image.

Relax again and think about something else entirely in order to return to a neutral state.

Run through the last sequence again and fully immerse yourself, or your hero, in peak the performance state and apply the same anchor again. This is to reinforce the anchor for later recall.

That is it really. Go back to your neutral state and then try out the anchor to see if it works. The idea is by triggering the anchor the desired state will be available to you instantly.

Try it now. For myself, I simply surround myself in a green light column and I am ready to speak.

In your scenario where you are the head teacher, when you come out of the heavy duty high pressure staff meeting, you would find a quiet space for two minutes, centre yourself then trigger your anchor and hey presto you will find yourself in a much more useful frame of mind and physiological state to meet the parents and deliver any bad news in an appropriate way.

This is another valuable and very powerful tool in your resilience toolkit. It is actually a meta-tool. A meta-tool is a tool which can make other tools. Staying mindful of your current frame of mind and then having different options readily available to you will be very empowering. After a while you will find you will be able to control your state almost without thinking about it. Take the time to develop a range of useful states which you can summon up at will. Remember, your brain, although it is hugely powerful, can be manipulated quite easily. You can manipulate it yourself in extremely useful ways so go ahead and give it a go.

It may be of great benefit for you to buddy up with someone you trust, or indeed a coach if you have one, and have them talk you through the process in the first instance. Keep the anchors fresh and current by triggering them once in a while and if necessary go through the whole process now and again to reinforce the resource.

As an aside, I used to hate dealing with bureaucracy and bureaucratic jobsworth types. You know the ones, they are massively inflexible and always reply, "I cannot do that; it would be more than my job's worth." Dealing with these people would really push my buttons. Anything I had to do which had me waiting in an automatic phone queue listening to lift music, or even a real queue now I come to think of it, would really get my blood boiling. Thinking back, quite a lot of things used to push my buttons. Told you I was just a regular guy. Nowadays, the way I deal with it is by using my "Battling the Forces of Evil" visualisation. It always makes my wife smile when I say, "I am just off to battle the forces of evil." In my imagination I am running a movie where I am the hero knight in white armour actually battling scary monsters. I am winning of course but it is hard work. This is a visual anchor for me and triggers a patient, knuckle-down and get this done and dusted frame of mind along with a relatively relaxed posture which reduces tension. It works for me and ultimately this is what counts.

As I mentioned earlier, we all make choices and taking full responsibility for your choices is a key factor in building your emotional resilience. Here is a little something for you to consider. When we are in a bad mood or a non-useful mental state and we stay in the state for any length of time, it is because we have chosen to do so. We can become so good at nurturing our bad and non-useful moods over long time periods, by placing them in our metaphorical mental greenhouses and watering them with negative thoughts to keep them flourishing, we can even start to believe they are our natural mental states. Right now, if you are in an irritated mood for some reason then you have a choice to make. You can choose to change the mood for something more useful or appropriate. If you do not change it then you are choosing to stay in the non-useful mood. You cannot blame anyone else because you are in control. How much time have you wasted by choosing to hang on to a bad mood or a non-useful mental state? Develop the habit of choosing to change this as soon as possible.

Flexibility and luck

Water is the ultimate flexible substance. It readily adapts its structure in response to changing external condition. It adapts its shape to the one formed by whatever container it is in. If you put your hand in water, you will leave no mark or indentation; it will simply mould itself around your hand. Water can push hard when required. If you ever get the chance to experience Niagara Falls in the famous Maid of the Mist boat you will feel some of the massive power water can exert.

I always recommend people model themselves on the example of super-flexible water. Push hard when required but be ready to adapt and flex in order to achieve the best outcome in any circumstance.

Focus in any endeavour is usually a good thing. When you focus effectively on something you can generally bring maximum resources and effort to bear on it and for longer periods of time. Good things get better and poorer situation can be tackled more effectively with enhanced focus and concentration. Many people are keen to develop their ability to focus.

Racehorse trainers deal with horses of all temperaments. Some horses are easily distracted and lose focus, especially when racing with other horses. Trainers will fit the head gear of such animals with small panels called blinkers (also known as blinders) which allow forward vision only. This serves to concentrate the animal's attention on the business of racing. The blinkers are only used when the horses are training or racing. The trainers remove them at other times.

We humans, however, have the ability to take things to the extreme. Too narrow a focus for too much time can lead to fixation on one activity, one path or one way of engaging with something. At best this forms non-useful habits but can ultimately lead to an obsession or a compulsion and this is not a good thing in my opinion. Many people go through life wearing metaphorical blinkers which they never take off. They then wonder why the same things keep happening to them again and again.

To get different outcomes you need to apply different inputs.

A key factor in being emotionally resilient is the number of options you have available to you at any time. It is fair to say the person with the most options for effectively dealing with things in any given situation is likely to be the one who comes out of the situation in the best condition.

Ask any good business consultant the one thing they want to hear most from a client, apart from "It doesn't matter how much you charge, it matters when you can start" and they will probably say, "We have always done it like that." This seemingly simple and innocuous statement speaks volumes. It lets the consultant know the individual, team or organisation is habitually following a process or system and they have long ago forgotten why. They are effectively blinkered. There is almost always a way for the consultant and client to revisit such a system or process and either improve it or eliminate it altogether. All this also makes the consultant look good and getting rehired is always a bonus.

In order to improve your mental and psychological flexibility and therefore your emotional resilience it is well worth developing a specific and hugely beneficial habit.

Develop the habit of asking yourself the simple question "Why?" I say ask yourself the question because if you start to ask everyone else this question all the time they will quickly get bored and irritated and you will soon have no friends. You can, however, ask yourself "Why?" as often as you like and even have more fun in life as a result.

Here is how it works. As you go about your day, give some thought to the things you do and the way you do them. Ask yourself "Why do I do this? Why do I do this in this particular way?" If you tend to eat the same thing for breakfast just ask yourself why. Is it because it really is your favourite breakfast or is it simply a habit you have grown used to? Consider all the myriad things you could eat for breakfast. What about your journey to work. Is there an alternative? Perhaps leaving a few minutes earlier and taking a different route would open up a whole new world for you; one you have never considered before. How do you go about your job? What routines are you stuck in? Why? What does your team or organisation do repeatedly which could be done differently? Why? Give these things some attention, ask a simple question and who knows where it could take you. It could be everything you do is the optimal way of doing things. This is great, at least you asked the questions and your confidence will be high.

When you get used to asking why you will even go beyond questioning the things you do and start to consider why you think the things you think. When this happens it opens you up to the possibility of habitually adopting an even more intriguing question. "What if?" I will leave you to think about this yourself.

I would like to finish this section with a short discussion on the oft misunderstood topic of luck.

Do you know someone lucky? Do you consider yourself to be lucky? Do you know or know of a person for whom life always seems to work out well? Someone who seems to get all the breaks, knows all the right people, makes all the right decisions and even has the whitest teeth in the room. How do they do it? What makes people lucky?

There is a formula for luck which I think works perfectly and explains a lot:

Luck = Readiness + Opportunity

Simple really, as many of the best formulae are. The bit many people get confused about is the weighting or relative importance they give to each of the two factors involved.

Most people assume opportunity is the governing factor. If you consider yourself unlucky is it because you feel you do not get many opportunities? This is a poor assumption because you get opportunities all the time. We all do. Even if you just got one great big opportunity and did not take it, would you still see yourself as unlucky due to lack of opportunity?

Many times we fail to see an opportunity for what it actually is. When we do see them we often fail to take advantage. Therefore, a more important question to ask yourself is "What prevents me from seeing and taking advantage of the opportunities which do come my way?"

The real key to the luck equation is your readiness. How prepared are you to take advantage of any golden opportunities which do present themselves?

There are many components to readiness and I will cover two of them here. I am sure you can think about many other aspects of readiness I have missed and I would encourage you to do so.

Firstly, let us cover your ability to recognise something as an opportunity in the first place. We have just discussed flexibility and this is a key aspect. If you have convinced yourself that getting a large amount of money quickly is the key to your success then you will be on the lookout for opportunities which potentially offer you this outcome. If you get one and you are ready to act, when you do act then you have a great result. The problem is genuine and impossible to miss opportunities like these seem rare when you are blinkered. Another downside is with your big one shot opportunity blinkers on you will probably fail to see any number of smaller or baby-step opportunities which could have potentially taken you to your goal and beyond if you had been able to identify them and been flexible enough to take the appropriate action.

The other advantage of the baby-steps approach is the sense of empowerment which continuous small victories gives to you. You get used to success, you feel luckier and you notice more opportunities to act on. A virtuous circle is formed.

Secondly, how prepared or ready are you to take advantage of any opportunities? Readiness covers a lot of ground so increasing your flexibility by having as many options available to you as possible will increase your chances of success when you do spot an opportunity.

Readiness means different things to different people. Here are some example scenarios to consider.

It could mean being ready with practical skills. If a job which you really fancy opens up in your department but specifies a skill set which you do not yet have, do you ignore it and put it down to bad timing or bad luck? You have failed to see an opportunity here. Instead, what if you see it as a way to approach your boss and get the needed skills training in place so you have the option for next time? What if you see ways to offer your existing transferable skills and learn the new task as you go? What if your keenness to move up in your organisation opened doors which you never dreamed existed? Exploring options can yield surprising results. If something good happened to you as a result of following up on this opportunity would other people say you were lucky? I would say you were simply more ready to be lucky.

Ready could mean you being fully in the game in the first place. Have you ever seen a new stand-up comic on television and wondered where they appeared from so suddenly? You might be good at telling jokes in the pub or at your sports club and think it is just luck the comic is on TV and you are not. They must have been in the right place at the right time to be spotted by a talent agent. Just dumb luck? Wrong. Most overnight successes are a long time in the making. The stand-up would have started for free at open microphone nights. They would have worked horrendous hours in front of horrendous audiences. They would have practised and adapted their material endlessly. They would have worked and worked to reach their goal of television exposure and the potentially high earnings and fame which come with it. They were in the right place at the right time to be spotted by a talent agent for the TV spot but they had to be at exactly that place at that exact time to "get lucky." Are you fully in the game to achieve your goals? Do you work hard enough to get good enough to embrace opportunities? Do you have enough options? Are you in the right place at the right time? Even winning a lottery jackpot, slim though the chances are, depends on you purchasing a ticket. Are you ready to be lucky?

Being ready could mean getting your mindset right. Taking some opportunities can involve major change. Change can be traumatic so having your mindset right and having enough emotional resilience in place to deal with the change and emerge in a better place is a huge plus. Everything in life costs something so having a mindset where you are willing to pay the price will allow you to take advantage of opportunities which others cannot or will not. I am not saying you have to sell your soul for a desired result but you do have to mentally prepare yourself to pay the appropriate dues, i.e. in time, energy, money, physical relocation or whatever else is required. Does this make you lucky? I say it makes you ready to be lucky.

How do you define luck? Take some time to carefully consider how alert you are to opportunities which come your way. Also consider how ready you are to take full advantage of them. If you are lacking options in any way then now is the time to start increasing them.

Your very next opportunity could be the one which takes you to the stars but only if you spot it and only if you are ready.

Case study - The bully

This first case study is about someone I have come to know very well in recent years. I like him a lot now but there was a time when I hated him and verbally bullied him mercilessly. The problem was, we were stuck with each other. To compound the situation, the more I bullied and berated him, the worse I felt.

I sound like a monster and in a way I was. So who was the hapless and innocent victim of my callous and continual verbal assaults?

Sadly, the victim was me. There have been far too many occasions in my past when I was my worst tormentor.

Allowing my destructive and toxic inner voice free rein to chatter away in any way it fancied, I literally used to mentally beat myself up for no good reason and this would effectively cripple my psyche. My self-image and self-esteem were shredded.

Whenever I made a mistake I would call myself a loser, a failure, stupid, useless and any number of other negative names. These were personal attacks on my own identity. The very core of my being and who I was. I did not seem to let up for a second.

Even in the rare moments when I was not attacking myself directly, I used a general internal language of doom, failure and negativity. "You'll mess up sooner or later." "You'll just get laughed at if you try and fail." "You'll fail at it eventually." "People like you don't get the good breaks." "Don't trust anyone because they're all out to get you." I could take any situation and reframe it in a negative way. I had the skills of a master of the reframe but I used it in reverse.

Most of the time I kept this bottled up and I functioned well enough in social situations. I was often considered the life and soul of the party, especially with a few drinks inside me.

At work there were negative people all around me. I did not know then what an emotional sinkhole they could be. You can only resist them for so long and it was all too easy to join in with their misery. Out loud and just like them, I tended to blame everyone else and the world for my problems. Inside my head and heart, I constantly blamed myself for my failure to be positive and my weakness for being dragged down by others.

Do not get the wrong idea here, I was not seriously depressed or mentally ill, just miserable and at the time I probably assumed everyone felt roughly the same way. Certainly, most of the significant people around me at work appeared to feel this way so it just became a normal state of affairs. A habitual low-grade and inexplicable misery brought on by uncontrolled negative internal chatter. I had no clue then about the concepts and techniques I discuss here in this guide. Neither I nor the people around me at work did any self-improvement back then. It was not an available option.

So the bottom line was I simply did not know how to fight back against myself. I wasted a lot of time and emotional energy wrestling with these inner demons.

Maybe it was just easier to attack myself than face the world at the time - who knows. Generally, I was not feeling very happy in the working environment and I was probably not a very nice person to know or be around back then.

The one shining light in all this was my lovely wife. She must have had positivity and resilience enough for us both. She has taught me a lot over the years and must be a truly great judge of character to see my potential through all the negativity. A lady with natural resilience and great patience.

When I do look back and reflect on that period in my life, the saddest thing for me is the total waste of time, energy and emotion. Hindsight is a wonderful thing of course and but I could have had so much more fun if I had known how to go about things differently. Regrets are pointless and I try to avoid them at all cost. Would I even be the man I am today without having gone through it all? Who knows? Our finer qualities are often forged in trying circumstances.

All of the above is now thankfully and rightfully in the past and later on in my life I came to realise I did not have to fight back at all. Fighting this voice directly is actually a battle no-one can win; the harder you fight the worse it gets.

Here is the key thing I learnt. We all carry on an internal conversation. We all have a near constant internal dialogue which cannot be silenced and cannot be fought directly but I now had a way to remove the negativity.

The answer turned out to be very simple. Sometimes things are so simple and obvious we do not see them until they are pointed out to us. I was privileged to have some very good teachers and mentors available right when I needed them and I was aware enough at the time to pay close attention to them.

You cannot control the talking of the voice but you can control the words the voice is allowed to use and the way it speaks to you. You can turn it from an enemy to a friend.

It is taken a while and it has taken a lot of practice to form this new habit. I have now turned my inner voice into my best friend and ally. I have to keep it under supervision because it can easily revert to its old ways if left unwatched. It now supports me and nurtures me. It builds up my self-image and self-esteem. This simple change along with the other ideas in this guide have made a huge positive difference to my life and the lives of those around me.

Am I special or lucky? Not at all. I have worked with other people who have used some or all of the techniques to get themselves where they want to be in terms of resilience and mindset. I can only recommend you give these things a fair go and decide for yourself.

Section 2: Success & Failure

Resilient water is infinitely adaptable. Throw a rock in a pond and see how permanent the ripples are. All ice melts in time and all water vapour condenses when the conditions demand it. Water knows not success or failure and cares nothing for them. Permanence is a myth and the more flexible you are the more emotionally resilient you will become.

Introduction to section

Failure is a taboo subject. Failure is bad. Success is great but failure is to be avoided at all costs. When and why did failure get such a bad reputation?

I have even been told by certain managers and bosses over the years, "Failure is not an option."

I have bad news for them. Like it or not failure most certainly is an option.

I do have good news for you though. What will offer you far more in the way of useful options, is how you choose to deal with and respond to the concept of failure; as well as your relationship to the concept of the fear of failure.

In my experience the fear of failure causes far more damage and creates more emotional negativity than most actual instances of failure. It can create a paralysis which prevents people trying new things. Fear of failure creates guaranteed failure due to things never getting started at all. If they are started they are often attempted in a half-hearted way; the fear of failure is built right in and can become a self-fulfilling prophesy.

Here is an example many of you will be familiar with. Babies have a powerful almost overwhelming desire to learn to walk. Amongst many other built-in desires, they have a need to stand up and learn to use their legs and walk. They keep falling over yet they try again and again. They get frustrated time and time again but they do not give up. They do not give up and resign themselves to failure because they do not understand the concept of failure. Giving up is not an available option because they have not been taught about failure yet. They do not yet know it even exists let alone they have to have a fear of it.

You read it correctly, the fear of failure gets taught to us, and usually at an early age. Our parents, siblings, teachers, colleagues and just about everyone around us, inform us about failure and we develop our understanding of it through their input. We are born with many personality traits which shape the way we develop as people and we learn many more as we grow up and mature. Some of these are useful throughout our lives, some are useful for a while then get changed or dropped as we move on and some are not useful at all but we keep them anyway. Fear of failure then is definitely a concept we are taught by others. It is how we are taught about the concept of failure and how we respond to it determines how it affects us in life. Each of us has an understanding of, and relationship to, failure which is unique to us and it comes with useful or non-useful conceptual baggage.

The good news for you is you can ditch some or all of the non-useful baggage and replace it with the useful variety.

So two incredibly important question to ask yourself are: What exactly does failure mean to me? What can I do to transform my understanding of and responses to failure?

Here are two lines from the poem If by Rudyard Kipling:

"If you can meet with Triumph and Disaster
And treat those two impostors just the same"

It is a superb work which captures the overall concept of resilience brilliantly and I recommend reading it regularly. I have placed a copy in the virtual appendix but you can look it up online easily enough.

Kipling was right on the money. Triumph and disaster are indeed imposters and should be treated the same.

We will look very closely at this whole idea of failure and success and transforming your conceptual baggage in the next section.

"That's all very well and good." I hear you cry. "How about some help with the success side of things?"

Funny you asked. We are also going to take a good long look at how to greatly improve your chances of achieving success by setting and completing goals.

To finish off we will look at why perfectionism is a sure-fire success killer and why you would do well to avoid it.

It is only data

As I said previously, failure and the fear of failure are concepts we are taught by others and how we are taught about them affects us throughout our lives. Each of us has a unique personal understanding of failure and it comes with useful or non-useful conceptual baggage.

The baggage I am talking about has come from many sources. All our lives we experience events, interactions and situations which can leave an impression on us. How we interpret and store these experiences determines their baggage value.

Whenever we experience something we experience the something through our five main senses or sensory systems. The fancy terms for these sensory systems are visual, auditory, kinaesthetic (or kinaesthetic), olfactory and gustatory but most people know them as sight, hearing, touch, smell and taste.

As a small aside here, the kinaesthetic sensory system is itself made up of a number of sub-sensory systems but we will just stay at overview level here. As I always say, feel free to dig deeper into this fascinating subject because you can never know about too many interesting things. It keeps life fresh.

We get all of our information via our senses and our brain processes this sensory data and tries to make some sense of it. This is how we perceive the world. Our perception is therefore our reality. There is a huge amount of sensory information entering our systems at any one time; far more than we could consciously deal with on any sensible level. For our purposes, we just need to know our brain passes incoming sensory information through a series of sorting processes or filters in order to handle and make some sense of this information. Any information or understanding gaps are filled in as best as our brain can manage from our existing store of available relevant information. The brain will also carry out a series of comparisons between the current experience and certain stored or reference patterns in order to try to classify the experience and respond to it in the most useful manner. For want of a better term I will call these responses programs. Most of the time the response programs run without us even being aware of them and we go about our lives happily enough.

Reference patterns are important. These are either patterns we are born with or patterns we develop over time. A reference pattern can be strongly encoded or imprinted by repetition over time and when coupled with strong emotional associations at the time of imprinting. Suppose a pattern is formed when we are young and it was imprinted along with an emotional association. If it were repeatedly topped-up over time it would remain strong. For example, if we were told by our parents being good and smiling got us presents, and we did in fact get presents to back this up, then we will likely continue to be good and smile until something or someone changes the behaviour. The reference pattern, in this case the possibility of getting a present, led to us run our "get presents" program. We all have these reference patterns and response programs and most of them will be beneficial or at least harmless. Not all reference patterns or response programs are useful. An extreme case might be a phobia or a very powerful fear and such a high level of fear can be debilitating. For example, the fear of wasps. This fear can occur if you are stung at any time of course but it can happen to children who have never been stung in their lives. If a parent shouts and screams and panics when a wasp is near this emotional association can be enough to imprint an unhelpful pattern. It will probably be reinforced every time a wasp attends a picnic. Now whenever the child sees a wasp they run the "flap and panic" response program. At best this can be annoying to the people around about and the wasp but, at worst, highly likely to result in a real sting for the child. The mind is a powerful thing but it is also prone to unintended or unhelpful responses now and again. If you do suffer from strong phobias I would advise seeking the help of an experienced professional and investigating the many ways you can lessen or even eliminate the problems the phobia or phobias cause you.

We also all have habits ranging from good to neutral to bad. People tend to notice the bad ones more than the good ones in my experience. Habits are strongly imprinted patterns and response programs which we use without thinking too much about them. We discover how deeply imprinted they are when we try to change them. Ask anyone who has tried to give up smoking or stick to a diet.

We also develop beliefs and values about things we feel are true or false and what is important in life. Once again, these are learnt concepts. Learnt first-hand, or experientially, directly through our senses or passed on to us indirectly by significant people or other strong influences in our lives. Values and beliefs are reference patterns too and we have our response programs for these as well.

Finally we get to look at failure in light of the new information above. We considered the scenario of babies learning to walk and noted the fact they have no real concept of failure. I believe we can understand this more easily now. They have the desire of wanting to walk; they may also be trying to copy their peers and parents. They will develop an initial reference pattern to falling over but the only response program they have when this happens, apart from some occasional tears and howls of frustration, is to get up and try again. If the parent supports and encourages the child at this point, the desire to walk increases in response to the encouragement. The encouragement pattern leads to a "trying harder to walk" response program.

It does not take a great leap of the imagination to see these early reference patterns can be reinforced positively, as above, or negatively if the parents offered little or no support and encouragement.

Any activity we undertake has to be judged against some criteria in order to ascertain whether the activity succeeds or fails.

This is what Rudyard Kipling referred to in the poem If. This is an important point to understand. Success and failure are subjective attributes. One person's failure could be another's success. Criteria can be set internally and we measure ourselves against the target. The criteria can also be set externally by other people or situations and we are judged accordingly. Can we trust these criteria to be fair or even accurate? How are these criteria arrived at?

Some criteria are set by society at large and based on years of collective knowledge as to what is good or bad. These are generally called laws and although they are still subjective the authorities prefer you adhere to them.

Rightly or wrongly, criteria will be set for us all the time and we cannot avoid being measured against them. We are either above the mark or below it. Success or failure.

How do we know which side we are on?

In any experience or interaction with the world we take in our sensory data and try to make sense of it. When we respond or react in some way we check our sensory data again to gain information relating to any changes or effects which our response created. This is called feedback and it is fundamental to our ability to function effectively in the systems of which we are a part.

The feedback we get from the world informs us if we have succeeded or failed.

If we are somehow rewarded for success we will strive for more of it. We will have had some positive feedback, either as praise from someone or something significant to us or a strong positive internal dialogue or self-generated emotional effect. If all we knew in life was success after success there would be no need for this guide or even resilience itself for that matter. I do not know about you but my life certainly does not work like this.

Failures happen. Small failures, big failures and even catastrophic terminal failures happen. It is an inescapable fact of everyone's life. Life is an inherently risky undertaking. A life lived without risk is a poor sort of life. If you never try anything you will never succeed at anything.

It is our relationship and response to these failures and successes, which has a huge bearing on our emotional resilience.

We all have a different natural response to failure; let us call it a baseline failure response. There is little point going over any old ground and blaming people or events in our past for issues we might feel we have now. We discussed this in part one so get over it. We need to take full responsibility and be in the active stance or in control of what we do from now on.

We know we cannot alter, contest or ignore all of the criteria against which we are measured. What we can do is examine and control the way we determine and respond to feedback on failure or success then take steps to alter things where possible and if needed.

Reinhold Niebuhr's Serenity Prayer sums it up well:

Grant me the serenity to accept the things I cannot change,
The courage to change the things I can,
And the wisdom to know the difference.

Ask yourself this question, "What exactly does failure mean to me?" Take some time over this one. It is a thought experiment which demands a considered and honest answer.

If you came back with largely negative answers you are not alone. Most people generally see and experience failure in a negative light. If you already have a positive relationship with failure and answered in an upbeat way, then good on you. Keep it up and push for even more success whenever you can.

Many of us have been taught to see failure as a problem or disaster to be avoided at all costs. Something to be feared and hated. The thought of an embarrassing failure puts many of us off trying new things. Failure can represent a lack or loss of control.

Over time some people can get used to accepting failure as their lot in life, they can struggle to succeed at anything. Failure is a known quantity and they have become comfortable with the idea and the associated emotions. They feel no need to try too hard because nobody expects them to do well anyway. What is the point? They might say to themselves, "If I succeed they will just expect more next time and then they will just be disappointed." They create self-fulfilling prophesies and even develop a real fear of success itself; when extreme this behaviour is known as a Jonah complex. These people believe they will fail and start to value not trying something over trying something because it is their default response program. It is a sad cycle which they seem unable to break out of on their own.

So, what can you do to transform your understanding of, and responses to, failure?

Here is the main thing to remember. Feedback is simply data. All data is fundamentally neutral until some meaning is attached. When you say you have failed at something you have attached meaning to the feedback data you have received. When you have been told by someone else you have failed, and then accepted the fact you have failed, you have attached meaning to the feedback data received from the other person. Their criteria has now become your criteria.

Often when we say we have failed, or accept from others we have failed, our self-esteem can take a knock. We weave this new information into our personal narrative and it immediately begins to run as part of our self-image movie. If we allow this to happen again and again we can begin to see ourselves as failures rather than just having failed to meet certain criteria or outcomes in one particular context. This can be psychologically debilitating over time.

This accepting the failure criteria of others scenario happens all the time. Much of it has to do with how much store or faith we put in the judgement of others as well as the context within which the judgement was made. People make judgements about others all the time. We all do it; you, me and everybody; with no exceptions.

In order to break out of this cycle of automatically accepting failure criteria, our own and those of others, the key thing to do is closely examine the failure criteria you set yourself and the value you place on the failure criteria of others. In other words you need to examine your strategy or program for attaching meaning to incoming feedback data. Where exactly do you set your bars and why? Are you setting them based on your true inner values and the things you really want? Are you instead basing them on what you think you ought to do based on the expectations of others? You also have to ensure you look at it in a balanced and unbiased way. Maintaining balance is something we can all often struggle to do.

There is a full section on dealing with feedback and reflection as well as biased thinking in part three so I will not say much more here other than to observe; a great mindset to maintain when considering the topic of success and failure is one of open minded curiosity and willingness to learn.

Rather than simply labelling something a success or a failure, you are much better served by learning as much as possible from the experience as a whole. This is where your analysis and reflection comes in. You can now weave this positive learning experience into your self-esteem narrative and this will serve to bolster your self-image too. You are now a learner who grows more effective with every experience and not someone who is prey to every arbitrary benchmark which life puts before us.

You cannot do this with every benchmark of course because some, statutory laws of the land for example, are generally non-negotiable. However, by altering or disregarding arbitrary targets and the judgements of other, always make every effort to put your own stamp on the situation and learn as much as possible. Your self-esteem and emotional resilience will grow ever stronger each time you do this.

Embrace the feedback from every situation and label it as simply neutral rather than good or bad. Treat feedback as a generous friend who will provide huge amounts of information and provide valuable energy or fuel for your next attempts.

Here are two of my favourite quotes:

Alan Alda, the actor, director, and screenwriter, in his 1980 Commencement Speech delivered at Connecticut College, said, "Be brave enough to live creatively. The creative is the place where no one else has ever been. You have to leave the city of your comfort and go into the wilderness of your intuition. You cannot get there by bus, only by hard work, risking and by not quite knowing what you are doing. What you will discover will be wonderful: Yourself."

Friedrich Nietzsche, in Twilight of the Idols, 1888 wrote, "What does not kill me, makes me stronger."

Learning from all feedback is the key to transforming it into your ally.

Not learning from feedback is what I consider to be a real failure.

Goals

We are often told by the self-help gurus success is all about goals.

Goals. Goals. Goals.

It seems we are always being encouraged to have goals. To set goals. To achieve goals. We are constantly told all successful people set and achieve goals. The reason for this is goals are generally helpful and beneficial things to set and achieve. Setting goals works. When designed well and planned well a goal can indeed help you achieve your desired outcome.

The problem for many of us is nobody has ever shown us how to design or plan a goal effectively or practically. It can also be hard to know what to aim at in the first place. Many of us can dream up grand schemes and call them goals. Take for example our new year resolutions which we start enthusiastically enough then find our resolve rapidly crumbles and we completely give up. I have even heard coaching clients saying "I am not a goal achiever, more of a free spirit." This is just an excuse not to even try and achieve anything of substance. Have you ever found yourself saying anything like this?

This is about emotional resilience so why am I talking about goals?

The answer; setting the right goals can help you become more emotionally resilient.

How will goals help?

The following is an extract from Alice in Wonderland by Lewis Carroll (Rev C L Dodgson) which nicely captures why goals are so important and useful. Alice is talking to the Cheshire Cat.

"Cheshire Puss," she began, rather timidly, as she did not at all know whether it would like the name: however, it only grinned a little wider. "Come, it's pleased so far," thought Alice, and she went on. "Would you tell me, please, which way I ought to go from here?"
"That depends a good deal on where you want to get to," said the Cat.
"I do not much care where," said Alice.
"Then it does not matter which way you go," said the Cat.
"So long as I get SOMEWHERE," Alice added as an explanation.
"Oh, you are sure to do that," said the Cat, "if you only walk long enough."

If you wander about our glorious planet aimlessly you will be sure to visit many places, see many new things and meet many fascinating people. You will also see dreadful places and meet people you would rather not meet. You will also spend some of your time and effort going down dead ends then backtracking, getting lost or crossing the same path many times as you go round and round in circles.

Likewise, if you have a destination to walk to, Liverpool for example, and you start in Gloucester, it is no good to you walking in any other direction other than towards the north.

If you ever want to achieve or complete something you have to have an end result you want to achieve or arrive at and a way to get there. You need a destination and a direction to go in. It is not a difficult concept but you might be amazed at how many people expect to achieve a goal yet have no defined outcome or plan of how to accomplish it.

Setting effective goals with inspiring outcomes and a clear plan of action will help you become more emotionally resilient. Having effective goals will allow you to consider in advance any negative emotional events, and plan your response options to them, in context with your desired outcomes.

This is important to bear in mind. Whenever a negative emotional impact occurs you will find you have a range of response options available to you. Some of these options will be easier to take than others. In the absence of any direction or goal you will likely choose the easier ones. Let us be honest here, most of us would; we are only human after all. The easier options, however, might not be the best ones you could have chosen. Here is the thing though, when you have a compelling and inspiring goal, which you are fully committed to, driving you forward you will tend to choose those options which keep you to your chosen path. These options may be the harder choices available to you but, in the context of your goal, they will likely be far more useful to you in the longer-term.

Here is another thing. Humans are easily distracted creatures. You, I and everyone else will naturally shift our attention to whatever new shiny thing, perceived crisis, fun activity or even patch of greener grass which comes into our sphere of awareness. It is termed our monkey mind and I think this is a great description. Left to its own devices, this monkey mind will wander and latch on to anything it finds interesting. When we are focused we are capable of huge concentration and productivity so being able to force our attention on a desired outcome is definitely a good thing.

Setting and achieving goals answers this need for focus. Having a motivating and compelling goal, with which we can maintain direction, can control our monkey mind; making it sit still to ensure it gets on with the tasks in hand. Of course the monkey mind will not be happy with this arrangement but it is tough. Control it or it will control you.

For these reasons, I believe it is well worth spending time examining some goal setting concepts and various practical techniques for you to try out.

Goals will help with resilience and being more resilient will help you achieve your goals. I always like a bit of circularity.

There are many useful resources on goal setting out there and, as always, I would urge you to read and research as widely as possible in order to get the best from your self-development. The following sections on goals and goal setting are the result of many years of my own study, experiment and experience as well as my work with many coaching clients from many backgrounds.

Eustress

We discussed negative stress and its negative physical and emotional effects in an earlier section. Too much negative stress causes distress. When most people think about or discuss stress it is the negative aspects which they generally consider.

Many people are unaware of another type of stress which is actually a positive form of stress. It is called eustress. Here is a quick fire introduction to this concept.

Eustress is a term coined by endocrinologist Hans Selye. The "eu" part comes from the Greek meaning either "well" or "good" so the word eustress literally means "good stress."

All things are relative and, in any given situation, what can severely stress one person will not stress another. If I find myself near a cliff edge for example I get extremely nervous yet there are people who would love to climb up the same cliff purely for the exhilaration of it all. It is the same for eustress. They are in fact two sides of the same coin. If you drew a graph of stress arousal against performance for a challenging task you would get a curve. The left side of the curve would represent eustress and the part of the curve on the right would represent distress. There is such a graph in the virtual appendix.

If someone encounters a new situation or attempts a new task it will initially be a challenge. In our working environments you will find some people continually seek out fresh challenges for themselves and some people have challenges thrust upon them whether they want them or not. If you want to get the best from yourself or your staff it would make sense to maintain any stress in the eustress zone.

To define it more fully, eustress occurs when there is a slight gap between present state and target and the person is slightly pushed, but not overwhelmed. The immediate goal is attainable but is still a challenge. The real benefit of any challenge is to motivate a person toward overall improvement as well as achieving a goal. So eustress is a good thing but remember we can have too much of a good thing. Continually striving for objectives which are never attained can quickly lead back to distress; give yourself a break now and again.

As I mentioned earlier, eustress and distress are relative concepts and are mainly determined by how able individuals feel when rising to meet a challenge. If you are generally down on your abilities, then many tasks will create distress for you and vice versa. If you believe you can do something then generally speaking, and given the required physical or mental attributes are in place to do it, you can do it.

There is another term to add to the mix and it is the concept of flow. Mihaly Csikszentmihalyi, a positive psychologist, created the concept of flow, which can be described as those moments when someone is utterly absorbed in an enjoyable task or activity with no awareness of time passing or their environment. The state of flow is a highly productive state in which the person experiences their optimum performance. They display task absorption, activity enjoyment and an intrinsic or self-generated motivation toward the task or activity at hand.

How do you define or recognise this flow state? Well, if you have ever looked up from something you have been doing really well for what felt like a short time then realised several hours have passed and your tea is cold; you have been in a flow state and when it happens, it feels great.

Some people have been known to delay tasks in order to add enough additional eustress to the task because they are actively seeking the exhilaration of this flow state. Athletes talk about "being in the zone" and this is in fact another description of the flow state. Flow is considered a peak emotional and productive experience. Remember the eustress/distress graph I mentioned? Flow would be the represented by the area very slightly left of the peak.

So your mindset is a significant factor in determining whether you will experience distress or eustress during a given task. Optimistic people and those with high self-esteem will have more eustress experiences. A positive mindset increases the chances of eustress and a positive response to activity induced stress. Sadly, a negative outlook and low self-esteem will produce more distress.

In their private lives, many people engage in eustress generating activities such as playing or watching sport, physical exercise at the gym or on a bike, riding roller coasters or skydiving, gambling, etc... These same people may also be the ones who welcome and even seek out the chance to take on new roles or projects at work. They are often perceived as risk takers by their less challenge-oriented peers. Where would you say you are on the eustress/distress spectrum right now?

The goal success trinity

Many people have an idea or notion about something they would like to achieve and they call it a goal. They do not think it through fully and charge ahead with half a plan at best. They fail and get discouraged. They consign goals and goal setting to their mental waste bin. What are they missing? Have you ever done this?

There are three key elements which must be in place before you can even contemplate achieving a goal. You will need to plan a goal carefully in order to have a path to follow and we will discuss setting goals and planning in the next section. You will also need to monitor progress and review your position along the way too. You will need tenacity and staying power. These things are indeed all needed for goal achievement. However, if you do not have the three things discussed in this section in place all the planning, monitoring or reviewing in the world will not help you. Without the goal success trinity, as I call it, in place your goal will be dead and buried before it has a chance to succeed.

What makes up this goal success trinity?

The trinity comprises purpose, commitment and action; in that order. Let us look at each of these in turn.

Purpose is your goal fuel. Use good goal fuel and you will be rocket powered. Use bad goal fuel and you will struggle to move at all. Purpose is your great big why. It is the focus of your desire and motivation. If you do not have a great big why driving you forward and powering your ambition then you will fail. You may start out with good intentions and you may even take some initial action but inevitably you will run out of juice and grind to a halt.

For example, if you intend to diet and go to the gym three times a week to build muscle and lose two stone in weight in order to fit into your summer wardrobe you will probably start out well and even make a little progress. You will rapidly encounter barriers and run out of motivation because your purpose is weak. After all it is easier just to buy some bigger clothes, you like shopping anyway, your wardrobe needs an update and so on and so forth. You know all the hundreds of justifications we can give ourselves in order to give up.

What if, instead, you have just been to the park to play ball with your young child and you realised how out of condition and unhealthy you are? What if you are picturing yourself in six or seven years being too unfit to play at all? Your child might even be embarrassed to be seen with you on sports days or at the park. There may be worse to come for you and your family if you do not make a change. Now you have got some rocket fuel. You have a purpose. You are doing it for you and your family. You will not just aim for a thinner waistline, you will likely aim for an entirely new lifestyle in order to be there for your child and other loved ones. You will start your diet and you will go to the gym at least three times a week to hit your targets.

This is the true power of purpose.

Once you have a powerful purpose which gets you fully motivated, you need to add some commitment to the mix.

Commitment is the solemn promise you make to yourself to complete the task or goal you have set. Commitment signifies your intention to do something. It is like a contract so treat it as such and stick to it. Starting a goal with no commitment means it will be doomed to fail.

A key element in commitment is accountability. Saying what you will do and doing what you say. Accountability means taking responsibility for the results of the things you say or do.

One term used a lot in the goal achievement world is willpower. It is the ability to stick to our commitment and keep on with the plan no matter what distracts or hinders us. One huge problem with this is we humans are generally lacking in willpower. I am the first to hold my hand up and admit it; I do not have a lot of willpower. My clients do not have a lot either. Most people I know lack true willpower. We find it easy to let ourselves off the commitment hook whenever the going gets tougher than expected. We self-justify our inaction and chip away at our purpose until the fuel no longer powers us and we give up. We effectively rip up our contract with ourselves. I have been there and I know many of my clients have too. Have you?

One of the best ways I know of creating guaranteed accountability and massive commitment is to tell someone else about your goal. Even better, tell many people about it. Make it public knowledge. Tell as many people as you can. You will be reluctant to fail under these conditions and you will take full responsibility for achieving success.

Many people do not want to go public with their most personal goals because they feel people will think them greedy or selfish. I understand this and in fact I do not generally talk about my goals with anyone. If this is you then there is another hugely valuable tool available to enable you to generate high commitment and accountability. Write your goals down on paper. Write them down and keep them safe. Refer to them at regular intervals. The act of writing goals down means it is harder to con yourself with feeble excuses. It is harder to ignore our purpose when it is there in black and white; it is like a proper written legal contract. Do it by hand, not computer, as the act of writing by hand connects you more fully with your goal and increases your commitment.

The final ingredient in the goal success trinity is action. Action is what creates success or failure. Earlier we looked at feedback and how you use it to measure success and failure. In fact, they only exist in relative terms when measured against feedback. Well, without action there will be no feedback. You have to take some action. You have to create outcomes of some kind in order to measure their effectiveness.

Every journey starts with a single step and continues only with more steps. Establishing purpose and stating commitment are both forms of action. Once you have created purpose and commitment you can take action to plan your goal. You then need to take more action and commence step one, achieve step one, commence step two and so on. Action is an ongoing multi-stage process not a single event. The minute you stop taking action your goal progress will stall and your goal will fail.

Hopefully you can see how the three parts of the goal success trinity rely on each other and also create each other. Action takes work, work takes energy and energy requires fuel. Purpose creates fuel and commitment channels the fuel to power your action engine.

Later on we will take a look at some of the potential barriers and distractions which can erode your purpose and commitment and prevent you taking the right actions at the right times. For now, just be aware before any useful planning comes the goal success trinity of purpose, commitment and action.

Goal setting models

Goal setting and planning, like most things in life in my opinion, work most successfully when a process model is followed. A good process model ensures nothing is left out on the way to your objective. Of course, the results obtained are only ever as good as the process you follow.

The word model in this case is a somewhat fancy term for something which can be used (e.g. a system, framework, pattern, workflow, procedure, etc...) as an example to follow or imitate in order to achieve a desired and specified outcome.

We will look at three goal setting processes in this section and briefly discuss the merits and downsides of each before moving on and looking at an overall strategy or process you can use as is or adapt to create your best possible goals.

Get SMART.

The most common business goal setting tool is known as SMART goals. If you have ever had an objective set for you it will likely be based on SMART criteria. You may have been encouraged to set your own appraisal goals in this format too. If you have ever wondered about it, the term SMART was first coined by one Mr George T. Doran in the November 1981 issue of Management Review Magazine. Business people love acronyms and the word SMART represents goals generally taken to be Specific, Measurable, Attainable, Relevant and Time bound.

There have been lots of variations, such as the SMARTER goal which has Evaluate and Review tacked on the end, but they add little to the overall approach which is a controlled and conservative style of goal planning.

This SMART approach may be all well and good in the business world where by and large people want a small stretch but not too much of a stretch. The risks of project or task failure are sometimes very high so the taking of chances or risks is not encouraged by many managers. I personally view this cautious approach as a huge deficiency for both the organisation and the individual employee. Permission to try and to fail and to therefore learn is not usually given and we have discussed issues around this in an earlier section.

Specific goals are clear and unambiguous. They might include how, what, why, who, where and which elements. They work best when stated in the positive so do this whenever possible.

Measurable goals have criteria for measuring progress and identifying final success which serve as both guide and motivation.

Attainable goals which are realistic and achievable by the individual or team. There is usually a small to medium stretch to generate productive eustress.

Relevant goals are generally aligned with both the individual, the project and the organisation of which they are a part.

Time bound goals create a deadline commitment are often intended to establish a sense of urgency and focus.

For example, "I would like to get better at organising things," is not really a SMART goal. Too vague and unfocused. How can you measure or quantify your results? On the other hand, stating, "I am going to tidy the office stationery cabinet in order to improve stock control. The task will be complete when every item is in an appropriate and clearly labelled storage bin. Doing this will make everybody's life easier and I will make sure I do it by four o'clock this afternoon," would be an example of a workable, albeit conservative, SMART goal. It is not perfect; they never are and I am sure you could do better. Go ahead and give it a go.

Many people therefore, through their experience at work, are familiar and comfortable with the SMART goals approach outlined above. If they try and generate any personal goals at all, they are likely to design SMART goals. If the same timidity and safety based approach is applied to your personal goals they are likely to be weak and not particularly motivating for you. Are these goals you are likely to achieve? Actually, you will probably have a good chance of achieving them because they are generally quite conservative and safe. Are you super-motivated to achieve them? If you do achieve them are they going to rock your or anyone else's world? My answer to both the last two questions is an emphatic NO!

To sum up SMART goals, they lend themselves to a very analytical and logical approach. There is not much room for emotions or feelings in there so I suggest they work best for clearly definable and distinct work activities or project based tasks rather than life changing personal dream goals.

Is there any other process you could use which does take emotions and feelings into account?

Get well-formed.

Amongst other things, I am a certified Master Practitioner of Neuro-linguistic Programming or NLP for short. I love NLP and it has given me a radically different view of my life and my behaviour. NLP is becoming more and more popular and I would recommend you take a look into it. There is a wealth of information online and you will find a lot of useful ideas and tools you can use or adapt. As a simple description of a huge field of study, the early developers of NLP (Richard Bandler, John Grinder and others) closely studied several highly skilled individuals to distil the elements they believed made them so skilled and effective at what they did. Bandler and Grinder studied the physiology, attitudes, beliefs, language and behavioural strategies which their study participants used to achieve their outcomes. It turned out when the distilled elements were used, in similar circumstances and by other practitioners, results were obtained which were similar in quality to the highly skilled study subjects. This technique became known as modelling.

A key question these early NLP modellers asked was what makes some people more successful than others. They found the way in which successful people defined the goals they set themselves gave them a huge edge over most other people in terms of achievement. It became known as the process of Well-Formed Outcomes or WFOs for short.

By applying the WFO process, which consists of six questions, you can create a much more emotionally balanced and contextual goal which will blend more easily with your values and the values of other people around you. There are some similarities with SMART but also some crucial differences.

Q. What do you want? This is your desired outcome stated in the positive. State "I want to be healthy" rather than "I want to give up smoking."

Q. Is it really yours to achieve? This examines if you can start and maintain the process to its conclusion. If it relies on someone else doing something or it is something you have no control over then it will not make a good goal.

Q. How will you know you have it? This is where you run through, and store in your memory, the sensory specific evidence which will let you know you have achieved your outcome. What will you see, hear, touch, smell or taste?

Q. Under what context? Is your goal desirable in every context? For example, you might ask yourself when you want it or when do you not want it. Important questions.

Q. Is it a good fit? This is an ecology check which relates your goal to your sense of self. The closer it matches your identity and sense of purpose the more the outcome will attract and motivate you. Who else do you want it to work for?

Q. What might you lose if you achieve your goal? Giving up smoking might help your health but you may also enjoy being a bit of a rebel. What alternative goal can let you become a healthier rebel? Take the time to find out what is really important for you to keep and take forward.

The process of forming a goal using the WFO method works well for individuals but the approach works particularly effectively if you go through it with a trusted friend or even a coach if you have one. Have them challenge your answers at every stage to ensure you really have looked carefully at every facet. It takes longer but the result is often far better.

To sum up well-formed outcomes, they lend themselves well to emotional and values based personal goal setting. They can lead to bigger and more ambitious plans which look to preserve what you want to keep and maintain a balance with the needs of others. Having the ability to fully immerse yourself in a vivid sensory future space makes this kind of goal setting very satisfying and compelling. It can take a little practice and a willingness to experiment. Give it a go.

What about really big, mad, outrageous, chance of a lifetime goal setting? Is there a process you could use for this?

Try getting WACKY.

We discussed WFOs and SMART goals in the last section and I now want to discuss developing bigger and better personal goals. I developed this idea around 4 years ago and I still love the ethos behind it; I use it constantly on myself and with my clients when planning their huge success goals.

This may seem obvious but it is often forgotten or ignored; highly successful people set big goals. I contend if you are going to set a personal goal then you might as well set a big one too. I recommend you make it as WACKY as possible. The more WACKY the better!

Goals are the fundamental tool for personal and organisational development. After all, how can you know you have achieved something or even improved your situation at all if you have no target or benchmark to work from? We discussed planning SMART goals and developing Well-Formed Outcomes in the last section and now you will see how to use them beneficially in a wider context.

Setting bigger goals simply provides you more of a stretch, more eustress, more emotional resilience and more of a driver for your overall purpose. Using the WACKY format allows you to overcome any timidity or perceived limitations in your goal setting.

I always aim to stretch myself – it is the only way I know to grow and develop as a person and to be able to help others more effectively; this has always been my driving force and purpose. Partial failure of one of my WACKY goals will often be far better than most people's mediocre goals.

These WACKY goals are generally my over-arching long-range life goals so they will certainly contain lots of mini-goal stages which is fine. Many small (SMART and Well-Formed) steps will add up to a huge WACKY journey. It makes life interesting.

Here then is the WACKY goal setting process and I would recommend you go through this process with a trusted friend or professional coach to get the very best from it.

Let us start with the acronym.

The W represents wonderful. It is meant to be a great goal so if it does not fill you with wonder, what is the point? It has to be something which makes your imagination work hard. You want it to play on your mind and draw you on down the road less travelled.

The A represents animating. Again, if it does not get you fired up and raring to go then find another goal which will. You want your pulse to quicken when you think about it. It must create passion.

The C represents colossal. Make it big, bigger and bigger still. If it does not make you stop and think "hold the phone, that's big even by my standards, people will think I am mad" then rethink it and just make it bigger. Make it a huge hairy gorilla of a goal which if achieved will make you think "Yeah that was a good one!" If people saw your goal walking toward them on the street they would cross the road to avoid it. It will be a kick-butt ferocious slavering monster of a goal.

The K represents killer. Try to make it undeniably unique and special; when achieved it will be well worth any sacrifice and effort you made. Try to be a trend setter not a follower. Blaze a trail.

The Y represents yours. You have to set and own your WACKY goal with all your heart and soul. Do not adopt anyone else's goal unless it is a stepping stone to your higher objective. Ensure it is personal to you and you will pour huge energy into it. The bar is set high. In my case for example, roller skating backwards up Everest might excite someone but it is just not my goal. My personal WACKY goals are safely written down. Choose goals which mesh with your core values as an individual and unique human being.

Take some time to think about each stage of the goal process. Challenge yourself along the way or have someone challenge your assumptions and any self-imposed limiting beliefs. Look at the next section for question ideas and some of the things which may hold you back if not considered. Refine and drill down to what you really want.

Remember everything is relative so one person's big goal may seem small to someone else. Who cares? We are talking about you here. Your big important goal is the one to reach for.

When you have finished, make sure you write your goal or goals down.

Go through them again on a regular basis and please also bear this in mind as you do so. Goals are meant to be drivers for improvement. They are not shackles to keep you going headlong towards disaster. This guide is about emotional resilience. It is an inevitable fact of life, things change and flexibility helps with resilience. Be flexible with your goals too. If your priorities change then your goals can change as well. If you find the thing you had your heart set on no longer fires you up; find something else which does. Repeat your goal setting process of choice in the context of the new situation. You control your goals not the other way round.

That is it. This technique and mind set works but I am not going to tell you it is easy. Use SMART and Well-Formed goal setting for the smaller things but be WACKY for the big important ones.

If you are going to pursue goals in your life I recommend making them huge, awesome, life-changing, jaw-dropping, pulse quickening goals which are worth your effort and time. Aim for the stars and even if you come up short you will still have had a hell of a ride and be higher than most everyone else. You will have learnt valuable lessons and be more than motivated to try again. In my experience it is always far better to regret the things you have done than live a life regretting the ones you did not try.

Try and design some of your own WACKY goals for your life; you may be surprised where they take you.

So all three processes are now covered. Which one could be best for you to use?

I recommend using all three and the next section will describe a practical way to do this.

Bringing it all together

Hopefully you can now acknowledge having good goals will increase your resilience. Negative emotional events will distract you far less when you are focusing on a goal or goals. In fact, all distractions will have less impact when you have more focus on a goal. Therefore, it will pay you to develop some goals to focus on. If you want to come up with a personal goal which will motivate you and drive you forward then the simple answer is use all three goals setting processes together. Cover all the bases. Create a WACKY Well-formed SMART Outcome.

Here is the strategy which I adopt and the one which I encourage my clients to go through when setting their goals. It will pay you dividends when you create a goal for yourself or indeed help someone else to set one. Helping people is almost always a good thing.

You need a purpose for your goal; a great big why. Outcomes are important and as all three methods require an outcome, let us start there and let us start big.

Here is where the WACKY system comes into its own. Let your mind drift and think about the huge goal which brings a smile to your face and quickens your pulse. Do not look at details yet, look at the big picture. Do not even worry if it is actually achievable at this stage. The whole point is aim big. If you do not achieve this goal you will still achieve some amazing things just by aiming this high and trying.

Work through the WACKY stages and write down the big picture hairy gorilla goal you selected and refined.

This is the time to apply the well-formed outcome process to the goal. Do not think of this as a way to reduce or dilute the goal in any way. It is simply a way to refine it still further and ensure it definitely works for you and your values. What might you lose? Is there a way to preserve the things you want to keep from your current life? Add these things into the WACKY goal because the next phase will require this additional information in order to produce a workable plan.

Let us look at a seemingly simple example. Suppose you came up with the WACKY goal of winning a gold medal at the Olympics. Is this actually a WACKY goal for you? If you are already a top class sports person in a particular discipline and you already perform at an international level then it is not necessarily a huge leap to consider or aspire to win gold at the Olympics. If you are middle aged person like myself who goes to the gym two or three times a week simply to avoid getting any fatter then this goal would definitely be WACKY. My good lady wife just pointed out a better description of this goal might be "insane." No matter - let us look deeper at this from a well-formed outcome perspective. In fact, I will put myself in your position and do the WFO from my perspective.

As it stands the goal is positive but vague; we will need to work on this. Can I do it through to completion? Again, some work needed here. I will know when I have it because there will be a golden medal hanging round my neck. No obvious ambiguity regarding context so this is fine. It is a goal which my friends and family would enjoy and I would like them to feel a part of it too. What I do not want is to risk any serious injuries, move away from home for any length of time during any training and I do not want to have to live in a gym or pound the streets in trainers.

This is all a bit different now. Let us do a quick bit of realistic research here. I have just looked up the list of Summer Olympic sports and notice they almost all involve things which I am not built for, are too dangerous or I simply do not want to do. I am a good yacht sailor but Olympic sailing is all about dinghies and I like bigger boats. There are two interesting possibilities which I had not thought of until I looked at the list; archery and shooting. Both of these could meet my context and ability criteria. I actually fancy shooting because I have done it before and I could select rifle, pistol or shotgun. My family and friends could support me and might class any competition travel as a holiday. It could of course take me a long while so, as I am reasonably fit and age is not necessarily a barrier to shooting success, I will give myself until I am seventy years old to get it done. At the time of writing this there are five realistically possible Olympics available for achieving my goal. Let us draft the new WACKY but well-formed goal:

I will win an Olympic shooting gold medal before I am seventy years old.

It is not a great deal different from the original WACKY goal and I think it is still perfectly WACKY from my perspective. By applying the WFO process it has now gone from just being a potentially mad idea to something I can actually picture myself achieving. We will now look at planning how it could be broken down and approached in order to start moving along my theoretical, yet eminently achievable, path to Olympic glory.

Now comes a different tactic. Even though it is now well-formed this goal as it stands is still far too big. This is what makes it WACKY and interesting. For anyone to aim at such a big result right from the start is a long shot at best. The inevitable result will be failure and disillusion. This will not help with your resilience either.

The trick is to break any big project or complex task into bite-sized and manageable chunks. Big goals are no different. I will call each chunk a sub-goal. Each one of these sub-goals can be further broken down into sub-sub-goals if required. Remember the journey is often as important as the destination. Let us try and make the journey pleasant as well.

Some people are very detail oriented and are quite comfortable with the idea of breaking something into numerous smaller parts. The issue with them is there are sometimes so many options generated, they simply do not know which small step to start off with let alone how to navigate through them all.

Other people can struggle with the necessity of creating smaller pieces from a larger whole. They cannot create small enough steps to allow them to move begin their journey effectively. If they can do it at all the size of their first sub-goal is often still overwhelming.

Even if you are somewhere in the middle it can be hard to get a useful plan mapped out for a big goal. It can be so hard many people give up at this stage. They do not even get to step one and another great idea bites the dust.

Here is a method which will help everyone get it right.

It can be very difficult to select a first step. We worry, because we might pick the wrong starting point, we could be wasting valuable time and resources by either, heading off course and having to correct ourselves or worse, having to backtrack completely and start again.

Here is the key point. We know the end result is what is really important so why not start there and work backwards.

The concept of starting to design a plan from the end back to the beginning will be familiar to you if you are an engineer. Engineers would call the process Reverse Engineering and it is as good a name as any for what we will do right now. Reverse Goal Engineering.

It involves asking the same question a number of times until you find yourself back at your starting point. Do not try and assign too much detail here or even try to assign any times either. We will get to the real detailed stuff later on.

The question to ask yourself again and again is "What has to have happened in order to have reached this point?"

Get some paper and pens and physically follow along with this as you read. I have included representations of all my diagrams in the virtual appendix. You can find details about the virtual appendix at the end.

Take a piece of paper and either start on the right hand side or at the bottom and write down the outcome in a box. For example, in our Olympic goal scenario it would be me in the gold medal position. Asking the question, "What has to have happened in order to have reached this point?" my first answer might be; I would have had to qualify for the Olympics. Write this down in a new box either to the left of the first box or above it depending on how you started. If I ask the question again I might answer; I became one of the top competitors in Wales. Write it down. Keep asking and the following reverse sequence might occur: I became one of the top competitors in my region, I won my club championship, I bought my own competition gun, I became a member of my current club, I tried several clubs, I tried the sport and liked it and finally I did some research on shooting as a sport. These answers will now form a chain of boxes from left to right or top to bottom on your page. Good work.

Each of these boxes now represents a sub-goal. There is not much detail in them yet but there is no need to worry. Each step is important. An engineer might call these sub-goals black boxes. The concept of a black box in this situation is simply that there is a specified input and a specified output in order to keep the design process going; the actual transformation details and internal steps will be created or specified later.

Now, take another piece of paper and run the process again for each of the black box sub-goals on your first page. Follow the same pattern and start on the right or bottom as you prefer. I like to do them by hand with coloured pens. Some people like sticky note pads, some people like cards pinned onto a cork board. Design your own numbering or cross-referencing system. Feel free to do whatever you like as long as it gets the job done.

As a demonstration, let us pick the box labelled "I bought my own competition gun" and apply the series of same questions process to this. I might now get the sequence: Paid supplier and collected gun, chose supplier, chose gun, obtained licence, sorted security, tried options, did research followed by decided to get my own gun. These boxes can now be thought of as sub-sub-goals. Some stages may be simple enough to stand as they are and some may themselves be black boxes which will need further detailed breakdown work later.

Repeat the same question process for all of the new sub-sub-goal black boxes which require it so you will now generate more pages each with a series of steps relating to a particular sub-sub-goal. Obtaining a licence for example would likely have a number of additional steps of its own.

Keep going until you can simplify no more.

Do you see how this works now? You cannot predict everything in advance but you can see how a whole chain of steps can be built up. There can be quite a build-up of pages and stages but you are unlikely to miss anything critical using this method. If you do miss something vital it is relatively easy to slot the missing piece or page in at the appropriate place. The real beauty is you automatically get down to your first sub-goal, sub-sub-goal or even sub-sub-sub-goal which generates your very first useful step toward your overall goal. In my case it would be research shooting as a sport and even this could be broken down still further. To speed things up you can even run some sub-goals or sub-sub-goals in parallel; if they lend themselves to this approach.

This approach can seem a bit strange and unwieldy at first but it works every time. After a few attempts it becomes second nature. Go ahead and try it with any complex task you have to achieve, do not just save it for goal planning. Give it a go and you might become hooked.

Now you can go ahead and make each stage of your sub-goals or sub-sub-goals into SMART goals in order to get the details down and some timings established. At least do this for the earlier phases so you can get started. You can introduce more of the SMART stuff as and when required.

This system removes the tendency many of us have, myself included, to reach analysis paralysis. We do not need to become overwhelmed. We start with the big picture and work back steadily and confidently down to the details.

You have your big goal. You have confidence it is right for you. You have broken it down into manageable stages and sequential steps. You can now start achieving it.

Go ahead and produce your own WACKY Well-Formed SMART Outcomes.

Is this the end of it now?

No way! I never said it would be easy did I? You have to commit and take action - plans without action are just dreams. Dreams are easy to have and we all have them. Successful people make the plans, commit to them and take action. Resilience and purpose keeps them going. More on this in the next section.

Now a personal disclaimer. The idea of my winning an Olympic gold medal for shooting was purely for illustration purposes. I am certainly not about to do anything like it in reality; writing things like this guide is hard enough for me nowadays.

Keeping on keeping on

The list of potential barriers and hurdles standing between you and your goal, or even between you and the very next step of your goal, is endless. Much has been written about the myriad ways you can give up and admit defeat.

This guide is not intended to be entirely about goals so I will be brief.

If a problem, issue or situation is within your control then control it. Revisit your goal purpose, your commitment, your planning and take the appropriate action to remedy things. All controllable issues can be categorised as either being motivational issues or process issues.

Always remember to be flexible and remain true to yourself. If, after careful review, you no longer wish to pursue a particular goal then drop it and create a new one which ticks all your boxes; now pursue the new goal whilst being resilient like water. It is relentless yet neutral and it gets on with the job no matter what. If what you are doing does not work then try something else which does. Check out next section on the demon of perfection and then forget all about trying to be perfect.

If a problem is beyond your control then accept it and move on; there is only so much you can do. Things happen in life which are beyond anyone's control. Regroup and assess the new situation. Alter and adapt your goals to suit. Start fresh ones if need be. Again be resilient and flexible like water, not hard and unyielding like a diamond. Diamonds break but water does not.

Keep your inner voice on your side and working hard for you. As we discussed in section one, it can be your greatest ally or your worst foe and the choice about which is entirely yours. Keep things in perspective and remain patient. Your self-esteem is a critical part of emotional resilience so keep your inner narrative positive and working strongly in your favour.

Aiming at the far distant big goal can be hard to do consistently which is why we looked at planning sub-goals and even sub-sub-sub-goals and adding them in. I would also urge you to build in celebration targets and milestone activities into your goal and sub-goal plans and stick to them. Celebrate all your victories and achievements, large and small, and celebrate them often. Here is the thing with success. You have read how we can get used to failing if we choose to. We can get so used to little problems chipping away at our life and our self-image we can begin to accept it as the normal situation of our life. You need to understand this; you can also get used to winning by following exactly the same process. If you get used to lots and lots of small wins then the larger ones are not such a reach or a surprise. Make success your new normal. Seek it out and enjoy it whenever you get it.

My grandfather once told me, if I carefully lay one brick a day, before I know it I will have a beautiful wall. Lay your success bricks one at a time and you will eventually have a beautiful wall too.

We will discuss this more in later chapters but do not suffer in isolation. If you encounter a problem or obstacle try reaching out to your support network for help and encouragement. You may well be amazed at how much support you can get if you ask the right questions of the right people.

Review your written goals regularly and monitor your progress, commitment and plans to see if they are still in sync with your aims, values and situation. There may be new people in your life such as partners, children or friends and these new people can affect your values and life goals due to the new responsibilities or shared outlooks you have. Your former dream of bumming round the world drinking with your mates might need re-evaluating if you value your new relationship with the person who wants to settle down and raise children with you. This is fine of course and you can set new goals, either individually or as a couple. It is all good. Remember it is the act of goal setting and planning which aids your resilience and your new resilience can also help achieve the goals. The concept of setting goals is more important than any one goal in particular.

Having patience is a key attribute because some of your goals may take time. Having the patience to keep going along the chosen path until your goal is reached will serve you well. Patience is a key skill in life and emotional resilience and we will look at the topic in more detail a little later.

Another one of the key drivers to goal success is your ability to be tenacious. Tenacity is your ability to stick with something through thick and thin but you must also learn how to let go sometimes. Successful and resilient people know when to keep going and when to stop. We have talked about failure and the importance of learning from mistakes. Keeping going in the face of irrefutable evidence proving something is a bad idea is insanity. Tenacity can all too easily turn into stubbornness. Remember back in part one when we talked about flexibility. It applies to goal achievement as well.

If your goal feels way beyond its sell-by date but you are struggling to let go, try asking yourself the following questions: "Is my ego getting in the way?" A little embarrassment is nothing compared with wasting emotion, time and energy on the wrong path. "Have I simply made a mistake?" Do not carry on with a goal which was poorly chosen. "Who am I trying to impress?" Are you carrying on with a goal which was really meant to impress someone else? So, be kind to yourself and always do the right thing for you and those around you.

The demon of perfection

Here is an amusing little rhyme which makes a lot of sense:

Good, better, best
Never let it rest
'Til the good is better
And the better is best

It definitely sounds like a good code to work from in terms of overall improvement but here is the thing. Where do you stop? What constitutes best?

Do you find yourself failing to finish tasks or projects on time, or even at all, because you are always trying to make them better and better? Do you try to get things exactly right before you release your work or your ideas to the world? If you are great at setting goals or starting projects, great at taking initial action and moving along with your project but poor at finishing them because you keep on polishing before the big reveal then you are likely to be a perfectionist. If this is a trait you exhibit then it may help you to learn you are not alone; it is a big problem for many people.

Am I criticising people with a tendency toward perfectionism? No way, because I have been a perfectionist myself many times. I have gotten bogged down in all sorts of ways, especially when writing. I have to be constantly on my guard against the demon of perfection.

If you have been striving for perfection in anything then I will have to be the bearer of bad news; there is no such thing as perfection. It is a ghost, a phantasm, a myth and you have got more chance of finding a unicorn than of finding something truly perfect.

Seriously, it does not actually exist on any level which is useful to us in our everyday lives. We as humans certainly cannot achieve glorious perfection on anything other than a very coarse level of measurement.

We like to use the word perfect of course but what does it mean? You or I might talk about perfect weather or a perfect sporting pass for example, we might get 10 out of 10 questions right in a pub quiz and call it perfect, someone might be said to have a perfect body or have the perfect life. Some people might agree with us and some people may not. The statements above are all subjective, relative and impermanent. They are examples of how we normally use the term perfect. Now consider a farmer with dry crops. They might not see a cloudless sunny day as being perfect and in reality no one day can be said to be perfect for everyone. In the real world nobody has the perfect body or the perfect life. Beauty is a highly subjective property as is lifestyle choice. The pub quiz example is only true at the end of the particular series of pub quiz questions. If you wanted pub quiz perfection over a longer timescale this would require more and more study and fact memorisation. Perfection in the quiz now becomes more difficult and essentially pointless compared to the amount of effort required. You could not even risk entering a pub quiz in case you got a question wrong. You would have to keep going until you knew everything the quiz master knew or could find out - you would effectively have to know everything.

If this last example strikes you as absurd then you are right. If you are always striving to create the perfect project outcome, task result or idea presentation then you are being just as absurd. If you are trying to make something perfect you will fail. For example, consider this entire written work, a section of it or even this single short sentence. None of them will ever be perfect no matter how many times I rewrite them. I can simply do my best with them and then get them out into the world. If I want to get my writing finished, published and read then I can do no more. You would not be reading this right now if I was still polishing my prose.

What are some of the potential thoughts in the mind of a perfectionist? As a professional coach I have worked with a number of people who could not get things finished. Consider the following reasons for perfectionism; maybe you have some or all of the traits, use the same excuses or know someone else who does.

Many people will say they are trying their best to please others and this is what drives their perfectionism. Let us examine this more closely. Many people say, if something is not perfect, they will worry these others will be disappointed with an inferior result, output or idea. The question often asked is; is it not only right and proper you strive to provide the best output you can for the intended recipients of your efforts? Yes it is and notice the question asked about the "best output you can" and not "perfect" output. Trying to get something perfect for the benefit of others is laudable but ultimately misguided. What is not laudable, however, is the real result of this never achieved perfection. The perfectionist never provides anything at all. No one wins.

This claim about perfectionism being for other people's benefit is an out and out excuse. It is a way of transferring blame onto the unachievable goal of perfection when there is a real root cause. It is a way for the perfectionist to cover up the deeper fears they have inside them.

Generally, the perfectionist non-completer of goals and projects fears other people's reactions and judgements. They worry other people will either ignore them or, worse, criticise them. They worry others will think them weak or stupid for getting something wrong or incomplete. This could not be more wrong or self-defeating for the aspiring creator of brilliance which this type of perfectionist undoubtedly is. The inner critic rears its ugly head and voice again and your self-image and self-esteem takes another battering. Your ability to be emotionally resilient will decrease.

So what about you? If you find yourself tending towards being a perfectionist what is it you actually worry about? Do you fear failure? Do you fear success? Do you expect perfection in others? Do you really believe they expect it of you?

Whatever you fear, the reality is if what you have to offer or say is valued and valuable; people will value it for its own sake and not because it is worked, edited or polished to near perfection. To them it will just be. So pour your passion and love into your creations and ideas, get them out there and people will get them, value them and love them likewise.

There is a law called "The Law of Diminishing Returns." This states, beyond a certain point you get far less improvement in something relative to the amount of work invested to make the improvement. Remember the pub quiz absurdity? The law in action. To put it more simply, once you get something as good as you reasonably can then more work will not make any noticeable difference.

When we looked at goal planning I emphasised the importance of starting with the end in mind. Having a clear result and a vision of how a finished task or goal appears will help you to stop tweaking and polishing when it is actually achieved. This approach will help you tame perfectionism and start to embrace completion and distribution.

Most of the time, the things you may see as potential defects and shortcomings will not even be noticed by other people. Remember, other people are not perfect either. You also have no control over the things other people think and do. They are unique individuals. You are unique so be your own judge, judge yourself fairly and trust in your judgement. Remember, "You can please some of the people all of the time, you can please all of the people some of the time, but you can't please all of the people all of the time." As far as I can tell from my research this beautifully stated phrase is attributable to poet John Lydgate but do not quote me on this.

Make things as good as you can, by any practicable and reasonable measure, then get your work out there. You can always improve it later if you want to. People will give you feedback if you just ask them for it.

I know I can always edit this based on feedback from my readers but, if it is not being read by anyone because I have not published it, then it may as well never have been written at all.

What valuable work or good ideas are you holding onto because it is not "perfect" enough for you?

Stop worrying about things you cannot control, do the best you reasonably can and no more, stop blaming perfectionism, start taking responsibility and get your work out there for everyone's benefit. Your overall ability to be emotionally resilient will improve as a result.

Case study - Pete's story

An acquaintance of mine who I had known on and off for a few years, let us call him Pete to protect his identity, had been banging on for as long as I have had dealings with him about leaving his dead end job, writing his book and becoming a professional speaking sensation. These are great dreams of course and, when he first started talking about it, most people, including myself, thought he was the man to do it. His plans sounded amazing.

Pete would bend people's ear about his ongoing projects whenever they would give him the chance. His natural enthusiasm and obvious conviction of success were engaging enough to keep people listening for a while. He would even ask advice from people if he thought they could help him. Pete knew that, amongst other things, I was an author and a speaker so he asked me for advice and pointers several times and I know he also asked several other friends of mine the same sort of questions.

Here is where things started to go a bit pear shaped with Pete and his amazing plans. People began to see there was no progress and no output. Pete was still in his job and moaning about it as much as ever. He had no book and he certainly never spoke anywhere about anything. People were beginning to realise that he was asking the same questions again and again. They were starting to avoid him and his ever more boring dream spiel; only he did not seem to notice. He would just find someone new and unaware of his reputation to listen to his tales of unrequited stardom.

The last time I saw Pete he had asked me to have a coffee so he could "pick my brains a bit." He said he had some news about his latest book. All the warning signs were there but I ignored them. I am all for being helpful but if you are a coach or consultant and someone asks you this, be on your guard. They will want the world for the cup of coffee and think nothing of eating into your time and energy as if you do not have a life or a business to run. Am I sounding cynical? Maybe, but on the particular day in question I must have been feeling a bit generous; I met Pete for the coffee.

Straight away he started off on his plans for world domination and I thought, here we go again. I switched off a bit and totted up the number of years I had been hearing this. It was over four years. Four years of maximum talk and zero action. I was not there to coach him as he was not a paying client. I do not offer unsolicited advice but at one point he asked me what I thought he could do about all the dream killing problems life was throwing at him.

This was all like a red rag to a bull so it was now high time for some direct questions and a bit of a reality check for Pete and his never ending story. A question and answer or Q&A session ensued which went something like this:

Me:	Pete, how much time do you spend on actual book writing?
Pete:	I've not written anything in over a month because I'm reading a great book on overcoming writer's block and I'm getting some great information from it.
Me:	What about before then?
Pete:	I only write when I feel right.
Me:	So, how frequently do you feel right enough to write?
Pete:	Oh, almost every Sunday afternoon.
Me:	Almost every Sunday afternoon?
Pete:	Well perhaps one in three.
Me:	OK Pete, what you've stated works out at between one hundred and twenty to one hundred and sixty hours in a year and if you wrote just four hundred words an hour for each of those hours you could produce at least a forty eight thousand word first draft. Where is your first draft Pete?
Pete:	Well there's planning and outlining and, wait a minute,

| | can you really write at four hundred words an hour? |
| Me: | Pete, I write at around eight hundred words an hour and I ensure I write between one and two thousand words a day, each and every day, on my books, articles, speeches and product scripts as well as all the other work I do as a coach, trainer and speaker. Seriously Pete, how on earth do you think you can write something as significant as a book without putting in some writing effort? |

This was Pete's first problem. He had no idea of the work involved. He thought he could just sit down one day when the muse was upon him and produce a finished book. I do not know anyone who can do that, do you?

The Q&A session continued:

Me:	What about the speaking then?
Pete:	What do you mean?
Me:	Have you been working on your material and techniques?
Pete:	No, I was waiting until the book was published so people would take me seriously.
Me:	Pete, how do you know if you're any good as a speaker if you don't already speak yet?
Pete:	I hadn't thought about it really. Besides I was good at my brother's wedding and if people like the book they'll gladly queue up to hear me speak.
Me:	Pete, have you considered trying a Toastmasters Club to practice and improve your public speaking?
Pete:	Well I looked into it once a few years ago but they meet on a Wednesday.
Me:	Why is Wednesday such a problem?
Pete:	Wednesday is when my favourite soap is on and I get some great story ideas from watching the soaps.
Me:	Great to hear Pete, have you incorporated any of these

	great story ideas into your book outline?
Pete:	No of course not because this first book is going to be a self-help guide.
Me:	A self-help guide? A self-help guide to what exactly Pete?
Pete:	I haven't settled on a topic yet. Every time I get an idea and check it out on Amazon it turns out someone else has written something similar already. I have to abandon my outlines then and start again. It feels like everyone else is just one step ahead of me. My killer idea for the bestseller is out there somewhere though if I just keep looking.
Me:	Seriously? A best seller Pete? Good grief!

It was all getting better and better. Pete obviously had no commitment to work at his craft. We have all got to start somewhere but Pete wanted to start at the top. He seemed to have an excuse or external reason for every scenario. He actually believed the world was conspiring against him in some way.

One last stab at the Q&A before I gave up in disgust:

Me:	What about the job you hate then Pete? You're still there are you not? I thought all these plans of yours were motivated by your desire to jack it all in?
Pete:	It's a dead end position alright. The management has always had it in for me. They promote people over me when I've been there longer. They don't put me on any of the new and exciting projects.
Me:	Have you asked them why Pete?
Pete:	What's the point? They'll only say no.
Me:	Pete, do you work harder than the new people?
Pete:	Again, what's the point? They'll have degrees and MBAs and all that malarkey. The company did try to put me on a few courses but I managed to wangle my way out of them. I'm too old to be learning new things

at forty and besides, it would interfere with my writing too much. I wouldn't want to spread myself too thin now would I?

The last statement did it for me as far as asking more questions. I have worked with many paying clients who had motivational and goal achievement issues and they often had some real challenges. Good old Pete was a breed apart though and I was delighted he was not and never would be a client of mine.

The difference with my clients and Pete was simple. They wanted to make changes and they were prepared to put some effort in.

Pete was and probably still is a very lazy man. Pete simply wanted his dream to happen as if by magic. He understood little if anything about the potential effort and sacrifice he might have to make to write a book. He barely wrote at all yet had convinced himself he was a writer. After all, it was not his fault others had beaten him to his topic niche was it? He would not even miss a bit of low-grade telly to get up and help himself learn the speaker's craft. He was lucky to have the job he hated so much. He had avoided all their efforts to help him and then he moaned when others passed him on the way up. Pete may well have had influences in the past which created unhelpful reference patterns and helped develop his negative and self-destructive response programs but these were not entirely what was holding him back.

Pete maintained his hard done by hero attitude and wore it like a badge of honour. He liked the feeling he got when people thought he was a plucky go getter who would make his mark one day soon despite the many obstacles he faced. He had no real intention of making any changes. Success was the last thing he actually wanted. Change takes effort and action. Pete also added naivety, negativity and a quick-fix entitlement attitude to the mix. He is not alone either but he was a particularly memorable example of a lazy dreamer.

Pete finally asked me, "Do you have any ideas to help me get past all these life obstacles?"

"No." It was all I could think of to say before I made my polite excuses and hurriedly left.

These stories do not have to have a happy ending; I am a coach not a wizard. Maybe you think I am harsh and uncaring? I have to be resilient and stick to my values and nobody said life will not be hard now and again. Needless to say, I have not seen Pete since but I hope he finds his easy dream; however, unless he makes dramatic changes, I would be very surprised if he does. There was nothing I could say to help him right then. You can lead a horse to water but you cannot make it drink. He was, and probably still is, his own worst enemy. Only he can ever take the first three steps towards changing. Those steps are deciding to change, committing to change and then taking action to change.

Section 3: Look At It This Way

Resilient water is infinitely flexible. Water always finds the easiest way around any obstacle or barrier. Water never favours one option over another. Nothing stops water. Be like the water. If something is not working for you then try something else. Find a way to your own resilience.

Introduction to section

In this section we will look at a bit of self-analysis and why you must be ready and willing to do it often. It is important to know why, or at least examine why, we think about certain things in a certain way or sometimes why we do not think about certain things at all.

Thinking about thinking itself may be a strange concept for you. If you like jargon, we could call it meta-thinking but on reflection let us just stick to the plain English version. Have you ever thought about your own thinking before? Most of us have had passing thoughts about things we think about but rarely do we take the time to deliberately sit down and analyse our specific thought processes and situational responses with the intention of learning and possibly improving them. Have you ever deliberately spent time doing this? Most people do not do it with any deliberation or intention and if they do, they do not do it enough in my opinion.

In this section we will look at why such reflection is so important. We will also look at ways you can mentally trip yourself up or trap yourself in unhelpful thought patterns and how to start to avoid these issues. We will also look at viewing situations, outcomes and problems in wholly different and generally more useful ways.

It is all about creating more options for yourself and it is also about recognising the options you already have but cannot identify due to some limited ways of thinking. Remember the more options you have available to you the more emotionally resilient you are likely to be.

Feedback and reflection

We looked at the topic of feedback in section one and came to the conclusion it is just data. We get sensory feedback data all the time from our immediate environments. Our brains process and use this data, adding to it as best as it can from the existing knowledge pool if there are any major gaps, then convert it into what we assume is meaningful information about how we are actually doing relative to our intentions. This can be at a biological level, operational level and societal level. For example, am I still breathing? Yes - good. Am I driving OK? Yes - good. Am I acting normally at this party? Yes - good. I say we assume because sometimes we process things poorly and we can trip ourselves up mentally. I will have more to say on this a bit later on.

We can also expect and ask for feedback from others on these same levels. The thing about feedback from others is how subjective it is. It is based purely on the other person's understanding of their own environment as well as their understanding and perception of us and our behaviour when viewed through the filter of their personal view of the world. No matter how well-intentioned, at best it is tricky to know what to believe and act on regarding such subjective feedback and sometimes it is simply impossible.

Remember the story about the Emperor's new clothes? He responded poorly to honest feedback so people did not give him any.

Once upon a time there lived an Emperor so vain he spent his entire life looking for finer and finer clothing to wear and show off in. By and by, two clever swindlers arrived at his palace claiming they made the finest material and clothing in the world. In fact, they claimed, their clothing was so good and fine it appeared as invisible to all but the most stupid. The Emperor paid them a huge amount of money to make him the finest outfit in all the realm ready for the grand parade. The two swindlers now made a great show of pretending to weave their wonderful invisible cloth and made sure they told everyone only stupid people could not see it for what it really was.

Finally, the outfit was ready and the swindlers pretended to dress the naked Emperor in his wonderful new clothes. The swindlers left with all the money and the Emperor set off on his grand parade. The Emperor himself was struggling to see the material but he was far from stupid so he held his head high and marched proudly along.

The courtiers and ministers, not wishing to appear stupid, gushed and fawned over his attire as they walked behind him. The crowds also applauded and admired his clothes for they too did not wish to be thought of as stupid. Everybody in the land loved the Emperor's new clothes. Only an idiot could fail to appreciate them.

Only one small child, who cared little whether he looked stupid or not, shouted out the obvious fact that the Emperor was naked. One by one the crowd began to see this too and they shouted out as well. The Emperor shivered in the cold and began to suspect he really was naked and people really could see it. Still, he really did not wish to appear stupid and the royal procession had to be completed, so he marched proudly onward with the adulation of his courtiers and ministers ringing in his ears.

Be careful who you seek feedback from.

The best external feedback generally comes from sources we trust and respect. It can often come from those we know care about us and it can often come from those who know more than us about the processes being discussed. A world class sprinter would waste their time getting feedback on his training regime from me for example. He would however get a lot of potential benefit if they were to seek feedback from me on his public speaking ability.

You do not review or expect specific feedback for every activity or behaviour. For example, you breathe automatically and your body and brain exchange information about this without you even being aware it is going on. We only get conscious noticeable feedback when something is going wrong or we specifically focus on our breathing; during a sporting activity or whilst meditating for example. The situation is different whenever you complete something consciously and which you feel has a significant potential impact on your self-esteem and self-image. This is where we generally talk to ourselves and I trust you are training your inner voice to do this in a really nice way at this point. We often replay activities and behaviours in our minds in order to examine them.

We are in effect giving ourselves deliberate internal feedback in the same way other people give us deliberate external feedback, whether we want it or not.

Now here is something else to add to the mix. We are all unique individuals but psychologists and other well-meaning people over the years have noticed we also share certain broadly defined characteristics which enables people to classify us on various behavioural spectra. Humans love to classify things. People who study personality particularly love to classify people.

There is an old personality profiling joke which states there are only really two kinds of people in the world. Those who classify people into types and those who do not. It makes me smile anyway.

Personality profiling is a useful tool to aid situational and behavioural understanding. I enjoy studying it and it has been helpful to me in my growth. There are lots of Interweb resources available to set you on your way if this sounds like something you might want to dig deeper into.

One of the popular classification spectra, which has a direct impact on our discussion, is termed internal or external reference. At one extreme and in simplistic terms, an internally referenced person cares little for the opinions or feedback of others. They rely on their own internal worldview and judgement to make decisions about whether something went well or not. At the other extreme an externally referenced person is hugely influenced by the feedback and opinions of others. They will often not make any decision until they have consulted widely. Most of us are somewhere in the middle area. It is also very context dependent. For example, if you have a lot of experience in a particular subject or behaviour you may be more internally referenced about it but as a beginner in another field or process you may well seek external input and confirmation of progress more readily from people with more experience.

The amount of importance you may place on any available external feedback will vary depending on your internal or external reference criteria applicable at the time. This is a fairly straightforward and common-sense view. "So, what is the problem?" I hear you cry.

You have to make sure you reflect and analyse as usefully and effectively as possible. There are a few pitfalls which can trip you up if you are not careful. You may reach conclusions which are not necessarily correct or helpful to you. Believe it or not, the human brain is not perfect. My brain is definitely not perfect and I will bet money yours is not either. Your conclusions can be skewed by your own cognitive, recall and social biases. We will talk about some of these biases and a few other general thought traps in the next section.

You can also impact your ability to reach accurate conclusions by not spending enough time on quality reflection. Being in the wrong emotional mindset will not do you any good either.

This is a practical guide so let us have a quick high level look at a workable framework you can usefully apply to promote effective reflection and feedback analysis.

Before you do anything else, find or make the time you need to relax and fully focus on your reflection. I know time is a precious and sometimes scarce commodity but the value you will get from an exercise like this more than outweighs the effort of creating the time and space to do it. When you get proficient at this process you may only need a minute or two to effectively analyse your performance or feedback then continue refreshed and refocused. Try having a cup of your favourite beverage and, if you are able, try listening to some relaxing music to put you in a good frame of mind.

Speaking of mind frames, what would be the best state of mind for you to get the best from your reflection and feedback analysis session? I like to be honest, curious and open-minded. I want to be non-judgmental and non-critical. I want to be happy and relaxed. I want to be flexible and willing to change if necessary. Remember the exercise we did in part one on state management. This is a great opportunity to utilise those state management skills. You have been practising I hope? Take some time to develop the ideal state of mind and practice moving into it using your preferred anchoring technique.

Start to analyse your performance in whatever activity or situation you are considering. Ask yourself a series of questions. Here are some examples which I use but feel free to create your own as, after all, it is your reflection time:

Did I perform as well as I wished? Was my outcome expectation valid? Did I respond the same as I always do or did I try something new? What prompted my choice of action? What stopped me choosing an alternative? Was it a complete disaster? If so why and based on what measurement? What was good and what was not so good? Did I get the required result anyway? Did I work well yet not get the result? What result did I get? What could I change or improve on next time? What additional information did I learn which could be applied elsewhere? Who helped me? Who hindered me? Who surprised me? How do I feel emotionally about the experience? Did my emotions help or hinder me? What other emotions could have been more useful? Who or what could have been helpful to me? How can I increase my options for more flexible and useful future responses?

Questions generate answers and answers can prompt potential new and useful options.

Just let the thoughts drift across your mind. Do not react to them other than to consider them and their effect on your understanding of the situation or activity and your possible new responses to similar events in the future. Do not try and defend or justify any actions you took or did not take. Simply consider them all in a neutral manner to see if they were useful or non-useful.

If you have had feedback from others about the performance or the situation, now is the time to think about and analyse the feedback in relation to your own thoughts and feelings.

Ask yourself another set of questions regarding the external feedback:

How did the outcome appear to them? Why might it appear like this? What comments did they make? How do I feel about those comments? What might be the reason they made them? How can I benefit from any suggestions? Does the person have my best interests at heart? Did the person fully understand the situation? Did the person have information which I lacked? Could I benefit from the information? Could the person help me further? Could I be of help to the other person? Justified or not, do their comments hold anything of value to me for the future? Am I looking at the event or activity the right way? Was my outcome expectation valid in light of this external feedback? Am I being honest enough with myself here? What metaphorical blinkers or mental defences may I have in place? What false or non-useful beliefs might I hold which may be limiting my responses?

There is nothing wrong with reverting to our childlike state and repeatedly asking ourselves why, why and why again. Throw in a few "what ifs" and you are getting creative as well as reflective.

This reflection and processing time is the time when we can actually learn something about our experiences, abilities and our personalities. We already do it subconsciously and habitually but, if we started to do it deliberately and consciously, we could get so much more benefit.

Please note, when we experience any event or activity we will be swamped with sensory information from the experience. We looked at this much earlier and decided the data alone was of no real use to us. It is only when we assign informational value to the data, make connections and process it in our brains, that it becomes potentially useful.

This processing part has its own built in set of trip hazards and pitfalls for the unwary thinker and we will look at some of these next.

Thought traps and biases

This is all about emotional resilience so any information or techniques which help you maintain high self-esteem and self-image will be a good thing. Am I right? Of course I am. This section could enlighten you about a few potential pitfalls and mental trip hazards and can therefore help you avoid some of the mental traps and poor thinking which can leave you feeling bad about yourself.

When we discussed sensory data and your relationship to it back in part two, you read about your many internal mental filters through which every bit of incoming sensory data passes. These filters are made up of reference experiences, beliefs, values, assumptions, stereotypes, and other automatic responses which you either developed yourself or inherited from significant others. It is always worth checking in case one of your own internal filters is skewing your understanding of any situational analysis or reflective activity.

On top of this, there are some additional ways in which you can get side-tracked or misled. It is not easy being mindful. There is so much to think about. It might seem a more attractive option to just to drift along and see what happens. It is definitely an easier approach but will not do you any real favours. In the long run taking control of your thought patterns about events and learning from them will make you far more resilient and your self-esteem and self-image will flourish.

To start off we will revisit one of my favourite words - gumption. You may remember we defined gumption as shrewd or spirited initiative and resourcefulness. It can be used to mean enterprise, inventiveness and ingenuity.

I first discovered the term gumption trap whilst reading Robert M Pirsig's first book "Zen and the Art of Motorcycle Maintenance."

As an aside, I can highly recommend it to you. It is not for everyone but well worth checking out; you can decide for yourself.

A gumption trap is any event or mindset which causes someone to lose their enthusiasm and become discouraged from starting or continuing a project or activity. It is an event which knocks all the wind out of your sails and kills your creative energy. It is called a trap because the person in it tends to get stuck and go round in a negative loop. The drop in enthusiasm and initiative reduces the chances of success still further and the lowered degree of potential success reduces enthusiasm and further discourages the person and so on and so forth.

Pirsig himself described two main types of gumption trap; setbacks and hang-ups.

Setbacks can come in all shapes, sizes and varieties. A setback is anything which stops progress.

As an example, leaving for work and finding your car battery is flat is a setback in your efforts to get to work. If a neighbour can help you get it started reasonably quickly then it is just a minor setback. If you have an important early meeting it is more of a setback. You may need a taxi which comes at some expense. Later on you find the flat battery killed your engine control unit and a mobile mechanic or even a tow to the garage may be required. More money and an even bigger setback. Setbacks can generally be fixed. They can even be avoided with meticulous planning and troubleshooting in advance, i.e. having a spare car, performing more regular maintenance or checking it out the night before, etc...

Let us look at another example. Suppose you decided to surprise your wife and three children with an exotic adventure holiday of a lifetime. They have been through a lot recently what with your new executive career coming first and all. You are now in a position to start to make it up to them with some fun and gifts. You get all ready to book the surprise so you visit the travel agent to secure the tickets. You are asked by the travel agent to confirm everyone has their passports. You thought the children could travel on yours. Turns out the laws have changed and they need their own passports. OK, you think, no problem. I will just go home and check the passports then come back tomorrow and book the tickets. It is a relatively minor setback at this stage. One more day will not be a problem compared to how much fun you will have on holiday.

Back home, you check the family documents box. There is your passport and your wife's. The two older boys are yours from a previous marriage and their passports are there too. The youngest boy is your wife's from a previous marriage and there does not appear to be a passport there for him. You turn the entire box out with no luck. Now what? You cannot leave him out and you cannot apply for a passport without involving your wife which ruins a large part of the surprise. It has become a more major setback but it is not insurmountable. You decide to tell your wife. After all, she will still be delighted with the exotic holiday and at least the kids will still be surprised. You are going to sort this out come hell or high water.

When you tell her, your wife is indeed happy with the holiday idea so together you investigate getting a passport for the youngest boy. Oh no, it turns out the ex-husband, who is incommunicado due to being in deepest Africa as a volunteer missionary, has the boy's birth certificate in storage somewhere and you need this for the passport application. Ah forget it, what is the point. I bet you wish you had never had the stupid holiday idea in the first place. Now your wife is disappointed and you are super-annoyed. This now very major setback so you decide to drop it entirely. Camping again this year with no passports required.

The initially small setback has now become a full blown gumption trap. You might have to apply all your new emotional resilience tools to get over this one.

Spur of the moment decisions can be fun but, when they involve a reasonably complex system like a family, it is well worth your time taking a step backwards. Pre-checking and pre-planning your actions in order to minimise the occurrence of just this sort of resilience sapping setback ruining your plans and your mood, will save you a lot of grief.

Hang-ups originate from internal or external factors which can get in the way of you starting or completing an activity or project. Examples of internal hang-ups include anxiety, haste, anger, boredom, impatience and any number of negative or unhelpful states of mind and emotions. Add to this list the potential failure to realise or accept you might not have all the information or skills necessary to succeed with the project. Additionally, factor in the reality you are not always aware about how certain aspects of the situation or problem might be more or less important than you actually believe. This last item is especially interesting as relative importance can change in response to changing context.

I will give you an example of this hang-up gumption trap from my past.

Many years ago, one of my first cars was an old wreck of a thing. It got me where I needed to go and the engine was actually quite reliable but it was not pretty to look at. Money was tight so I thought I would save a few quid by servicing the engine myself. I even splashed out on a proper workshop manual for the car. I had all the tools I needed and I felt confident of success; I was pretty handy with most DIY jobs. How difficult could it be?

It was only a minor service and I managed the oil change and the air filter change. On the home stretch now; I just had to do the spark plugs. My focus had initially been on saving a bit of money and the activity of servicing the car was a small step towards my goal. As I put the last spark plug in and started to rotate the wrench, it felt a bit tight. Never mind, I had an extension bar in the toolbox and this gave me more torque on the wrench. It started going in again slowly. All of a sudden there was a snapping noise and it started spinning freely. I got a couple of bloody knuckles for my efforts too. I pulled out the wrench with most of the spark plug still in it. The bit which was not there was embedded in the top of my engine block. I found out later I had cross-threaded it and then sheared it off. I did not have the mechanics touch to tell me the tight fit was a potential problem and I would have done better by taking out the plug and re-seating the thread. All of a sudden that half a spark plug took on a whole lot more importance and significance in my world than it had done previously. It used to be a relatively inexpensive piece of metal and ceramic but now I might have killed my car with it. The broken plug was a real hang-up. My gumption deserted me in an instant.

It cost me a lot more than just the towing fee to the garage and the huge repair bill. I was lucky they could actually fix it at all. The biggest cost was hidden and it was the negative impact to my self-esteem. It was embarrassing to have to admit my mistake and I also had to acknowledge there were some things I might not be good at. It was a hard life lesson.

To this day, even though I have many mechanical and technical skills coupled with high self-esteem and confidence, I have an extreme reluctance to touch anything relating to engines and always pass it over to expert and expensive mechanics.

Looking back with the twenty-twenty vision which hindsight provides there were many points during the situation where I could have avoided the damaged plug outcome. The minute it stuck I could have sought help or advice from a more experienced person. By taking a quick break to think through the reasons for a plug sticking like that may have yielded an answer. I could have studied the workshop manual troubleshooting section over a cup of tea. Dealing with hang-ups can be as simple as taking a short break from working on the problem or a specific aspect of it and re-evaluating one's position in relation to the job at hand. Altering the distance can alter the perspective.

Let us look at cognitive biases now. We all like to consider ourselves as logical and rational thinking creatures. Generally, we feel we are able to look at any subject dispassionately and come to a reasonably unbiased and fair conclusion when called upon to do so. Unfortunately, after many years of research by leading behavioural psychologists and experimenters, it turns out we humans are actually extremely biased. We are often completely unaware of our biases. We do not apply them deliberately. Some are learnt, some acquired and many are innate or intrinsic. We can, however, take them into account, once we become aware of them, and check our conclusions are not adversely affected by them. Gaining the ability to test for bias and to adapt your thinking accordingly can be hugely useful to you and I recommend you always keep an eye out for these sneaky little thinking traps.

This is not meant to be about psychology in any academic sense so I am not going to launch into a list of all the many cognitive (thinking) biases or the many social and recall (memory error) biases which have been identified. There are a lot actually - a quick check on Wikipedia listed around one hundred and seventy. If it is your idea of fun then get stuck in and have a look. Personally I find once I start looking at lists like that I begin to feel I exhibit all of them. It is like looking in a medical dictionary, if you are not careful then pretty soon you start to think you have every exotic ailment ever discovered.

I will select a few of the more relevant ones and we will take a quick look at them. You can then begin to check your thinking for any errors based on or caused by these biases.

You can in fact use these biases to help persuade others to your way of thinking. Please also note it is a double edged sword, it cuts both ways and these same biases can be used against you by unscrupulous salespeople or other influencing professionals, such as Interweb marketers. I will mention ways this might be achieved with each bias description.

As another aside, one non-fiction book I would encourage everybody to read at least once in their lives is *Influence* by Robert Cialdini. It is a genuinely fascinating and well-researched examination of the six main inbuilt, yet subconscious, triggers we all have. You will be amazed how savvy advertisers can use these six main triggers (or biases) to compel us to do their bidding. You can use them too if you are so inclined.

The focusing effect or focusing illusion is a cognitive bias which occurs when you place too much importance on a single event aspect. This can cause errors in your ability to accurately predict the likelihood of potential outcomes; both positive and negative.

Humans are generally drawn to the most notable or conspicuous things in our immediate mental and physical environment. As a result we can exclude less conspicuous things. This can skew the amount of relative importance we place on data and information. We also focus more things which relate to our highest priority beliefs or issues operating at a particular time.

As an example, let us suppose you really love cooking yet have a particularly small kitchen in your house. Now you might well decide to move house in order to get a bigger kitchen. If you have a choice between several houses you might well be much more in favour of the one with the biggest kitchen, even if the house itself had was not the best overall choice for you. You might say this applies in all areas of life and I would agree with you, we like what we like after all. With major financial and life decisions, ignoring any logical skewing created by such a focusing bias could be very costly long-term.

To offset this natural cognitive bias, when you are making any decision, pause to identify all the factors involved first and take care to give them a rational and balanced importance weighting. If you want to use it to persuade or influence someone try to get them thinking about a particular facet of the topic ahead of time. In the house example above, if you were the sales agent and knew kitchen size was important, you could send pictures in advance showing the large kitchen. This could then be a major sales influencer for you when you want them to decide to buy and might cause them to overlook some less desirable features in the house. Unethical? That is sales ladies and gentlemen; buyer beware. Consider all facets equally and do not become blinkered by your own though processes and biases.

The confirmation bias is a tendency we humans have to hunt out, interpret or remember information in a way which serves to confirm our beliefs or thoughts. We gather or recall information selectively or, when we interpret it, in a way which backs up what we want to believe. The bias is stronger in emotionally charged or deeply held beliefs. Once upon a time everyone knew the world was flat. It looked flat which sealed the deal for most people. In fact, if you disagreed you were likely to be burned at the stake. Now most people know it is basically round. For my purist readers, the Earth's shape is technically an oblate spheroid because both poles are slightly flattened. I am quite happy to think of it as round.

People will even hold to strong beliefs despite having clear contrary evidence being presented to them. Positions can tend to fully polarise during heated and seemingly irrational arguments. These entrenched and dogmatic stances are due in large part to the confirmation bias. There are many theories on offer as to why humans have these biases. If you like, you can look them up and examine their various merits. My point is we have them so do not get caught out.

A big danger of confirmation bias is it can contribute to over-confidence in personal beliefs and can maintain or strengthen beliefs in the face of contrary evidence. Reference my spark plug exploits in the gumption trap section above. I over-estimated my abilities at some cost to myself.

Have you ever made your mind up to do something and no

power on earth could talk you out of it or convince you to try something else instead? Did you find everything you saw, heard or felt confirmed your thoughts and drew you towards your choice? Decisiveness is often considered a good thing but beware because you may be ignoring other valuable information.

As another example, consider you are someone who has just purchased an expensive new item of exclusive designer clothing at a discount. To convince yourself you have made a good choice, you will likely look for the same garment in a more expensive store or on-line shop as confirmation. You may even look to see if you can find another just like it in order to further convince yourself it is also as exclusive as promised. We humans also hate to be wrong and this amplifies the effect. This strategy has the risky issue where you might actually find it cheaper and more common in many other places but then you will probably choose not to notice this information because of your confirmation bias.

To minimise the effect of this bias get into the habit, before and after any decision is made, of considering all the evidence you are presented with, even if it goes against your choice. If it stops you making a poor selection, consider it a great outcome. If you find you have made a poor decision, then at least you will have learnt a valuable lesson which could help you to make a better decision next time.

How about using this bias to your advantage? Well you could try this approach. After you persuade someone to take a certain action or change their belief about something, help them feel good about it by providing examples which confirm their good decision to be influenced by you. Beware of people trying to feed you confirmation evidence in order to coerce you into a poor decision. Another sales tactic with potentially dubious ethics. Consider all the available options equally and you will be in with a shout.

Finally in this section, we will take a look at the self-serving bias. This is one where we strive to maintain our self-esteem at all costs. I also call it the "I am never wrong" bias. Some people have a tendency to take personal credit for success (self-enhancement) and deny any responsibility for failure (self-protection). For example, you may hear a student say how they successfully achieved a particularly good exam result because of their superior intelligence and preparation yet assign the reason for failing an exam by blaming poor teaching or unfair exam questions. They may well have had great teachers or coaches helping them in their preparation but the person with such a self-serving bias will not acknowledge these factors. As an aside, if you are any sort of coach or mentor (and I include being a parent here) this all too common occurrence can be quite disheartening. The resilient approach is to be philosophical about it, give yourself an internal pat on the back for a job well done and build on your success for next time.

We are discussing the importance of reflection on performance via analysis of internal and external feedback and you have to be honest with yourself. Ignoring or blanking out negative feedback is a form of ego protection and a self-esteem enhancer but it does you no long-term good. When you are honest with yourself you will not take any credit when you do not deserve it and you will not apportion blame when it is unwarranted or undeserved. You will gain more credibility with the people around you.

Blaming other people and external events is another bad habit you would do well to eliminate from your response toolkit. Blaming hands over power to someone else or to an external event. You are saying in effect they or it caused something to happen to you. This might feel better in the short-term but serves to lower your resilience and the more you do it the more people will tend to see you as a weak person. Choose to take responsibility for what happens in your life and for what you make happen in your life. It is the right thing to do.

As I mentioned earlier, there are myriad ways our thinking and thought processes can skew the way we see and respond to things. Do some research and investigate some of the others. Forewarned is forearmed.

Take the time to relax and reflect openly and honestly on your situational performance and any internal or external feedback you have in relation to it but be as aware as you can possibly be in assessing your reflective thoughts against possible thought traps and cognitive biases.

Reframing and redefining

There is always more than one way of looking at something either as an outcome (reframing) or a problem (redefining)

By now you may well have noticed how the effective and useful choice of the language you use, and the way in which you talk to yourself, plays a key part in maintaining and enhancing self-esteem and, by extension, building emotional and professional resilience.

We will look at two new concepts in this section: reframing and redefining.

Utilising both these techniques will increase your available options and expand your resilience toolkit.

Let us start with reframing. Reframing is a somewhat fancy term for looking at something in a different way. I liken it to swapping picture frames on a painting or photograph. Different combinations of frame and image mounting can drastically alter the way we perceive the painting or photograph. New colours may seem to appear as if by magic. Once strong and dominant colours may appear to fade away, thus altering the overall look of the scene. Nothing has changed in the actual picture but our perception of it certainly has.

Reframing is generally associated with outcomes or results. Have you ever had a situational outcome or activity result which was not what you expected? Was it a bad result? Was it a good result?

Remember way back in part two when we looked at success and failure? It turns out using success and failure is just our own way of assigning a particular criteria range to incoming sensory data and then saying this or that combination or outcome was good or bad in relation to that criteria. Sometimes the criteria even get set by other people. They influenced our viewpoint regarding the success or failure of our outcomes and results. It is all very subjective.

The key thing to remember about subjectivity is simply this; it is so subjective. The old saying "beauty is in the eye of the beholder" sums this up beautifully; in my eyes anyway. When something is subjective the rules against which the sensory data is compared are fluid and flexible. They can be changed by the subject; you in this case. Can you imagine how powerful this could be for you? You have real control over the way you look at data. You have real control over the information you process. You have real control over the value you perceive and the value of the generated information.

As a quick example of reframing, imagine you are employed by a large business and considering the situation where you have just been rejected after applying for a promotion. It was a promotion you really wanted. You felt ready for it after you recently gained a good business qualification and you put a lot of work into the application. You have just heard feedback from your boss about why you did not get the position. The feedback you got explained how a stronger candidate had applied. The feedback also indicated your application was very good and the only thing you really needed was more hands-on experience with higher level projects. How do you feel initially? Are you mad at your boss? Are you mad at the company? Are you mad at the other candidate for taking your job? Are you disappointed with your performance? Do you feel the feedback was unjustified and you were never really in the running? Had you already mentally begun spending the higher salary? Are you not going to give them a chance to shoot you down again by not re-applying? Be honest, we have all been there. I have had these same dark thoughts and worse on many occasions in the past.

What is the solution from a self-esteem and resilience point of view? How do you change these negative thoughts into positive ones? When you take the time to reflect and look again at the feedback and take the statements at face value you can begin to reframe the experience. You did your best with the application. You made no mistakes and you presented your case well. This is a definite positive. Your process for completing applications has proved to be a good one. You would be highly confident in using it again. You could confidently help other people you know with their job applications. The fact they noted you needed more hands-on experience with higher level projects was, given more honest reflection, a fair comment. Much of your knowledge is actually theoretical and based on your recent college experience. Maybe you actually dodged a bullet. You may well have got the job if the other candidate had not applied and might well have found yourself out of your depth. It is good to be dynamic and forward thinking but careful planning and consideration can help you avoid the pitfalls of impetuosity. Ask your boss to ensure you get the hands-on project experience you need. You will be in a far better position to re-apply and who knows, ask for a raise at the same time. Companies like to keep quality staff happy.

It is an iterative process. Iterative is a fancy word for going round and round. Here it means you can keep reframing things until the new view makes most sense and is most useful to you.

So that is reframing. It does not mean putting on a happy smiley face all the time and it certainly does not mean ignoring negative feedback and burying your head in the sand. It does mean reflecting on the data, information and feedback you get then positively and purposefully viewing it in a different way to generate new perspectives and perceptions. You are then positively controlling your subjective experience. It is not always easy so, when forming any new habit, start slowly and get it in the muscle over time. It is well worth the effort.

Let us look now at redefining. If you are tackling or responding to a particular situation or scenario in what you believe is the best way possible yet you are struggling to get the outcomes you desire it could be as a result of not fully clarifying or correctly understanding the initial problem or situational conditions. Redefining is a way of altering your problem definition in order to understand it more fully or even in a completely different way. This new view may increase your response options or highlight a gap in your knowledge or skills. Acting upon either of these new bits of knowledge could improve your chances of a successful result.

There is nothing more dispiriting or gumption destroying than spending or investing huge amounts of time, energy and money into solving a particular problem only to discover it was the wrong problem. Time spent fully clarifying and redefining any issue is time well spent.

There are two useful ways you can redefine or clarify a problem or scenario; you can alter the language you use to describe or state it and you can alter the basis or location of it. You could in fact do both, it is your redefine after all.

It is easier to illustrate this with a practical example I think. Suppose you want to lose a few pounds before your holiday, which is two months away. It is a scenario I can certainly relate to. If you state the problem in terms of how can you lose weight quickly you may start enthusiastically with a crash diet and enrol in some sort of tortuous exercise program at the local gym.

Theoretically this plan will work. If you can avoid physical injury, eat less calories than you use, stave off food cravings, maintain your enthusiasm and make time for all the gym sessions then you will probably lose weight. Is it sustainable? Take a quick look at the dieting and fitness industry and you may notice a few other people may be struggling too. In fact, the diet and fitness industry effectively relies on people adopting these unsustainable approaches. They actively encourage them in order to maintain their customer base.

If you did lose the weight this way you would likely put it back on with interest after your holiday. You might even begin a cycle of boom and bust regarding your weight. You did it with the best of intentions but it is not great for your self-esteem, self-image or your resilience.

If you take a step back and redefine the problem, you may arrive at an alternative issue statement. Consider restating the problem along the lines of how can you develop more healthy and long-term lifestyle and dietary habits which will help you stay at your optimal weight whilst still enjoying yourself.

This is a huge shift in emphasis. By redefining the problem and the problem statement you have opened up a host of more sustainable options. You could replace poor quality unhealthy food with better alternatives and eat the same amount. You could walk to work or use the stairs more. Take a short walk at lunchtimes or in the evenings after work. Minimal chance of injury and you get to explore the neighbourhood. What about involving the family and making it fun? The money you save in binning the gym membership and the dodgy Lycra jumpsuit could go towards a future holiday or some other enjoyable reward. The list could be huge but the point is it will be sustainable. You will feel better about yourself and you will have developed more emotional resilience as a result.

As a final larger and more practical example which highlights the possibilities for reframing and redefining, consider an unexpected snow day. This is a day when it has snowed so much overnight when you wake up all the roads are closed and there is little real possibility of getting to work, school or anywhere else. How do you view this snow day?

Much depends on your prior plans for the day and how you think about the situation.

If the money you need to earn at your work is vital, then you might perceive the blanket of snow as a complete disaster but stop and think about it for a few minutes. Ask yourself some questions. Will anyone else be at work today? Can a few phone calls serve to smooth things out with your clients or employer? People are generally very understanding. You did not make it snow deliberately did you? Can you do some work from home in order to maintain progress? If you do not have it already, ask your boss or client to send stuff through electronically for this purpose. In my experience it sometimes works out, because of a little bonus quiet time spent on some paperwork or an ongoing project, you can get far more accomplished than you can at the busy office. If you are self-employed perhaps you have insurance for this type of occurrence. If employed, could you take a holiday day in order to more fully relax and enjoy the experience?

With a little reframing and creativity, it might even be possible to come out of the situation better than ever? You could get to know some new neighbours you have never met by organising a snow clearing team. Visit some elderly neighbours to see if they are coping. You could do some internal house maintenance which might save money on contractors. You could do your accounts, read a good book, learn a new skill or even plan your next sunshine holiday.

Most children love snow. From their perspective it is a no school day with maximum fun to be had. Take the opportunity to reconnect with your kids. If you do not have any kids then reconnect with your own inner child and build a snow person or have a snowball fight. Go sledging. Wrap up warm, take a walk and delight in the majesty of the snow covered landscape around you. Have some fun.

The original problem statement was "Damn, I cannot get to work today and I will lose money." A redefine might be "How can I use my time to create equal or greater value in my life to offset the loss of income?" I am not saying you will manage to do it but this sort of "What can I achieve?" attitude is far more powerful and creative for you than maintaining a "Look what I have lost" mentality.

The snow day could actually turn out to be the best thing which happened to you for a while if you can redefine the problem and reframe the outcomes.

It can be easy enough to help someone else get things in perspective. We have all had times when a distraught spouse, child, relative or friend has been convinced their world has ended. We are often able to help them see things with more clarity. Imagine how much better your own life would be if you could easily do it for yourself.

Reframing outcomes and redefining problems make for a more resilient life experience.

As promised in the introduction, I will now revisit the tongue in cheek reframe I mentioned back then. I said "If I have made you laugh or smile at any point in this tome then I will state I definitely intended to include humour. If you have not laughed or smiled at all then the story I am sticking to is I fully intended to write a serious sombre guide to professional resilience." This is a reframe which is slightly different in style because I said it ahead of the outcome. I will term it a pre-frame but you could also call it covering all the bases.

Experiment and have fun.

It all depends on your point of view

If something is not working then try something else.

The statement above is worth turning into a poster or screen saver and putting in plain sight so you can be reminded of it as often as possible.

Hold the phone though. Were we not always told, when growing up, sticking to your guns and staying true to your goals and beliefs was a fine attribute to have? What about, "If at first you don't succeed try, try and try again." After watching a cave spider stoically and repeatedly spinning its web after many a web-related disaster, Robert the Bruce, king of Scotland, is meant to have told his troops this fine phrase shortly before beating the English at Bannockburn in 1314. However, as the tale was told over 500 years later by Sir Walter Scott you might want to take this with a big pinch of salt. Historical accuracy aside, this tendency to stick to your guns is known as tenacity or steadfastness and it is viewed by many as a laudable attribute which marks you out as special. The exact definition of the specialness is often left unspecified.

As I mentioned in the goals section of part two there is a point where tenacity becomes stubbornness. There is a point where a tried and tested process becomes blind unyielding dogma. There is a point where strong focus on a particular goal or outcome becomes something to be achieved despite any and all costs; an obsession. These extreme positions do not assist with improving resilience. They actually reduce resilience by removing options.

From a very high level perspective, some call it the helicopter view or macro view, it is right to focus on a long-term overall objective or goal. This improves resilience by providing a path or direction to bounce back to when one encounters a negative emotional event. The long-term objectives will naturally create medium-term objectives and processes. They are interconnected and linked. Both these kinds of objectives needs to be reviewed from time to time to check they are still desired and relevant. At both these levels, if it is not working then try something else still applies.

I believe the biggest positive effect comes from applying the concept of "if something is not working then try something else" at the small, local or micro level. These are the day to day and even minute to minute objectives, strategies, plans, goals and intentions which we create or encounter every day of our lives.

Do you enjoy conflict? Most people do not. Do you handle conflict or potential conflict situations effectively? Again, most people do not. If you have a strategy for dealing with conflict and you apply it to a right here and now event, let us say you have to tell a notoriously aggressive staff member they cannot have the extra hour at lunchtime which they asked for, it is a good idea to monitor and check the strategy is actually working for you. If it is not working, then it is time to try something else.

We all get stuck in our ways. Humans like to operate on auto pilot. We save time and mental energy by using comfortable routines and automatic responses to the events unfolding around us. By and large these get us through our day unscathed but we can sometimes have resilience and gumption sapping issues when our auto pilot responses fail to get us what we want. I will refer to these real or potential issue generating situations problem spaces. These problem spaces are likely to be situations which can change rapidly or develop in unexpected ways. They can throw us off balance and might well leave us with a negative emotional impact.

It is all well and good talking about trying something new but what something new could we try? How on earth do we begin to think about getting hold of something new to try? What can we do about increasing our options?

189

In the section on state management we looked at a great technique for controlling your emotional state and physiology; giving you some new options and tools. We also looked at feedback reflection and how valuable they can be to you. One obvious downside of feedback and reflection in this situation is it tends to occur after the fact. The situation has occurred and the best you can hope for is an improvement next time. Will this next time be exactly the same? Probably not.

You could ask for advice from, or model, more experienced people in order to increase your options before an upcoming event and I would always recommend you do this as an ongoing skills improvement process. There are so many unknowns in any encounter or situation it is often difficult for someone else to help you perfectly in advance.

What you need is a technique which helps you before the problem starts.

The technique I am going to suggest here works well after the fact, in order for you to analyse a situation and provide yourself some feedback and reflection, but more importantly here, it works well to arm yourself with some new options prior to engaging with an upcoming situation. It will allow you to explore a problem space or potential problem space in advance and may yield some useful ideas, tools or strategies which you can either start with or switch to depending on what occurs. It will help you create your own options in order to try something different.

It is all about your perspective or your point of view. As stated earlier, we all have a unique view of the world and our relationship to it. This view is an amalgam or aggregate of our innate personality coupled with our entire life experience right up until today. The concept of perspective is an interesting one and is often misunderstood or simply overlooked altogether. Have you ever said,

"Try to see it from where I am standing" or "Why cannot you see it from my angle?" I am sure you have had other people say these kind of things to you too. How did you respond? Did you immediately start to try and see it from their side? In a heated debate you would actually be very unlikely to do this without a lot of conscious effort and focus. If we are honest with ourselves, we tend to see things only from our own perspective. This perspective is limited and sometimes it is extremely limited.

I am going to provide you with a technique which originated in the Neuro-linguistic Programming (NLP) field and, as I mentioned earlier, I am a big NLP fan. The technique is known in NLP as perceptual positions. Here I will outline the basic technique and theories then encourage you to try it out and get a real feel for it.

Our own perspective, where we see the world and the people and events we interact with, from our point of view is known as first position. You are going to access two other positions or perspectives when using this technique. Second position is looking at the situation from the point of view of the other person or people involved and third position is looking at the situation as an outsider would. Third position is always a neutral and balanced position. The process would be to run through the scenario in first position, then second position and then third position before giving yourself some information and re-running the scenario in first position with new insight. I recommend using actual chairs or locations and physically moving between them on each run through; it all helps. I realise this sounds clunky and a little odd when stated like this so the best way to illustrate it is by running through an example fictitious scenario.

Let us look at the scenario where, as mentioned earlier, you have to tell a notoriously aggressive staff member they cannot have the extra hour at lunchtime which they have asked for. The background to the scenario is this: One member of staff belligerently asks for an extra lunchtime hour off every two weeks, and during a busy production time, as if it is their due and they get very upset and awkward if they do not get their own way. There is another manager besides yourself and you have both decided to take a stand and refuse the next request despite any protests. The other staff do not get this perk; why can the rules be bent for this individual?

The real problem for you is you hate the conflict. After the inevitable shouting match and the employee storming off in a huff, you are dreading all the pouting and the sulks. They will not do anything wrong in work they will just do everything with a bad attitude; very passive aggressive. It actually gets everyone down but hey you have to be seen to be in charge and being a leader, right?

This time is going to be different because you have just read a fabulous new guide to emotional resilience by a brilliant and soon to be world famous author. Okay, okay, I did say it was a fictitious scenario but I can dream too you know plus it is my creation. You want to go into the meeting with more strategy options than normal; in the hope the tension and the conflict are reduced. You might even achieve a good solution for everyone concerned.

You find a nice quite place to run through the process.

You have positioned two chairs opposite each other just as they would be in real life. There is also a third chair a little way off to one side. You sit in one of the pair of opposite facing chairs and you picture the scenario taking place from this first position. Remember this is your normal point of view. You visualise the employee sitting opposite in the other chair. They have their arms folded and they are leaning back in the chair. It is an arrogant stance and they do not seem to have much respect for you as a boss. They are a bit red in the face and apart from asking for the time off they are not really saying much. They have not even given a reason for the request, just a demand for time off. You start to sense your own physiology. You are leaning forward and punctuating your words with short hand gestures to add emphasis. You are rushing a bit in order to get the words out and you feel like your shouting just a little. This is actually fine because you hope this will assist you in getting your point across forcibly and establishing your authority. You feel a little flushed. Maybe because you are anticipating some trouble. They suddenly rise and you lean back quickly. They storm out and you realise you are very tense. This is pretty much how it has gone in the past and you do not expect anything to change in the upcoming meeting.

As an aside, when you practice this sort of visualisation it may surprise you how well and realistically you can take on the physiology. Our brains and bodies are very closely linked and it can get quite intense.

You relax once more then run through it all again from the second position. You get up and change seats; you actually sit down on the one opposite. This is a strange feeling and it takes some getting used to at first. You mentally put yourself in the position of the employee. You can actually look across and see yourself talking. You cannot read the thoughts of this other person but you can take on their body language and their tone of voice. Strangely, from this second position perspective, your crossed arms and tilted back posture actually feels somewhat defensive. You state your request and hear the negative response from yourself in the opposite chair. Looking across at yourself talking you see your red face and choppy hand gestures. The words you use are delivered rapidly and in a forceful tone; you actually appear quite angry. You look like a bit of a ranting mad person from this perspective. From this second position point of view you get the real feeling that saying anything is in all likelihood pointless and might actually make the situation worse. It makes sense to leave even though you have not got what you wanted. You stand up and leave the room. You watch yourself recoil in the seat opposite.

It takes longer to relax now but you get there. You get up and go and sit in the third chair. This is the third position perspective; the position of the outside observer. You can see the first and second position chairs clearly. Now you run through the scenario again. You still cannot mind read position two but you can take note of the relative physiology and voice tone of each participant. After position two delivered their request, you see yourself leaning forward to respond, red-faced and talking rapidly. All the while your hands are forcibly and aggressively emphasising each point you make in a loud domineering voice. You see the red-faced employee leaning back with their arms folded in absolute silence before they suddenly get up and leave. They appeared to be overwhelmed by your position one onslaught. You see yourself, in position one, recoil then start to relax and calm down once the employee leaves. The employee's request for time off was refused and as a neutral observer you have seen something of a one-sided exchange. In position one you did almost all of the talking and left no space for the employee to get a word in. There was no chance to start a dialogue of any kind. You get the feeling both position one and two could be compensating for fear of something and position two might also be frustrated or even embarrassed.

As the neutral observer, you are now ready to give yourself, over in position one, some advice and insight. You tell yourself you never asked why the other person wanted the time off. They had no real opportunity to say anything to support their request. You tell yourself how angry and aggressive you appeared and how defensive the employee appeared. You tell yourself to try and start a true dialogue and actively listen to the other person's side of the story. Even if they do not respond as intended at least you will have been more like the leader you want to be.

You consider these offerings from your neutral observer self. Could the other person actually be scared of me? I thought it was me who was scared. Is their aggression just a defence tactic? Are they embarrassed by something? Might they be willing to talk if a more trusting environment was created? Have I learnt something about myself? I did not realise how bombastic I was. What if I approached the next meeting in a wholly different way? Would the employee react any differently?

You physically move back to the position one chair and, after a brief pause to relax once more, you re-run the exchange but this time you incorporate the new ideas from the neutral observer you.

You listen to the employee's request for time off as before but this time you pause, lean back slightly in your chair and you say the following: "I realise your request for time off during our busy period is important to you otherwise you would not have asked. Let us get a cup of tea sorted out before we get too engrossed. Now to start us off, can you let me have some background information as to why you need the time off? We can then examine all the options available to us."

Has the response of the employee changed at all? Has their body language or tone of voice altered? How does your physiology feel?

You obviously cannot know how they would respond in reality but you can try visualising different scenarios based on your new insights. Spend some time visualising several variations to see how you feel when using them. Changing your perspective and genuinely examining the perspectives of others can be powerful stuff. The insights you will gain will genuinely be your new own unique insights because you are the one who will tell yourself about them.

Go ahead and give it a go. Your personal and professional resilience can be improved by giving yourself access to more options and more resources. You will go into situations with more confidence and this in turn will give other people in those situations more confidence in both you and your abilities.

I recommend you practice this technique by taking the time to first analyse some recent problem space events in order to see if you can gain new insights about the outcomes and what you could have done differently. This might give you some fresh information to complement your now normal reflection and feedback approach.

The next stage will be to try out the technique "live" by applying the perceptual position strategy to an upcoming problem space event. If the exercise yields you some potentially useful alternative approaches then give them a go if and when the opportunity presents.

As with some of the other techniques I provide you with, whilst it is fine as a solo activity, it can be more useful at first to have a run through with a coach or trusted friend. They can talk you through the process and allow you to concentrate on the exercise.

This can provide a powerful and emotional experience and it can yield some surprising insights, see the following case study, and I use this technique a lot both with myself and my clients.

Have an open mind and experiment away. Always remember if something is not working then try something else.

Case study - Denise

A number of years ago when I was starting out as a coach I was, like many new coaches then and now, keen to try out the many new and exciting techniques I had learnt. An early client of mine was a lady I will name here as Denise in order to protect her identity.

Denise was a single mother bringing up a daughter who was now sixteen years old and becoming more independent by the day. They generally bumped along reasonably well together under the circumstances but Denise was telling me the problem was an inability for her to communicate with her daughter on such issues as boyfriends and going out. Every time they talked about anything along these lines it invariably ended in a shouting match with tears and tantrums on one or both sides. It was not a good situation and the pattern was becoming fixed. Denise was concerned her daughter was making poor choices yet would not listen to any advice despite her best efforts. She felt she was losing the mother daughter bond and was starting to fear initiating any conversations at all given her current results. She felt her daughter was being selfish and unreasonable.

Shiny new Mr Super Coach to the rescue. Ta dah! This seemed to be a classic opportunity for some perceptual position work in order to formulate some new communication strategies. I believed these new strategies would enable Denise to alter the approach she used to gain her daughter's agreement about the boyfriend and going out issues. I was feeling a little bit smug at that point.

Denise liked the idea of perceptual positions and seemed quite open to trying the exercise. I set up my three chairs and Denise settled down in the first position as herself talking to her daughter in a visualised replay of a recent confrontation over her staying out late.

Denise had chosen not to vocalise any of the content and this was fine. I could clearly see her running through the scenario and her physiology spoke volumes. Denise indicated she had reached the end of the dialogue and when she had relaxed a bit she then sat in the position two chair to replay the scenario from her daughter's point of view. Remember, this whole exercise was meant to allow Denise to gain new thoughts on the situation and some potential new communication insights and strategies.

Imagine my surprise when Denise completely broke down and started bawling her eyes out. Mr Super Coach was a little taken aback at that point. This reaction was not in my coaching manual.

Denise calmed down a bit and what she said next amazed me.

The minute she had sat in her daughter's perspective position and visualised the way she looked, sounded and behaved as herself sitting opposite she had a flashback to her teenage years and suddenly felt she was her younger self being lectured and shouted at by her own mother. She realised she was becoming her mother and this completely overwhelmed her, hence the tears. This was a big moment for her. Her mother had actually passed away suddenly a number of years earlier and she had never had any thoughts like this before. She felt awful because she had been putting her daughter through the same horrible experiences which she had been through herself.

We decided to finish the session for the day but Denise was adamant she wanted to explore further so the next appointment was planned and arranged.

The next session contained much less drama. Denise first ran through some scenarios with herself and her mother and whilst there were some tears, there were also a lot of questions answered for her. Her mother had also raised Denise alone and when Denise experienced the encounter from her mother's perspective she could sense the same fears which she herself felt for her own daughter.

She also revisited the previous day's exercise with this new insight and found it was as she realised. No tears this time but a lot for her to think about. We finished the coaching session and Denise had big plans to chat with her daughter and apologise. She had realised and, more importantly and usefully acknowledged to herself, her controlling attitude came from fear. Her efforts to protect her daughter and bring her closer were actually serving to drive her further away. She was determined to let her daughter run her own life and to try and support her rather than smother her. She had felt smothered as a teenager by her mother's own fear based control tactics and was not going to repeat the scene.

Denise has since told me she and her daughter now have a much better relationship. They have to work at it and like many family relationships they have disagreements now and again. Denise can also now think of her mother from a different viewpoint.

We never did get to the third position perspective.

I learnt so much from this particular coaching experience, when I look back and reflect on it. I believe it fundamentally changed the way I approach the whole subject of coaching for the better.

You see, I realised I had an inbuilt bias regarding coaching techniques. I had assumed the way these techniques worked on the coaching courses was the way they would work in real life. The coaching training room environment is hugely artificial and, as everyone there "gets it," the sessions tend to go as planned; you do learn things but you also do not learn things if it makes any sense. It therefore came as a genuine surprise to me when the real world was actually different. People do not conform to a standard approach. Denise had no idea what she was supposed to do, think or feel during the exercise and she approached it with an open mind. I approached it thinking it would achieve the outcome I believed was best and would help Denise the most, i.e. new communication strategies.

Denise was delighted but I felt like a complete fraud. Denise gained a dramatic breakthrough which enabled her to make great changes but my superhero cape was in tatters and my halo was now round my ankles. I believed I had simply got it all wrong. The techniques had not gone as planned and it was more luck than judgement which saved the day.

I was working hard at the time to help all my clients yet my love of the many process techniques and my using them to achieve specific ends had blinded me to being more open-minded and flexible in my approach. I thought of myself as a fixer rather than a change facilitator. The sessions with Denise triggered my light bulb moment and I finally and fully acknowledged good coaching is all about helping the client discover their own resources and insights and not about, even with the best of intentions, guiding them down the path I considered best for them. This had actually been mentioned many times on the coaching courses but I chose to ignore it at the time. The sessions with Denise gave me the kick in the backside perspective shift I needed to move on. To this day I still firmly believe she helped me more than I helped her.

Denise had in fact become more resilient by identifying and letting go of her fixed belief about how a mother rightly behaves. I became more resilient by letting go of my fixed beliefs and learning to embrace failure; recognising it as information pure and simple.

I now find I learn something new and useful whenever I coach or train any client. It may not be the exact thing I thought I might learn or achieve but, when I reflect, reframe and examine my thinking for traps and biases, it will almost always be of benefit to me.

Section 4: Action Stations

Resilient water adapts quickly to changing conditions. Water is always doing something. Water exists happily in many states. Water has an option for all the scenarios it can encounter. Water is relentless, tireless and patient; it always gets the job done eventually. If you adopt the same attitudes and behaviours you will develop your emotional resilience.

Introduction to section

There is a great emphasis and perceived value placed nowadays on people taking action. We hear action is good, action makes you dynamic and action makes you a strong decisive person. We have many expressions referring to this need for constant action, for example, "Don't just stand there, do something" or "Strike while the iron is hot" and even "Actions speak louder than words."

Do you ever feel rushed into doing something you know is a poor quality choice because you are often so short of thinking time? This is either because you are pushed into taking action of some sort by others or you feel compelled to do something just because you see everyone else doing something and do not want to be left out or fall behind. When you are short of planning and thinking time do you tend to go straight to your fall-back or default strategies? Do you figure they worked in situations similar to this and just hope they will work again this time? On many occasions this strategy will work and most of us do it all the time anyway. There are, however, occasions when it will blow up in your face and cause all sorts of problems. Ever had days like that? Me too.

I am all for taking action when the plan or strategy is felt to be a good one and based on correct thinking with a solid goal led direction and I will have more to say on this later.

There is also a huge amount of pressure on you to make correct decisions. Failure is generally thought of as "not an option" in our modern success or nothing culture. We have already looked at the concepts of success and failure in part two. You can even become paralysed with doubts and uncertainties, it is often called analysis paralysis, when you try to cover all the bases and guarantee success ahead of time. You can end up not starting anything at all.

If you see someone sitting around apparently doing nothing, how long is it before someone in charge moans at them or tells them to jump to it and get the work done? Not long in most work situations. Be honest now, how often have you thought of such people as lazy because they are not actually doing anything?

We are all conditioned to think like this but is it useful for us to continue to think like this?

Film directors love to shout "Action!" to commence the start of any filming session or "take" to use movie parlance. The hero of the movie delivers their witty one-liner then springs dynamically into motion to thwart the bad guy and win the leading lady's heart. The problem with the movies is they are unreal and drama is at best a fictitious version of real life. Even biographical or historical movies are unreal in the sense they are condensed versions of reality in which all of the boring bits have been cut out in order to create a watchable film.

Real life simply is not like the movies. You cannot physically edit it later to cut out the bits you do not want to have occurred although, as I mentioned in part one, you can mentally edit the internal narrative of your life to create or improve your current self-image and level of self-esteem. You cannot actually undo real events so you feel pressure to get them right first time whenever possible.

Here then is the modern dichotomy or dilemma which can ramp up your stress levels and reduce your emotional resilience. Where on the wide spectrum between taking action versus thinking and planning do we get the best results? You do not want to fail but you also do not want to remain on the starting line.

Do you go for constant action and make myriad changes as you go along in the hope you are successful with more things than you fail at? Or, do you go for incredibly detailed research and precision planning in order to reduce the number of projects yet vastly increase your success versus failure ratio?

This part is all about reconciling these two extremes and getting you from overwhelmed and stuck and into purposeful forward motion. We will also look at your relationship with time as well as your patience threshold.

Overwhelm

What exactly is overwhelm?

Generally, overwhelm is defined by dictionaries in two ways: one is to bury or drown beneath a huge mass of something, especially water and the other is to have a strong emotional effect upon.

Both of these are apt for our purposes.

If we are honest with ourselves we have all felt overwhelmed at times. I have been overwhelmed with grief, happiness, joy, sadness, worry, work, bills, you name it and I have been overwhelmed by it at some time or another. I expect you have your own experience of being overwhelmed in some way. It is a powerful emotional experience and one in which we can often feel completely powerless to control either ourselves or the events going on around us.

Overwhelm can happen at any time and the old cliché about the last straw which broke the camel's back comes immediately to my mind. Whether you get there slowly or quickly a tipping point is reached when it all gets too much and you feel as if you are shutting down and losing control.

Some of the signs and symptoms of overwhelm might be intense displays of anxiety, anger or irritability; self-destructive or non-useful thought process such as intense worry, doubt or helplessness and such behaviour as crying, needless lashing out or experiencing an anxiety attack. During an anxiety attack for example, you might experience a rapid heartbeat, excess sweating, tingling in the extremities and shortness of breath or even chest pains.

Overwhelm can start when a big personal or professional change has occurred or is about to occur. This is a very common experience amongst the clients I work with. In many circumstances, even though the actual change may be relatively small and if encountered in isolation might not even be a problem, combining this with a high level of general stress triggers the overwhelm state. The change may of course be big enough on its own to fully overwhelm you. Even though change is inevitable, we discussed the similarity between change and bereavement in the Fundamentals section, we are almost always significantly affected by it in some way as we pass through the various stages of the Kübler-Ross cycle. Overwhelm combined with a change experience can be a powerful emotional stress inducer. Overwhelm can also influence how long people linger at various stages of the change process so understanding it and developing practical techniques for overcoming it might prove extremely useful.

In my experience people often get overwhelmed due to the way they perceive their current situation.

Overwhelm can cognitively, emotionally and behaviourally paralyse you and stop you making any further progress. You cannot think straight, maintain emotional balance or behave effectively. You can become stuck and feel like you have zero options for getting unstuck. I know from personal experience; it is a bad place to be.

There are many ways in which psychologists and other students of human behaviour like to classify or differentiate people. One of the ways is by looking at how people prefer to gather their information and make sense of their world. People are said to have either a big picture high level preference or they are said to have a close-up detail preference. These two preferences form the extreme ends of a continuous spectrum. Some people operate at the extremes whilst most of us prefer a point of view between the extremes. We can also change our preference based on situational context.

When highly stressed and at our tipping point, if someone or something takes us over the edge we can become overwhelmed and we often become overwhelmed at either one of the two spectrum extremes. Perhaps you can think back to the last time you experienced overwhelm and see if the idea rings some bells.

Big picture overwhelm can occur when it all just seems too big for the person to handle. It is the classic catastrophe scenario as far as the overwhelmed person is concerned. They see everything at once with no apparent end point. You will potentially hear them say things like, "It's all gone wrong!" or "It's a complete and utter disaster!"

Detail avalanche overwhelm can occur when there is too much information or too many apparent things to do or cope with. People do not know where to start or even how to make sense of the perceived tsunami of tasks or details. You will hear them say things like, "I simply can't see the wood for the trees" or "I just don't know where to begin – it's all too much for me!"

If you have ever found yourself saying things like this be aware you are not alone. All of us have a different tolerance to ambiguity or the unknown. Your ambiguity threshold is the point where the situation changes from dynamic but tolerable to confusing and stressful. When stress levels are high you can more easily become overwhelmed. During periods of sudden change or after a period of lower level but relentless change the likelihood of you becoming overwhelmed by situations and events is heightened. In general, the higher your ambiguity threshold is, the more change and uncertainty you can handle before becoming stressed, the higher your emotional and professional resilience will be.

Now some useful mindsets, attitudes, behaviours and practical ways to avoid overwhelm then get unstuck if overwhelm strikes.

Getting unstuck

If you are overwhelmed at any time the very first thing to do is simply stop and think. One of my favourite Buddhist sayings is: "Do not just do something, stand there." This statement only applies to situation which are not life-threatening of course. You always need to make a judgement call in life so if a speeding car, runaway train, crazy dog, armed robber, flash flood or any other dangerous item is coming at you then I definitely recommend doing something positive and quick to avoid it. Private and work situations which are not immediately life-threatening can almost always benefit from you stopping and thinking in order to calm down, get unstuck, reduce overwhelm and then act wisely and effectively.

Here are some helpful ideas for you to think about during this stop and think period. Overwhelm almost always creates an "I am stuck" feeling which is what prevents you making progress. You do not know or see where to begin in order to move forward. You are metaphorically and often literally stuck.

Firstly, getting unstuck takes energy. You will need all the energy you can muster so the first thing to do is acknowledge the situation and your anxiety about it. Here is a question for you? Has resisting your feelings of overwhelm ever helped you get rid of them? It is more likely that fighting your anxiety only made things worse. Just accept the fact you are anxious about being overwhelmed and feeling stuck and also be fully aware there is nothing wrong with this. You are human and we all feel anxious at times.

Overwhelm is often more about the way you perceive the situation than the actual situation itself. Certainly, altering your perception of the situation almost always helps the overwhelming aspects of the situation recede and lose their apparent power over you.

So, the second idea is you need to stop any feelings of panic in their tracks and then calm down. Easier said than done perhaps but nonetheless necessary. Panic is a sudden sensation of fear which is so strong it takes over control of your executive or conscious decision making processes. It can dominate and even prevent reasonable and logical thinking. It replaces it with the overwhelming feelings and sensations of anxiety and agitation which we often label as the fight or flight reaction. I talked quite a bit about our response to strong emotions earlier in the fundamentals section so will not recap here other than to say, the faster you overcome it the faster you will calm down and start to think more clearly.

One key activity to help us humans stay alive is breathing. It is something we often take for granted because our bodies do the thinking for us and keep it all ticking along below our normal level of consciousness. When you are stressed you might find your heart racing as well as your breathing becoming very shallow and rapid. This limits the amount of oxygen you can take in and generally makes the situation worse. Deliberate and regular deep breathing on the other hand, or other lung I suppose would be more accurate, encourages your body's automatic relaxation response to kick in. Deep breathing occurs when you use your diaphragm, a pair of muscles under your lungs, to draw air fully into the lungs. This allows maximum oxygen transfer which then lowers your blood pressure, slows your heart rate and clears the blood of stress hormones. It also reduces the lactic acid build up in your muscles and balances the levels of oxygen and carbon dioxide in your blood. So if you are feeling panicky and overwhelmed, stop whatever you are doing and take a series of deep breathes. It is a great place to start your calming down routine and will often do the trick on its own.

To take your calming down routine further still, try and physically step away from the situation if you can. Changing your distance from a situation alters your perspective on the situation. Altering your perspective can alter your perception of it and never forget, perception equals reality. Try having a relaxing cup of your favourite non-alcoholic beverage in a pleasant or safe location away from the source of your stress. Take a walk, listen to some suitable music, meditate, have a yoga or tai chi session or even go to the gym or run to take your mind and self out of the situation. If you find a quiet spot try singing or shouting at the top of your voice. Write down your troubles in order to offload them for a time. Whatever safely relaxes you is a good thing to do to complete your calm down.

The third idea is really a set of three linked ideas which all fall under the same general heading of adjusting your head.

Alter your self-talk, alter your mental attitude and focus on right now.

We spent some time earlier looking at your self-talk and I said I believed it to be the single most important area in which to make life-changing improvements. Getting unstuck is a golden opportunity to practice your new skills.

Take some time to listen to the language you are using. If you find yourself thinking phrases like these then you need to take a time out: "This list of tasks is ridiculous, I will never get it all done today;" "Nobody can reasonably expect me to cope with this issue, I might as well give up now;" "What is the point in even trying?" I am sure you would agree, given all we have talked about so far, these phrases are not helpful to you in any way.

Stop, consider and ask yourself, "How can I alter these to make them more useful?" For example, you could change the phrases above to: "Although this task list is long and I may not finish it all today, if I prioritise and seek some assistance I can get most of the really important items finished and tidy up the rest tomorrow;" "I need to take a short break in order to get my head straight. Which will help me gain perspective in order to tackle this issue. I am not going to give up on this one;" "If I do not try I will definitely never succeed. Now, let us break it down a bit then develop a workable action plan."

When we are in an overwhelming situation we often think in strange ways and we do not always have a mental state or attitude which is useful or productive for us.

Because you have taken the time to acknowledge the situation, breathe, calm down and check for quality self-talk, you can now also take the opportunity to look at managing your emotional state. What emotional state would serve you best? Anger, fear and frustration have not been helping so what else would? How would a dynamic and decisive mindset help you out? What about a problem-solving and curious mindset? How about a well-organised, positive and calm mindset? If you need a refresher on a method to do this please check back to the mindfulness and state management section and follow the strategy outlined there.

Good, you are calm and relaxed now with a positive emotional state. To really get you on track and help get you unstuck the trick is to focus on right now. Whenever we have an overwhelming situation the tendency is to look ahead at all the work to come. Even if you pick one task to have a go at you can still picture all the rest stretching out in front of you. Looming deadlines can still get us agitated again despite our best efforts. This situation will not help you. Those deadlines will still be there tomorrow or in two months or whenever, whether you are worrying about them or not. However, by fully focusing on the here and now and forgetting the future for a while, you can put all your positive energy and skills into planning the all-important taking action phase with minimal distractions and maximum effectiveness.

If you are finding this idea of focus does not come easily to you, I recommend using a quick but powerful visualising technique. Here is how I do it but feel free to adapt to your own preferences.

I visualise myself in a large well lit room and I am stood in front of a nice writing desk, you know, the kind a powerful CEO might have. The only things on this desk are a switched off angle-poised lamp and a clipboard with a sheaf of papers clipped to it. I cannot see the papers clearly but then the edges of the room begin to grow dark and this darkness rapidly closes in right up to the edges of the desk until all I can see is the desk itself and the items on it. By now, the angle-poise light has come on and it is very bright. I lean over the desk and can now clearly see the first paper on the clipboard is a checklist of steps for the taking action phase of the whole getting unstuck sequence. This is all I can see and the darkness hides all other distractions. I can now begin to work.

This visualisation technique really does the business for me. There does not have to be any logic to it. It is just a simple way for me to clear my mind and focus on the important things I need to get done to move on. Give it a go. Your mind is a powerful thing and you may well be amazed to find you can harness it as an ally rather than unwittingly let it work against you.

The fourth practical idea is to take stock, analyse your situation then go ahead and take some positive action to move yourself along. How will you do this? The good news is this will be the topic of the next section and, being a process kind of guy, I will outline a practical strategy for you to get unstuck by effectively planning some action and determining your first next step.

Effective action planning

In the last section I ended by saying the idea of taking action is the best way to get unstuck. It is actually more of a necessity than an idea because, in my experience, you cannot get properly unstuck without taking some action of your own. You could just wait calmly and see if anything useful happens due to someone else's influence. This is a very passive approach and having other people take control of your life is not much fun in my opinion. I am not saying it will not work but you may have to wait a long while and, if anything does happen, you will have very little control over the results or the direction it takes you and it could even end up worse for you. No, the only way to go is to take some direct action of your own. You have to do something. Once you are moving forward again you can always adjust things as you go in order to make more progress, right? Well, here is the thing. You do not just want to take any old starting action at this point. It is not simply a case of taking action for action's sake. You want to be a bit smarter than the average bear and take some effective action at this point. You want to take a useful action which will justify your efforts and leave you feeling good about yourself. This is what resilient people do.

Because you have gone to all the trouble of calming down and getting into a useful mental state you can now afford to invest a little more time in order to think carefully about your next move.

This is why I suggest you use the following three phase strategy which will ensure you explore all avenues open to you and choose a useful start point. Take stock, plan and then act.

Let us look at phase one which is taking stock.

The first thing to do is analyse the whole scenario and try to define or redefine exactly what you are stuck about. This involves taking a big picture overview of the overwhelming situation, your knowledge of it and your relationship to it.

Let us create a suitable example to use for this whole section. Suppose you are running your own printing business and you and your staff are already snowed under with work. Suppose further it is two o'clock in the afternoon on a Thursday and you have three tight deadlines to meet for several smaller volume but still very important clients. The real big elephant in the room is the Mega Insurance company order. Mega Insurance is your bread and butter account and you are relying on keeping their account because you have a number of loyal staff and things have been tough lately. Your staff have been with you through thick and thin. Mega Insurance have just put in an important order for promotional material which absolutely has to be ready for their big conference launch tomorrow. The price is good and you are sure you can make all the deadlines and get their order in too. A lot of it is already done and provided nothing goes wrong you will just get it done along with everything else by the end of today. Whew! It is exciting running your own business but it can also be tough being the boss in such a fast paced world.

At ten past two it all starts to go a bit pear-shaped. Danny, who has been with you for many years and almost never goes off sick, has come over all funny. He has had to take a rest in the staff room and Rita, one of the other team members, is with him now. You check to see if he is all right and he says he just needs a rest. The first problem for you is Danny is the only one, apart from you, who can work the Doodadprint Super-folder machine. Keeping this bit of kit running is essential for completing the Mega Insurance order. You start to feel a little bit anxious but, as he said he just needs a rest, you chivvy Rita back to work and tell Danny you will pop back in half an hour. No worries, he says he will be back on his feet in no time. You take over on Danny's station. You are not as fast as him but you are the boss so you have got to lead by example.

At half past two one of the big printers, which is handling another client's deadline order, makes a loud screeching sound and starts billowing smoke. Kathy, the operator, deals with it calmly and correctly by switching it off at the wall with a wooden broom handle then using the powder fire extinguisher. The fire alarm did not even go off. Once the dust settles and everything settles down, you see it is a complete write off but at least no-one is hurt. What the blazes is going on today? You quiz Kathy on what she did wrong to cause the breakage and she surprises you by flying off the handle at your questions. She then bursts into tears and runs to the staff room. Almost immediately she comes racing back to announce Danny has passed out on the floor and there is blood everywhere. This is getting serious. Everyone downs tools and races to tend to Danny. You immediately call for an ambulance as the first aider announces he has fainted and bumped his head when falling. The blood looks a lot worse than it probably is but head wounds can be tricky. The ambulance is definitely required so good call on getting one sorted.

The ambulance soon arrives to take Danny away and Rita goes with him. You tell everyone to take a tea break to calm down but your own nerves are shredded. You go back to the Mega Insurance order and ten minutes later, because your mind is all over the place and you are not focused, you make a simple mistake which churns out a thousand useless brochures. You stop the machine in a kind of shocked daze, put your head in your hands and think to yourself, "That's it then, we've blown it. I've blown it. I'm down two machines and two staff members, one of whom might die for all I know. I've upset Kathy and none of these orders will be done by tomorrow. My reputation's ruined. I can't deal with all this anymore." The staff see you in this dazed and miserable state when they return from break. They force a cup of tea into your hands and sit you at your desk. It is three o'clock now. Any of these things in isolation would be stressful enough but all at once they seem to be devastating. In just one hour your world appears to have collapsed around you. A good case of overwhelm if ever I saw one.

So, this can go two ways right now. You can give up and pick up any pieces later or you can take the time to think and get yourself out of the proverbial with a plan and some positive, useful actions.

Luckily, it turns out you are the resilient sort so you drink your tea and take a series of deep breaths to calm down. You take a quick walk outside the factory to clear your head and, whilst walking, you tell yourself you have dealt with far worse situations than this before now and come through in one piece so you decide to approach this in a logical manner and get out your trusty notepad and pencil.

Let us step out of the example for a bit. When you first look at the big picture it can seem a little bit, well, big. I recommend asking yourself a series of simple yet powerful questions to initially try and make more sense of it.

What are the facts of the situation? What is important and why? What resources have you lost? What resources do you still have? Can you replace or substitute these resources? What deadlines are in place? What is yet to be completed? Can you contact anyone else for help? Is there anything else you have not asked?

Please note, whenever you answer these questions you must get into the habit of challenging your own answers. Act like a coach would and keep asking, "Is there anything else?" Check your answers are honest, complete and logically sound.

Back into the print works scenario where you start to answer the questions.

First, what are the facts? The facts are: It is now three thirty in the afternoon on a Thursday. You have two staff down, two machines down and four deadlines to meet by tomorrow. The Mega Insurance order is the most important deadline but the other three are still very important to your business and need to be completed. Hold on a second. Is this right? You are actually only one machine down because you can still work the folder unit yourself. You made the earlier mistake but the machine is not broken; this is what overwhelm can do to your logical processes.

Second, what is important and why? Your business reputation is important because the goodwill you have built up has resulted in very loyal customers. Keeping your customers happy is important for repeat business. Your staff are hugely important because they have been with you through good and bad times and you cannot do anything without them. Your calmness under fire and your leadership skills are important because right now other people are depending on you to guide them. Is anything else important? Have you missed anything? You do not think so but you can always come back to it.

Third question, what resources have you lost? This is an easy one. Same as the facts above right? Wrong! They are only hardware resources. On reflection you realise you may have lost Kathy as a positive resource. She is still here but upset. In the panic of it all you effectively accused her of breaking her printing machine. She performed well under the pressure of the fire and did all the right things but you gave her grief without knowing any of the facts. You make a note. One of your highest priorities now is to apologise to Kathy and regain here support. You have also lost time which is one of your most precious resources.

Fourthly, what resources do you still have? You have all but two of your loyal staff with you. You have all the remaining machines except Kathy's printer. You have one and a half hours of regular work time left and the staff are still producing materials as fast as they can.

You get to the fifth question and here you pause. You realise only certain members of your staff can answer this and subsequent questions so you go back into the production area. You consider talking privately to Kathy and apologising to her but it suddenly dawns on you; you told her off in public so you would do well to also apologise in public. You ask everyone to gather round. You make your heartfelt apology to Kathy and she takes it well. She then asks for a situation update. You begin to read your self-determined answers to the first questions and get your first positive surprise of the afternoon. The minute you start to talk about resources and the broken printer,

Joe points out there is an older model in the maintenance area which still works and will pretty much do the job; it just needs a new plug and some ink cartridges. Brilliant news.

When you ask about the deadlines and what needs to be completed you get even more good news but not the type of news you expected to hear. You find you are not just getting simple answers to your questions or a response list of facts about what there is left to do or when the jobs need to be completed. What you are getting are probing questions, well-thought out summaries and some wonderful suggestions for moving on. You did forget one massive thing when you wrote down your resources. You had your staff marked down as mere working resources. You could and should have considered them as a planning and idea generating resource. They are potentially in the mire almost as much as you are and they are keen to help. They love the business too. You are not actually on your own as you first thought. This throws you and you take a moment to consider before the light bulb really goes off.

You decide to work through the question list as a team - the time you take to do this will pay back many times over in terms of ideas and collective brainpower. Is this not an obvious conclusion? Do not beat yourself up about it because in times of crisis we do not always think and behave at our peak performance. Always have your internal voice working for you.

Things are moving at a fast pace now and you have in fact moved naturally into phase two which is the planning phase. There is often an overlap between phase one and two as it is an iterative process. More ideas generate more questions as you form a workable plan.

It further turns out two of the smaller order deadlines are actually at end of business tomorrow. This gives you a lot more time to complete. One of your staff, Terry, has a brother-in-law who works at a competitor business, something which you did not know, and he took it upon himself to give them a ring. It turns out they have the capacity to complete the third smaller order work overnight; they will even do it at cost as a gesture of goodwill. All you have to do is send a courier round to collect and deliver it first thing in the morning. They are apparently interested in tendering for some collaborative work which could benefit both organisations and see this as a demonstration of credibility. Well, well, well.

The only problem left is what to do about the Mega Insurance order. Another staff member has already phoned the contact there and it transpires they absolutely need the materials by 1100hrs at the venue which is 50 miles away from your premises. It is getting very near home time now so you put it to the staff to offer some suggestions for managing this which they will be happy with. You leave them to chat for 10 minutes and wander off to have a cup of tea in the canteen. Rita at the hospital calls you and says Danny is fine but needs a week off; nothing life-threatening. More good news which you share with the staff right away to lift their spirits.

Regarding the work to complete, they are all keen to help out. Some staff can stay on until 1am and the rest have agreed to come in at 1am to take over and finish off ready for the delivery driver to take the Mega Insurance order to their conference venue at 9am. If all goes well it will work out fine. You make a mental note to give a very special bonus this year.

You now need to ask yourself five more questions: What is essential? What can you ignore? Who can you empower? What quick wins are available for boosting spirits? Is there anything obvious I might have missed here?

The priorities have pretty much decided themselves in this instance but one thing you can do for a quick win straight away is to send out for fish and chips for everyone staying on as a thank you. The rest will get a big fried breakfast thank you in the morning.

You double check everything then you agree your plans and

assign various people to the various tasks. You ring the other printing company boss yourself to thank them personally and you also agree to meet next week as a follow-up. Someone from each shift is assigned to order free taxis and food for everyone. You still need to work the folding machine but you also need some sleep in order to work it with a clear head. You reluctantly agree to go straight home and rest up until 1am. This will also prevent you fussing about and getting in everyone's way. It has been a long day for everyone.

That is it. You have taken action and you have gotten yourself unstuck. You have also discovered positive things about yourself and your staff which may well have surprised you. You have all been very resilient despite the seemingly disastrous situation which unfolded earlier on.

Right now, you might very well be saying, "Hold on a minute there Mr Big-time Author, that fictitious situation is all very well and good but what about the real world where I live? What about the real situations I find myself in?" Good question and I would ask something similar in your position. This scenario was indeed an illustrative construct and the ending was also a construct. You will note here I have selected the happy fairy-story type ending. It could have gone in any number of ways of course. For example, Danny could have died, the orders might never have been completed, the business could have closed, the staff may have given up leaving you alone to face the music and so on and so forth.

Here is my point. Situations very much like this, and very much worse of course, play out all the time in real life and they can always be handled in one of two basic ways. You can take control of the situation or you can let the situation control you. You might not always get a good result, such is life, but you will have a far greater chance of a successful outcome by choosing the resilient taking control route and following the general three phase process illustrated above. You will move away from a non-useful victim mentality towards a far more useful self-determining mentality.

All of the above applies to your personal life and life goals as much as it does to business and professional situations. Take the time to examine and analyse what you really want to do then start doing it. Use your head and your heart to help you decide; use your thoughts and your feelings. Ask yourself the right questions and give honest answers. Take some action and control over your life by starting your good but not perfect projects with the confidence you can shepherd them to their ultimate destination and get the results you desired.

If you want to get different – you have got to do different. Develop a workable plan and initiate some action. If it works do it some more. If it does not work go through the three phases again and then try another plan. Resilience often takes perseverance and flexibility.

GOYA

The Spanish artist Francisco José de Goya y Lucientes (1746 to 1828) was a painter to the Spanish Royal Court.

Better known simply as Goya, he was a romantic painter and printmaker and is regarded as both the last of the Old Masters and one of the precursors of the expressionist movement. One of his best known paintings is "The Nude Maja" (La Maja Desnuda).

Why on earth am I waffling on about a late 18th century Spanish painter?

What interests me is his name. When I want to get myself to take some action I think of Goya or more precisely GOYA.

For me, the letters which make up the word GOYA represent the statement and instruction to Get Off Your Arse.

We all need a metaphorical kick up the backside now and again. I know I do. Please bear in mind, I generally reserve this direct approach for myself only. There have been occasions where I have successfully encouraged and motivated certain people with this approach but, as we already know, you cannot change anyone else directly - you can only change yourself.

Sometimes all the rational and logical arguments and encouragement in the world will fail to motivate me. If you have ever been mentally stuck and unable to make progress with a task or project you will know the exact feeling. I can put a glittering and compelling goal together and break it down into the appropriate steps but, if the first step is one I do not necessarily relish or look forward to, I sometimes have to kick myself in the rear end and say to myself

"Get off your arse and ..." in order to get moving.

Here is a great quote, overwhelmingly attributed to Mark Twain, "If it is your job to eat a frog, it is best to do it first thing in the morning. And if it is your job to eat two frogs, it is best to eat the biggest one first."

I love this quote and I believe Mr Twain would have been a big fan of the GOYA approach. It quite marvellously captures the whole concept. Substitute whatever is putting you off starting your particular task or activity in place of "eat a frog" and get it done early. Get it done speedily and efficiently in order to move on to other activities. This quote inspired Brian Tracy to write his excellent book "Eat That Frog!" and I can heartily recommend it to you if procrastination is one of your barriers to success.

Whenever I find myself over-thinking a situation (analysis paralysis) or simply going round in circles regarding my next step or action, I tell myself firmly to "Get off my arse" and do whatever is needed to get into gear and into motion. Once in some sort of motion and making progress, no matter how small or simplistic, I find momentum builds naturally and it is far easier to make progress toward achieving my goals.

Here is a quick reality check. From many years personal experience in the "struggling to get started" state, I am the first to admit it is not the easiest thing in the world. Many of the people I work with are frequently in the same situation. Here is a technique you might like to try and adapt for yourself. As you will know by now, I always recommend maintaining a friendly and supportive internal voice but sometimes the internal boot in the backside is just what is required to get me motivated. I like to have my internal voice impersonate Mr BA (Bad Attitude) Baracus from the hit TV series "The A-Team" (1983 to 1987). He was hugely over-played by the fabulous Laurence Tureaud (professional wrestler Mr T). A tiny version of him sits on my right shoulder and delivers all the motivation I need to get off my backside and do something useful. Seeing his avatar and hearing his loud and over the top persona makes me crack-up laughing but it does the job. Humour is an incredibly important value in my worldview so I laugh and make things fun whenever possible. If you have not seen any of "The A-Team" series check out a few episodes to see what I mean about BA. He is my motivator; try developing your own.

What voice or character would get you moving? How could you change or amplify the characteristics of the voice or character to power up the motivational effectiveness and the humour?

Give GOYA a try and you might just surprise yourself.

Your relationship with time

If you feel constant time pressure in your life and work then you are definitely not alone. Nowadays everyone feels under pressure to manage their time well, produce optimum results within ultra-tight deadlines and never waste a second on anything remotely unproductive.

Just to make it interesting, you are also bombarded by advertising media which tries to convince you to believe unless you are fully in control of your life, having unlimited fun and high quality times with your loved ones whilst buying and using the advertised products to do it of course, there is something seriously wrong with you.

There is also a huge and profitable training industry niche which has been built up through delivery of Time Management courses. The reason for the demand for these courses is, no matter which course is delivered by whatever guru or fancy training business, no real progress is ever made with time management. Businesses still want to improve their time management so they buy more and more courses in the hope, eventually, one will do the trick for them. However, there is a good reason why no real progress is made and here is the scoop which you will not hear very often from the time management training industry, time management is actually impossible.

Doctor Who, the Gallifreyan Time Lord of UK television fame can certainly manage time. The Time Traveller hero of HG Well's novel "The Time Machine" could manage time. Marty McFly and Doctor Emmett "Doc" Brown in the movie "Back to the Future" could manage time. Even the various crews of the Enterprise in "Star Trek" could manage to control time now and again with their chronometric particles and other such useful devices. The key point to notice here is all these time managers are fictitious. They are made up. Imaginary. Not real.

We cannot manage time.

All we can do is maximise the quality and/or quantity of the things we do and the experiences we have in the seconds, minutes and hours of every day, week, month and year we get in our lives; time we will never get back once we have lived through it. These seconds, minutes and hours are one-shot deals and are never to be repeated. Phil Connors, Bill Murray's character in the movie "Groundhog Day", got many chances to go back and correct the past mistakes of a day but I am pretty sure you and I cannot because once again it is a made up fantasy movie. You get the idea I am sure.

In reality the time management courses are actually prioritisation and productivity courses. It is all they ever can be in fact. They will likely help you cram even more stuff into your busy day. They will try to help you prioritise the things you tackle in order to accomplish better results. They will try to help you eliminate non-productive or time-consuming activities and encourage you to develop good habits which help you cram more into less.

This guide is all about emotional resilience so I am not about to give you a huge list of time saving tips and a lecture on prioritising.

What I am going to do is offer you some insights on improving your relationship with time and your strategies for working effectively with the time you have. We all have our own way of relating to time and we all have our own stress triggers when time pressure is applied. Getting this time relationship right for you is a key factor in helping you avoid the negative stress of overwhelm. This will allow more options for you to take action, get unstuck and therefore become more resilient as a result.

From my previous personal experience, and from my experience of coaching many time-stressed people, the most common time stressor is simply trying to cram too much into too little time. This low quality scenario can happen in several ways. Sometimes our working environment dictates this outcome by constantly piling too much work on our plates. Sometimes we lack the ability to use our existing time effectively enough to achieve deadlines. Sometimes we create the situation ourselves by trying to over-achieve and offering or committing to doing too much in too short a timescale. However, the situation arises it can generate a large amount of negative stress for us and the people we work with and for. Have you ever had to wait for a vital item from somebody which only arrives in a last minute rush or worse, too late? Hopefully the quality is good enough but sometimes it is not. It is stressful and not a lot of fun.

Can you do anything to mitigate or better yet avoid the above situations? Can you really develop different relationships with time in order to improve your emotional resilience? I will offer you my thoughts on the subject and why I think many people have it all wrong at present.

All of the above scenarios, and many more involving conflict with time, are just as described; conflicts with time. People are working against time. Time is seen as the enemy to be battled against. This is wrong. The trick with time is, always has been and always will be to work with it and not against it.

Reading this, you might feel fully justified in saying, "Once again, that's all very well and good Mr Smart Alec Writer, but how exactly do I work with time and not against it? My boss may not have read this, by the way. Life happens all the time and gets right in the way of my timetables." I hear you loud and clear and these are words I have used myself many times over the years. With experience, what I now know is once you start to think differently about time and change your relationships to it, you will start to get more control and make better decisions around how you work with it. Others will see this change in you and begin to respect it, or at least accept it, and your self-esteem and emotional resilience will be greater as a result of the changes. It is not easy and will take time just as anything worthwhile does; and it is worthwhile.

Have you ever been so absorbed in a hobby or activity which has you so focused and had you so engrossed you lost all track of time? You know the scenario where your tea is stone cold, your loved ones have given you up for lost and it has gone pitch dark outside even though you started in the morning. You were in what psychologist Dr Mihaly Csikszentmihalyi calls the flow state. Essentially this flow state condition means your whole cognitive processing capacity was being used up on the task at hand. Time essentially appeared to stand still for you.

Do you remember the best holiday you ever had? Did it seem to go all too quickly? Great parties also are always over all too quickly. How about other wonderful and fun events in your life? Did they move fast or slow? Do you remember your school summer holidays? I do, the lazy days always seemed to stretch for months and it never rained. How were yours?

What about the opposite end of the spectrum? Ever had to do a chore or drudge task which lasted forever? Watching the clock made it worse did not it? The seconds stretched and stretched. The minute hand seemed to have jammed and the hour hand never moved at all. Time dragged and I will bet you really hated time itself right then.

Here is my first point. Time is plastic and can be deformed like a plastic. Time can be stretched or compressed; at least it feels like it can. It is our perception of time which creates this feeling and for us humans our perception is our reality. Our attitude and mental state at any given time can directly influence our perception of time and therefore our actual experience of time passing.

One of the most obvious things you can do with tasks which are boring or unpalatable is to perceive them as passing more quickly. Try to make them fun. Turn them into competitions or games. Redefine the tasks into something different and more exciting than the seemingly boring or pointless activities they first appear to be. Doing fun things appears to make time pass more quickly. Mary Poppins is a master of this. I know, I know, she is also fictitious but hey I am the author here. Mary Poppins knows how to turn drudgery into fun and I am a real big fan of her work.

What about extending the time of things you enjoy? What about stopping time altogether? Try to replicate the flow state mentioned above. Focus deeply and get fully in the moment. Become engrossed and absorbed in the task or situation at hand and be mindful of your emotional and mental states. What states will benefit you most? For me, a combined state of curiosity, concentration and relaxation works really well; states I use when writing. Find what works best for you. Reread the part one section on state management if it helps.

We all know there are sixty minutes in an hour, twenty four hours in a day and seven days in a week. In hours, this equates to one hundred and sixty eight hours in a week. We all have this amount of time and no more in a week. If we sleep for an average eight hours each night this still leaves us an average of one hundred and twelve hours to work, eat and play a week. Sixteen hours a day. This actually seems quite a lot of time but how many of us fully use those sixteen hours to get done what we want or need to get done? Not many I will bet. How well do you use your time?

At the time of writing I have been on this earth for approximately eighteen thousand five hundred days. Those days are gone. They are behind me and will never be repeated. Do not misunderstand me, I have had huge amounts of fun and have many brilliant memories of brilliant experiences. Now, if I am lucky I will have around eleven thousand days left. Many of these eleven thousand days will not be my best or most active days but I need to make sure I maximise and enjoy as many of them as I can. Does this appear to be a weird or morbid way of analysing a life? Well there is no getting away from it, if you are born you will at some stage die and it is a cast iron no quibble guarantee. Here is the trick, get as much good stuff done in the time between those two events as possible. How do your time equations look? Are you maximising your brilliant memories?

Here is my second point. Time for us is precious and finite. You simply cannot magic or create more time out of thin air; when it is gone, it is gone. Here are some things to consider as you ponder on this obvious but often ignored fact.

Do not procrastinate. If you want to do something there is no better time than now. If there is something boring or annoying which you have to complete in order to get to something good then get it done now. The delays you make are robbing you of your precious time resource. When we are young we feel we have all the time in the world. This is not true. If you have something you want to achieve or complete, then get started as soon as you can and keep going until it is done. The old saying about procrastination being the thief of time is true. The person being robbed of the time is you.

Be wary of time vampires. These are people who will carelessly or deliberately take up your time for their own agendas and give you nothing in return. You will hand over some of your precious time for someone else's use and get nothing out of the deal. Time spent with family and other loved ones is a great trade. Time spent having brilliant experiences is a great trade. Time spent doing good works which fill you with joy is a great trade. Time spent building a worthwhile career which delivers you a lifestyle you love is also a great trade. Time given to a time vampire is simply time wasted. Zealously guard every second which they try to steal from you. Educate them to understand your time is not there for the taking. Think about it every time someone says to you, "Have you got a spare five minutes?" It is never five minutes and it is never really spare is it. Take the time to identify these time vampires. They are often the people you would least suspect. A little here and a little there soon add up. Control your interactions with these time vampires whenever possible and you will have more time for doing what you truly value.

Do not waste time on any pointless activities or activities which you do not have to do.

Think about your work life. How many pointless meetings have you attended just because someone else (a definite time vampire) wanted a full house on the meeting day? How many pointless checks of your e-mail in-box do you make in a day? How many e-mails do you get which are nothing to do with you? How many do you send? How many wasted minutes on the phone waiting for someone to pick up? How many nuisance calls? How many quick Interweb searches do you run? The list could go on and on. How many drudge tasks do you undertake which would be better done by someone else? People often complain they have no time at work for all their assigned tasks yet they are constantly wasting the time they do have. If you are bored then find or create a project to do which challenges you. If you are tired by your current task, leave your desk to take a short but high-quality break and come back to it refreshed and energised. Do not simply search the Interweb or turn round to chat with colleagues about how tired you are; you will become a time vampire yourself. Can you outsource, delegate, negotiate or simply palm-off any tasks? I am sure you can find at least one if you look hard enough. Remember a drudge task for you might well be a development task for someone else. Do what you are paid to do and create real value with what you do. I constantly monitor my writing output with a spreadsheet and charts. It might sound lame and nerdy but I need this sort of thing to keep as focused and productive as I can be in this noisy time-hungry world we live in. If I did not do this, things would simply drift and my creations would never see the light of day.

Think about your private life. We all need to relax but how much of your time is wasted on TV or video games? Could you do something different with you time? What bad habits have you developed? If there are things you really want to achieve then why are not you working on achieving them? Why are you wasting your precious time? If I sound a bit evangelical about all this it is because I get incredibly annoyed at the waste going on. Be ruthless with yourself. When you feel more in tune with how well you use the time you have you will feel less pressured by deadlines, you will feel able to achieve more and you will naturally be more emotionally resilient as a result.

Here is an eye-opening activity which shocks many of my clients. I recommend everyone try it out and I especially want you to try it. Keep a journal, notebook or diary of every activity you do both at work and at home with the time spent on them. Be deadly accurate and honest because if you cheat you are just cheating yourself. Do this for at least a month and then tot up all the time you spend on each activity. Some of the time wasters will make you cringe. Eliminate them and use the newly available time to do more of what matters most to you. It is quite a liberating experience. I have clients who still keep the diaries going after the trial in order to keep fine tuning their use of time. They are now highly productive in their working environments and very happy and more creative in their private lives.

When you free up more time, and you will if you stop wasting it and stop others stealing it, here is one last pair of key ideas which serve my clients well in their efforts to become more resilient.

Key idea one is to commit fairly then try to over-deliver. These things need to be done together or it does not really work. The commit fairly part means you will always agree or negotiate fair time scales for projects or services which you are confident you will be able to achieve. Both parties will be happy with the deal at this point. This means you will rarely if ever let anyone down. Your promises will be kept with regard to your agreed deadline targets. Doing this part alone will make a huge difference to your emotional resilience due firstly to the fact people will perceive you as highly reliable and secondly you will feel in much more control of things. With enhanced control comes enhanced resilience. With the luxury of the correct and workable amount of time now available to you I recommend you now try to exceed people's expectation in some way which is still within your control to deliver but adds real value for them.

For example, many years ago, and in a previous working phase of mine, I knew a top class furniture maker. A discerning couple had commissioned this furniture maker to design and create for them a relatively expensive piece of bespoke bedroom furniture. The craftsman came highly recommended and the design he drew up was wonderful. The price quoted was fair given the design and materials and because the quality of the finished item was very important to the couple agreed to the fair delivery date of six months. Now, here is the thing, the furniture maker quoted the more than fair six months in order to be sure he could definitely deliver on time. In reality he completed the work in five months and also had one of his apprentices use the offcuts from the expensive timber to produce a practice piece. The apprentice actually made a small but beautiful one of a kind jewellery box. The furniture maker then decorated it with some rare veneers he had and also had the inside professionally lined with silk by another respected crafts-person he collaborated with. What effect do you think this extra but relatively inexpensive work had? Aside from the early delivery, the couple loved the jewellery box almost if not more than the furniture item because it was unexpected and just for them. The apprentice gained valuable new skills and the partner business also gained some income. Do you think the furniture maker was recommended by the couple? You better believe it. They ordered more furniture and told their friends about him too. This man never actually advertised for work. How could you start to run the commit fairly and over-deliver strategy in your life or work?

Key idea two is to focus on and complete one task, or indeed one discrete phase of any planned project, at a time. The act of focusing on a single activity until it is complete will get your overall task list completed much more quickly and with better quality results than doing many tasks at the same time. Forget the multi-tasking concept. Seriously, multi-tasking is one of the biggest productivity myths out there. It is very attractive to think juggling two or more tasks at once will make you super-productive but sadly, with everything save the very simplest of tasks, it is simply not going to happen. You will not complete twice as much in the same time. What you will do is end up with two or more half-baked outcomes in far more time. You may even have to redo your work. How will poor quality work keep your clients and co-workers happy? Will it get you respect, recommendation or even a pay rise? We humans simply cannot multi-task. All we can do is switch our attention rapidly back and forth between the various tasks. It is obviously more difficult to regain focus on the current task if you are switching rapidly like this. This is why it takes longer and the quality inevitably suffers. If your work and your results are important to you, do not try and multi-task. If you are under pressure to produce more output with better quality always carefully plan your work in advance then opt for the focus and complete approach. Spread the word.

Make sure you know what is important to you and spend as much time as you can on those things. What activities represent good time for you? For myself it is about personal growth, having fun with loved ones, producing quality work results, helping clients, achieving goals, writing, sailing and relaxing in order to recharge my batteries; these, and many others, are examples of good time activities for me. You do not always have to be busy to be investing in quality time.

To summarise this section. Make the time for the things which are important to you and the people you love. It is your time after all so do not waste a second of it if you do not have to. Get into the good time relationship habits as quickly as possible. You will feel more in control of things and your emotional resilience will grow.

Patience is a virtue

Another hugely important tool to add to your emotional resilience toolbox is patience.

Despite the impression everything in modern life either is, or could be, made available or achieved in an instant, it is not good for you in many ways. Nowadays we have and expect, fast travel, super-fast communication, fast food and fast just about everything else. We abhor delays of any sort, especially in communication. Delays have us worrying about the possible reason and imagining all sorts of dire outcomes, almost all of which are, well, imaginary. How did you feel and behave during your last traffic jam? Have you ever sent an e-mail and wondered why an instant response was not forthcoming? Would you like to feel or behave differently? We all feel time-poor and we often ignore any choice which is not "fast" even though the ignored choice might be the best one for us long-term.

This constant modern need for speed and instant gratification has encouraged us to develop an attitude of impatience in many areas of our life where patience is still required. Patience is vital in many circumstances and if you can become more patient you will become more emotionally resilient.

Some of the benefits of patience would include better emotional state control and reduced negative stress levels, better and more-effective decision making, being less demanding on yourself and others along with an enhanced ability to reflect on feedback leading to improved personal growth. I am sure you can think of many others. Patience is in fact a necessary component of many of the emotional resilience tools provided.

We all have a level of patience already. There will be a point where we lose patience with someone, something or some situation and I will call this your patience threshold. It varies with context of course. Your threshold at work it might be quite low relative to your threshold at home.

Developing more patience is clearly a good thing but it does not come easily to most of us and it is probably harder now than ever to be patient. Even if you feel you are quite patient, in my opinion it is always worth trying to raise your patience threshold still further. So, whilst it is all very well to waffle on about this, how exactly can you start to develop more patience?

Let us look first at what patience is and is not. Patience is a positive state of mind. Patience is your ability to mentally cope with waiting, delays or other frustrations without becoming angry, bored, agitated or otherwise unduly upset. Patience enables you to control your emotions and behave in a calm and controlled manner when presented with unexpected difficulties or unwanted challenges. Think of patience as a kind of guardian helper whose role is to constructively challenge your decisions, allow you to stay calm and stress free, exhibit empathy and understanding of others and keep you on track when pursuing long-term goals or projects.

Patience is definitely not to be confused with passivity. Patience involves taking full responsibility and control, taking an intentional stance and moving steadily toward a desired outcome. Passivity involves taking no responsibility or action at all and simply waiting around to see what will happen to you.

Based on the last section, when we discussed your relationship to time and the idea of guarding against the wasting of it, you might be thinking the idea of patience is in opposition to the idea of maximising time usage. This is a common misunderstanding regarding the relationship of patience and time. As I have said, patience is not about sitting around and wasting time waiting for things to happen. Far from it in fact.

Patience is more about mentally prioritising and organising things in order to get them done right. Patience is about taking care to invest a little bit of time effectively to ensure a lot of time and energy is not wasted further down the line. Patience is about checking and challenging your decisions and ideas as thoroughly as the situation allows and not simply charging ahead with the first thing occurring to you. Patience is about helping you maintain your big picture perspective and keeping you focused on your distant long-term goal. Even though you might break it down as we discussed in the goal setting section, you will need patience to keep going with the overall plan. Patience is also an attribute which allows you to empathise and understand others. This helps prevent your stress levels rising and helps keep you calm in moments of discord and upset. Above all else, patience is about anticipating and recognising the most opportune moment to do or say something and act appropriately when the opportune moment presents itself.

Here then are five practice tips for activities and exercises designed to raise your overall patience threshold. Pick whichever one suits your mood and give it a go. Go ahead and try them all if you like. They may well take a bit of time, concentration and effort so you will need to be, well, patient.

Practice tip one is to try a mindfulness day focused on impatience. I mentioned mindfulness way back in part one in relation to managing your emotional and mental states. You can be mindful about anything you choose. If you want to become more aware of your environment for example, you could set yourself the task of being mindful about the colour blue, square shapes, triangles, people with grey hair, dotted lines, certain noises or anything else which takes your fancy. You will be amazed at what you will notice. What you choose does not really matter. The key thing is to build up your sense of environmental awareness. With all this in mind, a really useful exercise in mindfulness is to focus on impatience. Notice times when you are impatient. Ask yourself what triggered it. Are you impatient with people, things or situations? What about all three? What does it physically feel like to be impatient? What is your physiology like? How can you turn this into a patient state? What about other people? How do they react or respond to your impatience? Are they impatient with you? How does it feel? Give it a go and prepare to be surprised.

Practice tip two involves deliberately delaying gratification. We all have our little naughty treats in life, you know, chocolate, sweets, doughnuts, cake, chips, beer or whatever. Let us assume yours is chocolate and you love to have your chocolate during your morning coffee break. The idea here is to practice delaying the gratifying experience of the chocolate by placing it where you normally do during the morning coffee break but not actually eating it. Look at it, focus on it, smell it even but do not eat it. How do you feel? Is this easy or difficult? Ask yourself whether you even want the chocolate after all. Would it perhaps be healthier to give it a miss? I do not want to ruin your coffee break so go ahead and eat your chocolate if you want to; I am not the nutrition police. Try this with other things you like and see if the results are the same. The point is you will develop the ability to take a brief time out before taking action. Who knows, it might well be that one of the time outs you take in the future as a result of this practice gives you the thinking time which prevents a self-esteem destroying rash decision. As an interesting aside, at Stanford back in 1972, psychology professor Walter Mischel ran an experiment where children were left alone with a marshmallow for a period of time. They were told, if they left off eating it until the researcher returned they would get another marshmallow in addition but they were free to eat the single one there ahead of time if they wanted to. As you might expect, some ate it and some waited. The more interesting results came during later follow-ups with test subjects. The children who were able to display delayed gratification tendencies by waiting also tended to do better on average, in school and in later life, than the subjects who displayed a penchant for instant gratification. It sometimes pays to be able to wait.

Practice tip three involves deliberately pausing before you speak or act. Very simple this one. During any normal or routine part of your day, start to take a deliberate pause, let us say two seconds, before you say or do anything. Mentally say one Mississippi two Mississippi to yourself in order to get used to the timing. Once the pause is created use the time to think about what you are going to say or do. Could you say it differently or even not at all? Could you act differently? You will be surprised at how much thought you can cram into those two seconds. Do other people even notice the short delay?

Practice tip four involves closely observing someone you know who is very patient. Watch how they behave with and talk to other people. Watch how other people respond to them. How do they move and act? How do they approach tasks and projects? How are they different from you? Now extend the idea to taking on some of the approaches and patient behaviours they use. How does your behaviour change? Do people respond differently to you? How do you feel about the whole experience? Can you learn anything useful from this? This process is technically known as modelling and it can be very useful and effective in developing useful new skills. Try it in other scenarios too.

If you feel you are always on the go, always hurrying and not taking enough you time then this might help. Practice tip number five is all about slowing down by taking up slow activities. Seriously, take up a slow hobby or two and carefully monitor how it impacts your overall pace in life. To me, for example, a slow hobby would be gardening. My wife usually dragoons me into doing the heavy digging, labouring and bulk planting phases and I also get to mow the lawn on a regular basis. I quite like the end results because, let us be honest here, you cannot beat a nice gin and tonic or two on the patio when the sun is shining. If I were to take up gardening full time as a hobby I imagine it would be very easy to become engrossed in the process. Designing the layouts, picking the plants, watching the plants grow to maturity, checking for pests, weeding, feeding, watering and all the other gardening activities. There are a lot of advantages to having a slow hobby or pastime. Time to think and reflect. The opportunity to lose yourself in a flow state generating task requiring patience and concentration. It could be anything you fancy of course. Jigsaw puzzles, wood carving, French cookery, cake decorating, etc... As long as it pleasantly slows you down from your too fast pace and allows you to relax and reflect it will be time well spent - not time wasted.

They say patience is a virtue and I agree. Being dynamic can be a good thing but I am a great believer in working smart, not hard. Having patience allows you to work smarter.

Case study - John and Sarah's story

This case study compares the real life outcomes of two different people and the varying approaches they took when faced with massive upheaval and change at work. Names, occupations and other significant details have been changed to preserve anonymity. The strategies they chose to adopt regarding change and the eventual outcomes have not.

John was a successful purchasing officer in a fairly large engineering design and manufacturing business. He was 45 years old and he had risen up through the ranks and to all intents and purposes he knew the business inside and out. He could hold his own in almost any technical discussion with the designers, engineers and the shop floor manufacturing staff. He liked the friendly and robust humour of the engineering environment where every day brought something new. He had built a great network of industry contacts and had a good reputation amongst his suppliers as a straight-talking fair dealer. John enjoyed his job and was good at it. The business appeared sound and as a result he was essentially looking to serve out his time and retire as early as possible.

Sarah was about the same age as John and she worked in a large commodity manufacturing facility. She had been with the business since leaving school but she had not really scaled the promotional heights. Sarah did know pretty well everyone on the site after all this time. She currently worked in a fairly low-grade administrative capacity in the HR department, had been moved around different departments her whole career and had a general grasp of how most of them worked. She had never made any upward progress but she was considered conscientious, reliable and good at her job all the same. She could not picture herself working anywhere else and, because the business was relatively profitable and stable, she assumed she would remain and retire at the appropriate time.

John and Sarah did not know it but the working world was about to change unexpectedly and drastically for them both.

John was called in to his manager's office on Friday morning. The business had recently bought another local company to add an in-house specialist steel coatings capability to their business portfolio. Several staff from the main business were to be transferred immediately to the new business in order to get the management and business systems in-line as quickly as possible. John was the chosen one for purchasing. He was distraught. There was no problem with travel, it was actually a bit closer to home and with better access. His problem was the fact that it was a different industry entirely. The key people there were chemists, process engineers and maintenance staff. Things and people he knew nothing about. The new factory was run as a long-run batch system rather than the one-off design and manufacture style of the main business. The whole process was run by just a handful of shift technicians who used computers rather than spanners and worked in quiet control rooms rather than a noisy shop floor. His manager was acting like this was a great opportunity and not a personal disaster. He was assured it would only be for a maximum of two years then he could return to his old job once the new systems were working smoothly. Two years! He knew he was going to hate it. New people, a new business style and not a clue where to begin. He would be like a fish out of water. This was all so unfair.

Sarah was also being told by her manager how a plant takeover would likely affect her. The news had come out of the blue a few days earlier. A large multi-national had just bought the business she worked for. Rumours were rife and many people including Sarah were worried about their jobs. Her manager was pointing out the new business was keen to increase productivity and reduce head count. They would increase productivity through a one year fast track program of multi-skilling staff, installing new technology and IT improvements and organisationally restructuring. A reduction in head count was to be achieved through natural wastage and by proactively eliminating some "dead wood" within the workforce. Sarah's head was spinning. Although she was struggling to follow much of what her manager was telling her it was becoming obvious she was considered as potential for the dead wood pile due to her general lack of transferable skills and overall reluctance to develop herself. Luckily for Sarah her manager was a good sort who did not want to see anyone on his team get left behind. He was keen to help her and he had already drawn up an outline plan consisting of some IT and modern business skills courses which Sarah could take within the next year which would enable her to upgrade her CV and keep herself safely in the running as the changes were rolled out. She had an ample personal training budget to work with and would benefit most by sorting out the course arrangements as soon as possible to ensure success. Her boss was also at pains to emphasise the huge range of support on offer from in-house mentors and trainers and urged her to take full advantage; the clock was ticking. Sarah left his office in a bit of a daze.

Two weeks later John was relaxing for a few minutes at his shiny new desk. It was in a communal yet quiet office area with a picture window overlooking the local park. Much better in fact than the cramped windowless cubicle he used to know and love. He sat there reflecting on the first week at the new premises, a week which had appeared to fly by. A marked contrast to his final week at the old building. Packing his desk to leave and tying up loose ends had dragged interminably. On his first day at the new site, his new line manager had taken the full morning with him to discuss the transition plans and it all seemed well-considered and eminently achievable in the timescale. John effectively had full autonomy to design and implement the purchasing systems required in order to obtain the desired outcomes and he also had an ongoing remit to improve them when he saw the opportunity. One week on and he had in fact done a lot of thinking. He was a lot less distraught than he had been.

Sarah on the other hand had done nothing. Two weeks on from her meeting she had not investigated any of the options her manager had outlined. "I've got a year," she thought. "A lot can change in a year. I'm too old and stupid to go back to school at my age. They will laugh at me. I've gotten this far so I can't be doing too badly. They're just trying to scare me. If I ignore it all they'll probably forget all about it. Even if I don't know any of the new systems they're always going to need good admin staff to do the routine stuff."

One month on and John had settled in well. The people here were actually good fun. The banter was about different things but still enjoyable. John had realised the things he was good at and the transferable people skills he already had, far outweighed the things he did not know. He had initially felt quite overwhelmed with the new situation then he took stock and thought about priorities. John knew he liked to retain as much control of his life as possible. He decided to primarily focus the bulk of his energy on the actual task he was there for; the purchasing system upgrade. There was a lot of groundwork which could be done which did not involve specialist local knowledge, so this became his priority. In parallel with this, he also spoke to as many of his new colleagues as spare time allowed in an effort to find out what he did not know and what he would need to know. It turned out the process operators undertook a structured study course via distance learning so, even though he had not studied for years and it was not even a requirement for his role, John signed up. He had all the on-site resources he needed in terms of engineering and process help and his previous experience added some interesting perspectives. He even set up a study area at home and his family helped by ensuring he had his quiet time. The chemists and operators were quite impressed when someone new was showing an interest in their area and from John's point of view it meant he could learn and understand the local language of the new factory in a relatively short space of time. This satisfied his need for personal control and would also ensure his need to know list would be dealt with much more effectively.

One month on for Sarah and things were pretty much back to normal. A week or so previously her boss had asked her how the development plan was going as he had not had any budget requests for training so far. Sarah managed to convince him it was all in hand. Shortly afterwards, it all calmed down again as she knew it would. Her co-workers kept discussing the upcoming changes but Sarah knew the real truth. The new owners would not want to rock the boat after all. Everyone knew change was tricky and best avoided. They probably bought the business because it was doing well so why fix something which is not broken. She hunkered down and doggedly carried on with her work and life as if nothing had changed.

One year on and John was loving his new role. The new purchasing systems had been integrated perfectly. All the new plant systems had been installed effectively because the business culture was one of information sharing. John had received help with his new system and had also been able to offer help to other departments when they were behind. It was a great team environment and John was a key part of it. Perhaps more importantly John had realised he was actually happier in his new environment. His wife and family had all noticed the positive difference. He was starting to think about not returning to his old role at all. As the chemical coatings business scaled new heights, new possibilities and opportunities were appearing all the time and John figured if he could change so successfully once, why not again? He was even considering studying for a degree in chemical process design in order to increase his options.

One year on for Sarah and it was a completely different scenario. Six months after her initial chat with the boss she had again been asked for progress reports on her development plan. She had done nothing because she felt there was no reason to do anything. She was informed the new manning structures were now being rolled out from the top down and, at her employment level, she would see real changes in around in three to four months. Her manager also chided her for her lack of action and expressed his genuine concerns for her future in the organisation of she did not make real progress in short order. Sarah finally acknowledged she would have to do something. She dug out the development plan and realised she had no idea how to find the information she needed on her own because this Internet thing was too complicated to get to grips with at her age. She finally went to the in-house trainers who pointed out such courses do not just appear out of thin air. She had missed several opportunities already and only half of the list was potentially achievable in the time she had. There was nothing they could do in-house. She found the situation was worse in the local colleges. The business she worked for actually had the best training resources in the area by long way. She was now beginning to panic. She was annoyed at her boss for not pushing her harder. "Why didn't he tell me it was so important? Why did they leave me to sort out these courses myself? I should've been told by HR and training when and where to go. This is so unfair." She blamed the HR department, the training department, the union who by now could not help her, the new owners and she especially blamed the original business owners for selling her down the river and causing all this grief.

Sarah never actually started any of the courses which were available and would have helped her continue. She even knocked back a last ditch offer of a fork lift truck driving course so she could work in the warehouse. Sarah was even asked to apply for several new roles under the restructured organisation but she refused and was made redundant almost fifteen months from the time her boss asked her to improve her skills. After a period of unemployment, she is now working shifts at a manual packing line in a food production facility and she hates the job. It is all she can get at anywhere near her previous wage but the hours and shifts are dreadful and she is exhausted all the time. She is bitter and feels let down by her previous organisation and she tells everyone she meets about how badly and unfairly she was treated. She is still doing nothing to improve her employment prospects and hopes to serve out her days packing salad pots for supermarkets, unless this new company lets her down as well.

John proved himself highly resilient. Although he felt overwhelmed and also felt the situation was unfair he took the time to talk to a few key people. He listened to what was being said rather than jumping to conclusions and he also realised he had many transferable skills and could learn the new things he needed to with the time and support on offer. He focused where he needed to focus and prioritised the need to know items. By talking and reaching out he discovered a novel way to get off to a flying start and integrate with his new colleagues. The whole experience has been highly positive for John and it is all down to his flexible mental attitude, carefully considered choices and good old-fashioned hard work. He has come through the experience stronger than ever and learnt a great deal about himself in the process.

Sarah displayed no resilience at all during this period of her life. She still displays little. She blames the world and all its relatives for her problems. She sees life as being fundamentally unfair toward her. Sarah takes no personal control of her actions and choices and she exhibits low self-esteem. She was offered ample help and advice, more than was required in reality. Her boss went out of his way to support and warn her but Sarah was just too scared to try new things, she was reluctant to put any effort into remedying the issues and she took no responsibility for herself. Whenever she feels overwhelmed she withdraws from situations and then blames others for the problems. She is adrift and direction-less and lets life push her this way and that with no effort at self-determinism; Sarah is a classic victim in a situation of her own making. Sarah has come through the experience in a much worse condition. She has learnt nothing and is doomed to repeat the process again and again with the same outcomes and increased bitterness and misery.

I have met many people over the years who respond in similar ways to either John or Sarah. It is a spectrum of course and many people are somewhere in between. Hand on heart, I used to behave and react to events and situations in much the same way as Sarah and sometimes far worse than her. I generally was not a happy man and rightly met with limited success. No-one is perfect but John has it generally right in my opinion. I strive to be more John-like every day and I am a lot happier. Which of the two characters are you most like right now? Which of the two characters do you want to be most like?

Section 5: Systems within systems

Resilient water is always in motion. Water never sleeps. Water has its own cycles and systems and is also a vital part of many other systems. Throw a stone into a still pond and the ripples spread outwards. Ripples can become big waves. You are formed of systems and you operate within systems. If you stay in constant motion relative to these systems you will be resilient like water. What stones do you need to throw in your ponds? What ripples can you create? What waves can you start?

Introduction to section

Systems are in us and all around us. They are part of us and we are a part of them.

When John Donne wrote, "No man is an island" [Private Meditation XVII in 1624] he was referring to the fact none of us can ever truly be isolated from a wider system of some sort.

A system can be usefully defined as a complex whole; a set of things working together as parts of an organised mechanism or an interconnected and interrelated network. It can also be usefully defined as an organized scheme or process; a set of principles or methods by which something is done.

I am fairly sure everyone reading this is a human and, as I am also sure you would agree, we humans are complex whole entities comprising many sets of things working together with the general aim of helping to keep us alive and producing more humans. I am not going to get into any deep philosophical debates here as to how all this came about; there are plenty of arguments about this already out there. Personally I am enjoying the fact it happened at all and I am happy to be a part of it.

Within your own body are some well-known major systems such as: Your skeletal and muscular systems which keep you from puddling in a heap and which facilitate bodily posture and movement, your immune and lymphatic systems which help combat disease, your cardiovascular and respiratory systems which pump blood and provide you with oxygen, your digestive and urinary systems which handle your nutritional inputs and waste outputs, your nervous and endocrine systems which handle sensory information and hormonal requirements amongst other things and finally there is also your reproductive system which handles the producing of more humans operation. These are the tip of the iceberg in terms of internal systems. Examine any introductory text on human biology and prepare to be amazed at what is in us and on us. We support many inter-dependent micro-sized living systems both internally and externally; some are beneficial to us and some not so beneficial. Even the cells from which our bodies are constructed are complex systems containing yet more complex systems within them. Scientists are finding ever more surprising things about us every day.

I have only mentioned us humans so far. Imagine how many systems go to make up the Earth and all it contains. We are a part of the super-system called Earth and Earth itself is part of a system called the Solar System which is a part of the galaxy known as the Milky Way and so on and so forth until we get to the system we call The Universe. I, along with most other people, am a bit hazy as to what The Universe is a part of. We might find out one day. With advances in science we can look at systems from the extremely large all the way down to the atomic level and far beyond.

So, from the inconceivably big to the vanishingly small you can see interconnected physical systems are everywhere; we are either a part of them or have some of them within us.

What about the systems we humans create? We love a good system do we not? We have our tangible physical and social systems such as local government services, security, military, transport, housing, trade, medical, communication, educational, manufacturing and so on; far too many to list but you get the idea. We also have our more intangible conceptual systems such as mathematics, religion, politics, science, measurement, etc... There are some crossover and therefore harder to classify systems too. For example: Is the Interweb a physical or a conceptual system now? Is international finance tangible or intangible? Government can be thought of as physical or conceptual at different levels. What about society itself? Is it a real system or just an intangible construct we all generally adhere too?

It is all very confusing but on a personal level, most of us are familiar with, and a part of, many if not all of these human-centric systems. We choose to be part of some of these systems and some of them are imposed upon us. Life can be lonely and hard when some of these systems are removed or our participation in them is impaired in some way. Some people even talk about "The System" as if it were an independent life-form with control and power over itself and us. We can often feel passive and helpless when we are in direct contact with some of these intangible systems.

One of the more interesting things to note is systems have to be defined by someone at some point to be a system. System definitions are a very human concept. Nature ticks along quite happily with no names for its many systems and often no definite boundary between one system and the next. It is we humans who feel compelled to identify systems and name them. We like labels. It helps us understand our world and helps us fathom out how it might work; both independently and as part of yet more complex systems we identify. Most of us tend to go with the flow and accept the defined systems as they are presented to us. We muddle along and accept our lot. Why rock the boat? You cannot fight the system, right?

From my experience, I now believe more emotionally resilient people take a keen interest in the systems of which they are a part and in the systems upon which they impact. If you want to be more emotionally resilient I recommend you develop a comprehensive and detailed understanding of where you fit within your personally defined systems and the wider world, how you impact on them and how they impact on you as well as assessing the usefulness of some of those systems and system definitions. If this sounds a bit heavy let me try and illustrate what I mean by taking a quick look at my personal human-centric systems and see if it helps with my explanation.

My nearest and dearest system involvement is with my family, closely followed by my friends. There is also my work system and my work colleagues and acquaintances. I run my own business so I have my client network and I also have quite a large professional contact network. These are all social systems. I know various people via social media, sports activity, hobbies and clubs as well as various other private and professional associations. I am involved in various financial systems. I am also a part of various levels of society from my local neighbourhood right up to, well, let us stop for the minute at my currently being a citizen of Europe. I engage in the local and national political system as a voter and I am part of numerous government systems which will include such things as licencing and passports, transport, pensions, taxation and health care to name but a few.

Some of these systems are tangible and immediate, like my friends and family, whilst many are more nebulous constructs which I am aware of but rarely come into direct contact with, like the pension systems. The popular expression "work life balance" is in effect the interaction and balance between two major systems of which we are a part. Considered individually, these are all rich and complicated systems in their own right but if you started to draw out a system of circles representing these systems and their relationship to me, you would see they also overlap with each other and with the systems of other people around you. Try it for yourself and you will see the interactions are hugely complex and diverse. These type of drawings are generally known as system maps. They can provide a useful bird's eye view of the interrelated systems of which you and I are a part and which are also a part of you and I.

As you may by now have realised, we cannot get away from systems. If we want to grow as emotionally resilient people we might benefit by learning a bit more about them.

Before we move on to the next section I recommend you take the time to create a system map of your own as good way of seeing the big systemic picture as it relates to you and your life. My own system map as described above is included in the virtual appendix.

This is where things start to come together. Each individual tool or technique is like a puzzle piece which can be combined with others to make super-tools or super-techniques. There are numerous new options available if you take the time to experiment and learn. Your enhanced emotional resilience can have far-reaching impact when you purposefully start to turn your attention outward.

In the next section we will look at ways you can affect, and be affected by, some of the many systems you are involved with. In the rest of this part we will look at the benefits of having some positive paranoia, some emotional intelligence and more assertiveness. We will also look at helping others and reaching out to your organic and extended networks for the help you might need.

Stones and ripples

Right at the start the metaphor I chose for illustrating resilience was water. Waves are often associated with water and I want now to examine the topic of waves in a little more detail. Any body of water can have waves on its surface. Waves are generally caused by two main factors: Wind and/or shock. Bang a glass of water down on a table and you will see some waves. This would be an example of the formation of shock waves; they will not last long when contained within a glass but they will be there. Look at any pond or lake on a windy day and you will see waves. Wind rushing over the surface of the water transfers some of its energy to the water. This energy forms the waves which tend to travel in the direction of the prevailing wind. The size of the waves is related to the length of time the wind acts on the surface, the wind speed and the surface area being acted on; all technically known as the fetch. Small bodies of water therefore only have small waves even in high winds.

The largest masses of water on our planet are of course the oceans. They are huge bodies of salt water which cover approximately seventy percent of the Earth's surface. Oceans can develop truly massive waves as the wind can act over huge areas of the ocean surface and over great distances. As these unimpeded and growing waves roll over the top of the deep ocean water they store up huge amounts of energy. Out at sea these waves can be big enough, especially in stormy conditions, but when they reach a shoreline they can rear up to enormous heights. The land slows the leading water down and the momentum of the following water causes it to build up until it eventually collapses on itself. Surfers love big waves and at the time of writing Garrett McNamara holds the world record for the largest officially confirmed wave ever surfed which is seventy eight feet or twenty four metres, set in 2011 in Nazare, Portugal.

Not all waves are created equal of course. Some waves simply get cancelled out by other waves and some waves get amplified in combination with others. Some waves travel a long way then break unobserved by anyone and having no noticeable effect on anything; almost as if they had never existed. Some waves get so big they are referred to as rogue waves and are said to have swallowed massive ships whole on occasion; leaving behind no trace. Massive and devastating Tsunami waves are often caused by seismic disturbances in the Earth's crust; either by submerged earthquake or by earthquake triggered coastal collapses.

This is a lot of talk about water and waves so what is my point here?

Under the right conditions and with appropriate support, waves can form, spread out and grow in power until they are capable of having a huge effect on a shore many thousands of miles away. In other words, given enough time and under the right conditions, even very small initial triggers can transform into high impact events with huge consequences. On a grand scale and right this very second, a large and far distant meteor may have been hit by a big asteroid with just the right amount of force to send it on a direct collision course with Earth. Do not worry too much about things like meteors or asteroids because space really is a big system and things can easily change; besides, Hollywood has already got a workable plan and the A-list celebrities are all lined up to save us if it does happen. On a more human-sized level, tiny changes right down at a cellular level within just one of the systems we are all made of can grow to have far reaching and sometimes terminal results for us as the host of the changed system. In 1961 whilst working on computer models to predict the weather, Edward Lorenz, an early pioneer of Chaos Theory, demonstrated the idea whereby minute changes in the initial conditions of certain unpredictable or non-linear systems could lead to massive and unknowable outputs further down the line. Come to think of it, humans and our human-centric systems are complex, non-linear and unpredictable so may lend themselves well to analysis and treatment as chaotic systems. My life has certainly been chaotic at times.

We examined the concept of change and our choice about responses to it way back at the start. Some change is self-generated and some changes are thrust upon us by outside agents. In water we could create waves by splashing or throwing in rocks. In our lives we can try to change the systems we are in by creating metaphorical splashes or throwing in metaphorical rocks. These would be like our self-initiated change attempts. Likewise, in the same body of water, waves can be created by the wind or by seismic events. These would be more like the changes forced upon us and our systems by outside agents.

We can create impacts, of varying magnitude, on all the systems of which we are a part. If you liken the systems we are a part of to various sized bodies of water, then some of our systems are no more extensive than a puddle. Some are like ponds, then lakes then all the way up to ocean size depending on our perspective. We can have an almost immediate effect on a relatively small system we are a part of; like our family for example. One forgotten birthday card or too sharp a word said at the wrong time and the emotional hurt can spread like wildfire. On our own, we might think, we can generally have little if any impact on a much larger system like the government. However, if we join forces with many like-minded others and sign a popular petition then we can potentially make a huge impact. At election time we can have a definite and clearly visible impact, at least on the political aspect of the government if not the bureaucratic one. If we eat or drink certain things or take certain medicines or drugs we can have an impact on many of the systems within us as well.

Sometimes these impacts can produce unintended consequences or express emergent properties. This is fancy talk for getting something you did not expect. Sometimes a good surprise and sometimes a bad one. Sometimes an extremely bad one.

The classic illustration of this concept is the Australian Cane

Toad introduction project.

In August 1935, one hundred and two Cane Toads (Rhinella marina; formerly Bufo marinus) from Hawaii were released in northern Queensland, Australia by the Bureau of Sugar Experiment Stations, now Sugar Research Australia. This introduction of an alien species was an attempt to control two native beetle pests which were causing significant damage to valuable Australian Sugar Cane crops. The troublesome beetles in question were the grey-backed cane (Dermolepida albohirtum) and Frenchi (Lepidiota frenchi). For various reasons they were proving hard to eradicate so enter the Cane Toad, mighty slayer of cane beetles.

Cane toads, it turned out, liked Australia and they bred happily. A little too happily in fact. Today the toad population is thought to number over two hundred million and is growing rapidly. They are threatening to spread right across Australia and they are causing widespread environmental problems.

The sad irony is, even after all this effort and environmental misery, there is no hard evidence they have had any significant impact on the very beetles they were meant to control. Hindsight is a wonderful thing of course and it probably seemed like an incredibly good idea at the time.

Be aware, it is perfectly possible to change any system of which you are a part, or even those which are a part of you, if you can apply enough thought, exert enough effort or marshal enough resources. What you cannot always do is predict the precise outcomes or results of these changes. I recommend you always pick your battles carefully and monitor things closely in case of any unintended consequences; it is almost always better to spot them early and avoid them rather than try to fix bigger things later on.

As I mentioned earlier, some waves get cancelled out whilst others get amplified in a wholly unpredictable manner. This will also be true for some of your systemic or personal change attempts. You may initiate a change in or on one system only to find it is snuffed out quickly by the actions or properties of another system. A simplistic example would be house building or house extensions. People often find, even though their grand plan is enthusiastically welcomed by their family and friend systems, they get blocked or denied building permission (neighbourhood and planning systems) or it is deemed too risky a prospect to get a bank loan (financial lending system).

Some other change ideas can get amplified by other systems. Let us hypothetically suppose you have a close friend with a rare medical condition which is very expensive to treat. You discover there is a charity dedicated to increasing awareness of, understanding of and the fighting of this rare condition. You decide to help by raising a little bit of money for this charity and announce you are going to do a twenty four hour charity walk. You tell your family and friends about the idea and ask them to sponsor you per mile completed. To your surprise this fires up the enthusiasm of a few of your other friends and they ask if they can join in. You say of course they can. You then mention the plan to your boss who is delighted to help financially and physically as he and a number of your co-workers join the group. Someone else knows the editor of the local paper and he interviews you for the weekend edition. This prompts a whole slew of volunteers. You are now swamped trying to organise all this but your boss steps in and offers some company admin support. The local radio station picks it up then the national media gets involved. What next? Pledges and donations are coming in from all over the country now. So many people have asked to join in and help you realise you need to think about financial management, a properly planned course, safety people, t-shirts, first aid people, refreshments and a thousand other things. All these positive things have happened and the project seems to have taken on a life of its own. You did not plan any of this, you just wanted to make a difference to your friend's life by doing a simple charity walk. It all happened due to outward ripples from your immediate systems impacting and creating waves in others which you never even knew about.

I would like to briefly introduce you to two more useful concepts: Your locus of control and your circle of influence.

Your locus of control is a fancy term which refers to the extent to which you believe you can control the events affecting your life. We talked about personal power near the start and this locus of control concept relates directly to your personal power.

Your locus of control is said to be either internal or external. Someone with an external locus of control generally and genuinely believes their decisions and lives are controlled by environmental or external agencies which they cannot influence and even by chance or fate; they blame others for their lot in life. Someone with a strong internal locus of control believes the results in their life derive primarily from their own decisions and actions; they also accept full responsibility for their own actions and decisions. It is a spectrum of course and we may have differing position on the spectrum in different situational contexts.

So far so good because emotionally resilient people fall easily and naturally into the internal locus of control end of the spectrum. If you are still operating in the external half of the locus of control spectrum then you now know where to place some of your change effort. I am now going to introduce you to the circle of influence which provides a useful strategy for moving your locus of control from external towards internal.

The idea of a circle of influence was introduced by Steven R Covey in his justifiably famous work "The Seven Habits of Highly Effective People" and I recommend you read it cover to cover.

Picture if you will, two concentric circles. You are to imagine yourself at the centre of the circles. The smaller circle represents your circle of influence and the larger one represents your circle of concern. Simply put the circle of concern contains all those things you could worry about but realistically cannot control such as wars, the weather, the national debt, your height, what other people say, etc... Your circle of influence contains all those things you do have influence over, either directly or indirectly, such as what you eat, how you vote, how you spend/invest money, your job, your emotions, your friends, how you drive your car, how you spend your free time, etc... If you invest time and energy worrying about things in your circle of concern you will achieve little and likely get very frustrated and stressed. This also leads to your feeling less able to influence anything. Your circle of influence shrinks and you may start playing the blame game. The recommended alternative is to focus your energy and attention working on positively influencing the things within your circle of influence. This will begin to create a series of victories; both large and small which will boost your self-esteem and lead to a more emotionally resilience outlook. As you grow more accustomed to influence and develop your influencing skills your circle of influence will grow. You may find you gain influence, either directly or indirectly, over more areas of your life than you ever thought possible. I have included a suitable diagram in the virtual appendix.

Do not misunderstand the conceptual power of the circle of influence. It does not limit you in any way, rather it serves to focus your attention on what you can change and work from there. For example, I mentioned the national debt as potentially being in your circle of concern. The implication being you have no direct control over it so do not worry about it. This does not stop you from deciding you will set a big goal to have a direct impact on the national debt at some future point. You could hypothetically achieve this in a number of ways. You could become so rich and powerful you had the ear of the Governor of The Bank of England and the Chancellor of the Exchequer. Alternatively, you could become the Governor of The Bank of England or the Chancellor of the Exchequer. You could even become a renowned economist and have an effect on fiscal thinking which could change the world due to your novel ideas on monetary policy. The options are many but my point is this. You still have to take a first step then a step at a time to get from where you are now to where you need to be. Your circle of influence is the place for each step. As you achieve each step the circle of influence becomes wider to encompass your new skills or achievements.

We have now looked at numerous ways you can increase your self-esteem and emotional resilience. We have looked at how you can effectively change yourself; emotionally, mentally and physiologically. You can change yourself if you are prepared to put the work and effort in. You have to make the choice and it is yours alone to make.

Here is the thing; you cannot change anyone else directly by force of will. If you are in a position of authority or physical superiority of course you can compel people to act in certain ways but there will only ever be short-term compliance and never any real or lasting change.

Personally therefore I can only choose to change myself. I cannot change anyone else directly. I can encourage them to change and I can even create conditions conducive to making that change happen. I can speak to them and try to persuade them to change. I can provide tools and techniques to assist with change. I can even help them make their own changes if they want me to and they request my help but I cannot directly change them myself. So it is with you. You can only create conditions suitable for change and help someone else to make their own changes. The actual decision to change is always down to them.

If it seems like I am labouring this point a bit it is because it is an important one to grasp. The urge to try and change others directly is strong in many people. Resist this urge.

So you cannot change anyone else directly but you can certainly change yourself and you can directly affect some of the systems around you. This may then indirectly encourage or enable others to make their own changes. The systems you both interact with often overlap.

Awareness of the systems of which you are a part, how they work and how they interact can help you understand how best to make any changes and also the best potential point in the system to apply your change effort. Being able to take control and make changes in the world around you, and perhaps more importantly believing in the idea you can do this, will give you many new options and opportunities. Noticing and taking some of the more beneficial options and opportunities will make you far more emotionally resilient.

The more tools and ideas for autonomy and emotional resilience you are exposed too, from any source, the more these new options will appear to become available to you. You will start to develop a new system you can both interact with and be a part of; an emotional resilience system.

Due diligence

I mentioned in the previous section about unintended or unwanted emergent properties appearing as a result of the change activities you undertake. You can also get personally unwanted developments emerging from situations or projects initiated by others which at first, and on the surface, appeared perfectly reasonable to you. Many times these problems occur due to the influence of systems outside of your awareness and theoretically beyond your control.

I speak from past experience and I am sure you have had your share of it too. It often occurs even when the other person has the best of intentions but has an alternate agenda.

As an example, many years ago I was a carpenter involved in the construction industry. On occasion I would work with employment agencies and they would contact me when suitable work arose and then take a percentage cut of my rate as a finder's fee. I preferred to do certain types of work, such as the final fix interior woodwork known as second fix joinery, which I was good at. There were also types of work I definitely did not want. Generally, this system worked well and I would go along to the site to complete the contract as agreed. At one agency my contact, let us call him Dave, had been great for a while by getting me the type of jobs I liked and at the pay rates which suited me. Things started to slide a bit and the rates began to drop and a few of the jobs even turned out to be not quite as anticipated. As a travelling site carpenter you get used to thinking on your feet and going prepared for most eventualities but there is a limit on how many tools and other bits of equipment you can reasonably take to a job in order to cope with this. I always needed the best information I could get prior to any trip away from home.

Things finally came to an end for the agency and I one

November when Dave rang up and said he had an emergency and could I do him a big favour. Someone had let him down and could I go up to Scotland for three or four weeks to finish off the final phase of the contract joinery. He was unusually vague about the exact type of work involved but said it was perfect for me and all indoors. There was even quality accommodation already sorted out, I just had to see the site manager; and the rate was very high. I had always had a good working relationship with Dave and felt I could at least trust him one more time. He also asked if I could pick up two other local lads for the trip and he would pay the petrol as a thank you. I had a few days of private work on so I arranged for someone else to do it whilst I went up and earned the big money in Scotland.

I picked up my two passengers at very early o'clock in the morning and we were off. They turned out to be an electrician and a plasterer and they had been given the same job information as me; which equalled not much. They had however been promised the same good rates and the same clean indoor work.

Eight hours or so later, we arrived at the site. We had driven past it several times in disbelief. There was a huge empty field in the middle of nowhere with one site hut and several excavating machines; nothing else but wind, sleet and three by now very concerned tradesmen.

We went to see the site manager in case we had the wrong site after all. He said he was expecting us and started showing us the plans for the concrete foundation formwork and steel fixing. We tried to explain what Dave had told us and he said Dave told him he was getting two formwork joiners and a steel fixer. Whilst I could do formwork joinery it was not what I was best at and the site manager certainly was not overjoyed ay having an electrician and a plasterer on site before anything had even been built. Just to rub our noses in it there was no accommodation arranged either. Dave had told him we had our own caravan. He let us use the site phone but Dave was out of the office for some reason and no-one else there seemed inclined to help.

It was too late to go back home so we decided to stop in a nearby hotel, have a few beers and plan the various ways we would physically punish the elusive Dave when we got hold of him. We eventually got home the next day and, to the great credit of other lads, they chipped in for fuel. We were all down two days plus the cost of a hotel and fuel money. You can imagine the atmosphere in the car.

A few weeks later I heard this on the grapevine. Several months before our particular incident the agency involved had in fact quietly put all their staffing agents on a commission only pay structure. This was obviously an effort to make themselves more money by getting more contractors placed in work. They did not expect contractors like myself would even notice the transition.

Unfortunately, the first real outcome was Dave's money went down and the only way he could make it up was to place as many contracts as possible. This meant he chose to lower rates and send people all over the place to jobs they did not want and under false pretences. Dave had left his job just before we got home and the agency went into liquidation a few months later. No contractors would work for them even when they reversed their policy and openly apologised. Trust is important. They failed to anticipate the emergent condition and contractors like me were the unwitting victims of their remote system change.

I was annoyed with myself but, on reflection, there was no real possibility of seeing such an outcome. Work and money are sometimes hard to turn down when you are self-employed in a tough industry. I was far more careful from then on but I still got my fingers burnt every so often despite the extra vigilance.

During my more recent time in the chemical process industry, I learnt a great deal more about checking things thoroughly; I had to because it can be a very dangerous environment.

Many people feel it is a personal insult to have their work checked. In the chemical industry it is encouraged. When you take over a piece of equipment, especially under maintenance conditions, it is a requirement to physically check and confirm what you have been told during the handover. Mistakes can and do happen in such dynamic and fast-moving situations so failure to carry out these checks could be disastrous. I in my turn had people check on what I had done or told them I had done and this was fine with me. Nobody I ever met in the front line of this industry felt remotely insulted by this careful approach. Staying alive is a good thing.

I still follow a personal ABC mantra which was taught to me by the older and wiser workers during my time in the chemical industry: Assume nothing, believe no-one and check everything.

If you want to reduce the number of times you get caught out or misinformed, either deliberately or unknowingly, I suggest you adopt a similar approach. Double or even triple check facts and assertions via other trusted sources. Challenge opinions or statements to test their veracity and/or accuracy. You can be polite about it of course but do not ever let potential embarrassment or fear of offending anyone else's precious ego get in the way of your own peace of mind. Having trust in other people is important but so is due diligence. You owe it to yourself and others. People have to earn trust and they have to maintain it with some demonstrable consistency. In my experience if something sounds too good to be true it probably is not true. There are a great many unscrupulous influencers out there armed with some powerful and persuasive techniques and you would do well to always be on your guard. Once again I will recommend the book *Influence* by Robert Cialdini; it is a must read for everyone in my opinion. Feel free to challenge me on this. I would expect nothing less.

You must of course be comfortable when other people check your work and/or assertions; it is only fair after all. Doing all this can sometimes take real courage. If your self-esteem is solid this will present no real problem for you. In my experience, most people get bent out shape about having their work or activity checked when their self-esteem, self-image or self-belief is low; your checking or challenging them appears to be undermining these resources still further. It is, however, their personal baggage and not yours. If they mention their concerns at all, you can consider softening the effect by pointing out you have been caught out before in a similar situation which resulted in bad feeling on all sides. Tell them you respect them and value your professional or personal relationship far too much to risk a similar occurrence down the line; all for want of checking a few small facts, challenging a statement or questioning a prediction.

Your own self-esteem, self-image and self-belief levels will all rise as a result of you taking such control over your future success and your emotional resilience will rise likewise.

There is one more concept I would like to introduce you to in this section; the concept of groupthink. It dovetails nicely with the idea of checking or challenging people. Psychologist Irving Janis wrote a very interesting book titled *Group Think* in 1972 (revised in 1982) which examines some fascinating case studies exhibiting this phenomenon.

If you have ever worked, or been a part of, any team or group, the group or team would likely have made some decisions around actions to take or directions in which to move. Most decisions or directions taken are appropriate but if you have been around teams or groups long enough, you may well have been puzzled or even alarmed at the quality of some of these group decisions. If you have ever worked outside of a group or team which is making such strange or alarming decisions, you may well wonder what could allow a number of individually rational and intelligent people do such counter-intuitive things and make such obviously bad choices.

Groupthink is essentially a psychological phenomenon which results in an impaired group decision making ability by virtue of there being too strong a desire for maintaining group harmony. Group members voluntarily minimise conflict to such an extent to preserve this cohesive environment they simply do not challenge any erroneous or irrational thinking. It gets worse, because the group feel so harmonious it often believes the decisions made by it are superior to those made by people outside the group. When groupthink is in operation the group greatly overrates its own abilities and underrates those of the outsiders. There is massive peer pressure within the group to ensure everyone conforms and no-one disrupts the status quo.

If you are involved in any groups or teams which you feel might be exhibiting this characteristic groupthink behaviour you essentially have three choices: You can live with it and carry on as if nothing is happening, you can try and change it from within or, you can take the necessary steps to move away from the team or group. These can all be emotionally draining options and many clients have come to me feeling trapped and worried about how to move forward.

All three options have pros and cons. If the situation is not actually as problematic or causing as serious an amount of harm to anyone or anything as you first thought, then you could consider staying. Only you can decide if the activity is sustainable or indeed a good use of your valuable time. Alternatively, you might decide to try to change the situation. Be aware, for the reasons given in the description of group thinking teams, this could be hard work and potentially stressful. You will need to start with high reserves of resilience and self-esteem to succeed. If the work the team or group is supposed to be doing has high value for you or others, you might feel morally obligated to try and make changes. If this is the case, then I applaud you for your integrity and courage. Any group or team is a system after all and making changes to any system can have unpredictable results. Take things a single carefully considered step at a time and ensure you always protect yourself and those close to you. The third option is to move to a more conducive environment and if this is practicable then it is generally the option I would recommend. As above, proceed carefully; one step at a time. If you can ensure the transition goes smoothly and everyone will be happy this is great. If not, and as this is a practical guide to emotional resilience, make sure it goes in a way which works best for you and yours.

Getting back to my ABC mantra of assume nothing, believe no-one and check everything, the very best way to do this is with questions. Ask lots of questions then ask some more. Never stop asking questions. Ask yourself questions and question others; always listen to the answers carefully.

Ask the questions in as considerate yet assertive a way as possible. Make it implicit and clear to people, the answers are important to you; explain why if it helps. Never take anything at face value.

Ask yourself if what you or others are assuming is actually correct or valid. Ask questions to validate other people's statements or assertions. Ask questions to clarify any potential misunderstandings or clear up any confusion. Ask yourself if you have personally checked everything you are able to in any given situation. Question your own motives as well as those of others. Question your mindsets, attitudes, beliefs, approaches and methods. Question your internal and external language patterns. Question what the media is really telling you or not telling you. Question all your sources of information until they prove trustworthy and useful. Ask what can be done to improve situations or solve problems. Never settle for, "That's the way it is," if you can possible avoid it.

Think of this as emotional due diligence and adopting this form of questioning and positive paranoia as positive habits will do you a world of good.

Asking confident and meaningful questions, for all the very best reasons, and being able to accept and purposefully use the answers you are given is one of the key signs which indicate you are becoming an emotionally aware, emotionally resilient and confident person.

Emotional intelligence

I want to discuss a concept known as Emotional Intelligence (EI). In his highly popular 1995 book of the same name Daniel Goleman called it the master aptitude; the book is well worth a read.

Daniel Goleman brought the idea of EI to great prominence but in differing guises its history goes back somewhat earlier. Work around the subject of EI can be traced back as far as Charles Darwin and in his 1872 work The Expression of the Emotions in Man and Animals and from the 1920s through to the early 1950s various people examined and wrote about the concept of emotional thought versus logical thought. Ideas about EI were further developed during the 1970s and 80s through the work and writings of Howard Gardner, Peter Salovey and John D Mayer and, since Daniel Goleman's work, there have been many more volumes written on this popular subject.

Nowadays, EI is increasingly being seen by business organisations as a highly relevant and useful way to both understand and assess people's behaviours, management styles, attitudes, interpersonal skills, and leadership potential. Many organisations now rate a high Emotional Quotient (EQ) score as being more important than a high traditional Intelligence Quotient (IQ) score. If you are interested there are various ways of checking your EQ, some are free and some are paid for. I will leave it up to you to decide which options work best for you. You may well have come across the terms EI or EQ at work so it is worth briefly covering the subject here and also examining how awareness of it dovetails nicely with our exploration.

No matter which way you look at it, EI really boils down to just two elements which cover our entire emotional and social lives:

Understanding and managing yourself.

Understanding other people and managing your relationships with them.

Ultimately, everything we have covered is about the skills, mindsets and thought processes which will contribute to a healthy EQ so there is not much to add in this section apart from two key things to think about: your overall balance and your overall level of EI.

Let us look at balance first. For a bit of visualisation practice try to picture an old fashioned set of scales; the type you might find in an "olde worlde" sweet shop or pharmacy. Picture one with a pivoting balance beam like a seesaw and having a pan or dish on either side. The pans are suspended by chains hanging from the ends of the pivoting balance beam. Anyway, on the one side you have yourself and the way you manage yourself and your place in the world and on the other side you have other people, your understanding of them and your ability to manage relationships with them. When the two sides are at the same level you have achieved a balance between them.

What are some of the potential problems associated with an EI imbalance? Let us do some supposing at the extremes:

Suppose, although you are an incredibly self-aware individual with a good understanding of where you want to be and go in the world, you have a limited ability to empathise, little understanding of other people or their motives and you simply do not know how to relate to them appropriately, you will have a hard time dealing with others no matter how much you would like or need to. You might be seen as an isolated distant loner, cripplingly shy, aggressively angry or someone so difficult to relate to it is simply not worth the bother. People will be unlikely to want to get to know you better. Depending on how you actually related to others you could be perceived as being totally passive or acutely aggressive. Worse yet, you might vary constantly in your approach due to your inability to spot appropriate emotional feedback from others; this unpredictability confuses people and leads to all manner of interpersonal problems. You would likely be someone with a lot of love to share and no ability to share it. Unless you truly desire the life of a quiet hermit or an angry dictator, you could end up feeling very unhappy, emotionally imprisoned, lonely and friendless. Your self-esteem and emotional resilience would be very low. You would need to tone down your inward facing aspects and work on your ability to understand other people and manage your relationships with them in order to bring about some balance.

Now suppose the situation was reversed. Although you can empathise with the emotions of others, read their physiological feedback and relate to others with seeming ease, you have no real sense of self, no real sense of your place in the world or even where you would like to be. In this scenario your whole life will be driven by other people, trying to please them and providing the things they want. You will feel as if you have no moral or personal value compass to guide your decisions. You will likely feel empty and adrift inside. On the surface, you will be seen as an approachable and dynamic social chameleon, you will probably be very popular with a lot of casual acquaintances and you will be someone who gets on well with others in most situations. People who do try to get to know you on a more deeply emotional level however will find the hollow emotional shell inside the superficial you and ultimately they will be repelled. People may discover you are essentially passive with a strong desire to please others and they may be able to manipulate you very easily. You have no real way to avoid this scenario if it happens and you may even welcome the control, no matter the negative intention behind it. Once again you could end up feeling very unhappy, emotionally trapped, lonely and friendless. Your self-esteem and emotional resilience would again be very low. You would need to tone down your outward facing aspects and work on your ability to understand yourself and manage your emotional self in order to bring about some balance.

These are obviously extreme examples to illustrate a point. Most of us never get to the extremes mentioned above but, if the EI imbalance was not noticed and checked, things can and do spiral out of control sometimes; it can happen to the best of us. You might have your own thoughts on the potential issues which could develop. My point is this, we all have large and small EI imbalances at different stages of our lives and in different contexts and it will never be perfect.

The other key thing to be aware of is the overall level of your EI. Having it balanced but at an overall low level will not do you much good either. You might well be incredibly intelligent and rational in the traditional IQ sense but you probably will not function particularly well in the self-awareness and social management arena. You will have a poor grasp of your own self-worth and direction and others will likely struggle to work or communicate with you. Ideally, if you do actually want to see improvements you will have to work hard and bring both sides of the balance up as evenly as possible.

There are no magic techniques to achieve better EI, apart from using the right tools, seeking the right path and working damn hard on your personal growth. For me the key to improving emotional intelligence is, and always has been, through openness and honesty. In the first instance you need to be open and honest with yourself. Work with a coach, mentor or other trusted guide, if you have access to a good one. Spend time going deep into your heart and mind and you will start to find the answers you need inside. Secondly you can start to work on understanding other people and how to build and maintain appropriate relationships with them. Other people are essentially the same as us. They generally have similar fears, similar dreams and similar emotions so use this thought as a starting point. This can take time, courage and commitment and you will make mistakes; remember, learning from our mistakes is ultimately how we learn anything worthwhile.

I will offer this last observation and I will be interested to hear if anyone has experienced this situation first hand or in fact believes it is complete rubbish and I am talking out of my you know what. It has been my experience, and the experience of a number of my clients, that after a lot of personal growth work and at a certain level and with good balance, your EI becomes self-stoking. The world is like a mirror and what you project outward comes reflecting right back to you. As your own EI level improves and becomes more balanced the people you relate to and deal with will see this fact. They will react and respond to you more positively and the positive feedback increase your EI thus effectively setting up a virtuous circle. Your EI suddenly seems to rise with no apparent additional or conscious effort on your part. Fear not, I am not talking about Zen enlightenment or religious epiphany here, just the fact you suddenly become very positively self-aware and highly confident in your own ability. Your deft management of other people and your skilful handling of once problematic social or work situations, seems almost effortless. Stress drops away and the world seems a nicer place altogether with the future bright and about to take care of itself.

I like to think of this moment as the emergence of the mastery of your emotional resilience and your emotional intelligence. If and when you get it, believe me, it is a great feeling and you will be glad you put in all the hard miles to attain it.

The ancient Greeks had the phrase "Gnothi seauton" inscribed above the entrance portal to the Delphic oracle. It translates as "Know thyself." EI has been around for a long time I think.

Assertiveness

Assertiveness is one of those words which it seems everyone has heard about, but when pressed, no-one can easily define. We are often told, especially in an organisational context, to be more assertive but what exactly is it we are supposed to do more of? What makes someone more or less assertive? How assertive are we right now? How assertive must we be?

There are many on-line self-evaluation questionnaires available so if you want to find out your level of assertiveness or your preferred interpersonal or influencing style then feel free to try them out. Some are free and some are paid for; some are useful and some are not.

I am going to cut right to the chase and assume most of us, including you my friend, could use a little more assertiveness in our lives. This is quite a big section as assertiveness is a key element in your emotional resilience toolkit.

Before defining and looking at developing it, let us look at some of the positive behaviours associated with being assertive:

The ability to choose when and whether to say yes or no to people, based on what you actually want, rather than meekly agreeing to other people's agendas.

Deciding upon, setting and then sticking to clear personal and professional boundaries as well as having the confidence to defend your stated position even if it might provoke conflict.

Being able to give and receive honest constructive feedback with the right open-minded and balanced spirit; positive and negative.

Understanding how to negotiate with integrity when two parties seek different outcomes.

Being able to talk openly and honestly about yourself and being able to openly listen to and empathise with others.

You will no doubt notice from the above descriptions of positive assertive behaviours it is a key part of your emotional intelligence. Being more assertive during your interactions with other people allows you to maintain or even take back emotional control when once upon a time you would have left the interaction feeling diminished, drained and emotionally impoverished.

With the above in mind, in this section I am going to provide you with a useful working definition of assertiveness and will also provide you with some simple and practical techniques for developing and applying it. You will find increased assertiveness will help you preserve and even increase your levels of emotional resilience.

For our purposes we can reasonably say assertiveness involves being completely clear and open about how you feel, what you need and how it can be fairly achieved. This requires assertive communication skills, assertive body language, confidence and the ability to interact calmly without attacking or yielding unnecessarily to another person.

Learning to be more assertive will help you to express your thoughts and feelings freely, speak up and defend yourself, know and stand up for your rights, negotiate reasonably and control your emotions effectively during periods of interpersonal conflict.

Right here and now I want to give you the key concept which needs to be understood before moving forward. Assertiveness is a state of mind. It is an attitude. It is a way of thinking. Sure, there are some great techniques which I will share with you and they will help you achieve more success when you behave more assertively but you have to develop an assertive mindset in order to carry them off. Because of the work on state management we did earlier the good news is you can summon your new and useful assertive mental state whenever you desire with relative ease.

Let us examine some of the main ways we can interact with others and the ways they can interact with us.

From the list of positive assertive behaviours given above it is evident that knowing what you want, setting clear boundaries and staying true to yourself are important elements. You might also have noticed two other key characteristics. One is openness and the other is consideration for others.

For our purposes, openness means someone's willingness to disclose to someone else their thoughts, feelings, past experiences, reactions and so on. Some people give away very little information about themselves, others reveal moderate amounts and others speak of their thoughts and feelings fully and directly.

An individual's degree of consideration for others means their willingness to assign to others the same rights and respect they assign themselves. Again, some people have little respect for the opinions, feelings and reactions of others, some have moderate respect and others defend and try to preserve the rights of others as strongly as they do their own.

If you combine these two elements in a high/low format you end up with four possible different combinations of interpersonal interaction and influencing style which I will label as aggressive, assertive, passive and passive-aggressive:

High openness and low consideration gives aggressive
Low openness and high consideration gives passive
Low openness and low consideration gives passive-aggressive
High openness and high consideration gives assertive

These are extremes and you will likely fall somewhere in the middle or have a similar preference for several styles. They are also context dependent as with so much of life. For example, you might be an extremely passive individual in work and far more aggressive at home or you might be assertive with your good friends and far more passive-aggressive with your work colleagues.

What you believe about yourself and your preferred influencing style is one thing of course. It is more important to understand and control the interpersonal style which other people perceive and receive from you. It is also very important you understand and recognise the styles adopted by others so you can deal with them more effectively to maintain your emotional control and resilience.

Aggressive behaviour results when someone employs a high degree of openness but gives little consideration for the thoughts and feelings of others. Aggressive behaviour may be demonstrated when someone is behaving in a domineering, pushy, self-centred or overly self-promoting way. Extremely aggressive individuals may be abusive, threatening and authoritarian. Their non-verbal communication may take the form of staring, glaring, frowning, finger pointing or other angry postures, gestures and movements toward others. Aggressive people often try to communicate an impression of superiority and disrespect. Aggressive people tend to adopt an "I win you lose" approach to life. By being aggressive we put our needs, wants and rights high above those of others and our aggressive behaviour nearly always violates the rights and feelings of others. Taken to the extreme, aggressive people are all too often outright bullies. Aggression is the result of poor emotional intelligence and low levels of self-control. At first glance it would seem the aggressive types have very high self-esteem but in reality the opposite is true. They create an artificially high opinion of themselves and, using the idea about attack being the best form of defence, defend it at all costs with their aggressiveness. We have all encountered this type I am sure; not pleasant but at least visible and often consistent.

Passive behaviour is inhibited, it subjugates the self and it always seeks to avoid conflict. Passive types do this by trying too hard to please others. The passive person therefore ignores their own needs and feelings to try and satisfy the needs and feelings of others; as a result, they can often experience feelings of low self-esteem, frustration and sometimes emotional withdrawal. They turn anger and other potentially negative feelings inward. Other people are provided with more rights than they provide themselves. By being overly passive and indirect, communicating a message of inferiority and allowing the needs and rights of others to take preference over their own they often end up feeling like a victim and this comes with the associated victim mentality. Other people will often perceive them as victims too and respond to them in like manner. We have all encountered this type I am sure and it is sometimes hard not to take advantage of their weak behaviour. Passive people tend to adopt an "I lose you win" approach to life.

Passive-aggressive behaviour results when a person is neither open nor considerate of others. Passive-aggressive individuals find subtler, more subversive and more insidious ways of conveying their feelings and reactions. For example, a passive-aggressive manager may start to quietly exclude an unsatisfactory employee from crucial activities as a way of encouraging them to seek another job, rather than talking directly. A worker who is unhappy at the promotion of a colleague might start a gossip or smear campaign against them rather than be open about their true feelings. They seem to go out of their way to secretly undermine other people rather and drag them down than build themselves up. They are often being nasty or demeaning to others in order to feel less bad about themselves. Their efforts usually do not work because in my experience passive-aggressive types almost always have low self-esteem and low empathy levels. Passive-aggressive personalities tend to support and adopt the "I lose you lose" approach. Unfortunately, I am sure we have all encountered passive-aggressive types or been on the receiving end of their passive-aggressive behaviour. They can be toxic people to deal with in any situation and later I will discuss some practical ways to handle them.

Lastly, an assertive person is both open and considerate of others. They are self-revealing and self-respecting yet able to communicate their thoughts and feelings in ways which respect the rights of others. They treat the opinions of others as equal and valid. They seek to negotiate outcomes which allow all parties to get what they need. They work from a foundation of the "I win you win" approach. They have a high level of EI and solid self-esteem.

To be assertive then is to be active, direct and honest. Being assertive communicates an impression of self-respect and respect for others. It allows for us to influence, listen and negotiate in ways which allow others to choose whether to co-operate with us or not. This behaviour leads to success without retaliation or recrimination and encourages open, honest and sustainable relationships built on trust. You and others have needs to be met, rights to be respected and responsibilities to uphold.

In my experience, most people err on the side of passivity at work. You know, the old "No need to make a fuss and anything for a quiet life," approach.

Surprisingly often, my clients will cite the fact they are being taken advantage of by someone else either at work or in their private life; and their self-esteem and resilience are low as a result. When I challenge them to fully examine and explain the background it often transpires they have set the problematic and non-assertive ground rules early on in the relationship.

It is all about how you have educated people regarding their interactions with you. Yes, you read me right, in most cases you will have educated other people yourself and they now interact with you in the way they have been taught to by you. In almost all situations, you are one hundred percent responsible for the current situation you find yourself in.

For example, I once worked with a client, let us call him Steve, who was always being told by the same person to refill the ink and paper on the office photocopier; this was six years and several substantial promotions on from when he first started in the office as a wide-eyed and enthusiastic trainee administrative assistant. This situation was obviously upsetting him and it negatively impacted his mood whenever it repeated. The other person involved would discover the photocopier was out of paper or ink then go to Steve's desk and instruct him to fill it up again; no explanation or a "please would you do this," just an instruction to do it. The possibility of Steve being busy did not seem to matter to this person or indeed the idea someone else, at a lower operational level than Steve, might be better suited to the task. According to Steve, when he started work in the department, around six year ago, he was keen and eager to please. Always looking for jobs to do, he was more than happy to fill the photocopier for anyone who asked. The apparently ruthless and heartless villain in this ongoing scenario, let us call him Reg, was a senior manager from another department and was based in another office area situated on the same floor. Reg used the photocopier a lot. Steve was seeking help about this perceived victimisation by Reg; the implication was Reg personally had it in for Steve.

Steve seemed amazed by what I told him next. I told him it was the natural and wholly expected outcome of his own behaviour over the previous six years.

Steve still seemed keen to assume Reg had it in for him personally and asked me why on earth I was taking Reg's side. I explained I was not taking sides at all. I then asked Steve a couple more questions. Had he ever refused to complete the task? Had he ever said he was too busy and directed the manager elsewhere? The answer to both was a sheepish no.

Here was the story as I saw it from Reg's perspective.

Six years ago the administration assistant Steve happily accepted the role of photocopier replenishment technician. This worked out well for Reg as he did not have to do it himself or, as Steve's desk was close by the machine, go far out of his way to get it done. Whenever Reg found the machine empty he would always go to Steve and have him replenish it appropriately. Steve always completed the task without complaint so Reg continued to go to him whenever he needed to and he will go to him again the next time the machine is empty.

In actual fact, I explained to Steve, Reg is not a villain at all. He is actually behaving assertively from his perspective. He is not being aggressive or manipulative. Whenever he finds a problem with the machine, he considers his time too valuable to spend on the task of refilling it so delegates it to someone nearby who always accepts and completes the task efficiently and without complaint. He quite simply had no indication of any kind his actions are causing anyone a problem so therefore has no need or desire to initiate any changes in his own behaviour.

Steve's mouth opened and closed a few times but no sound came out. He was trying to justify himself and blame Reg but he simply could not think of anything to say. He thought about it all quietly for a few more minutes. Finally, he asked, "So what can I do about it?" This was real progress.

The answer, of course, is for Steve to become more assertive. If he wants to change the situation he must re-educate Reg to not expect him to fill the photocopier on demand. Let us look in more detail at how we can all achieve this.

Firstly, take a few minutes to consider how many of the assumptions other people make about you and the things or tasks they appear to impose on you, are actually created, allowed and maintained by the way you have educated people and responded to them over the years. It is a huge clue you have created such a situation whenever you find yourself saying, "Why do they always ask me to do this?" or "Am I the only one who ever does anything around here?"

If you are honest about it the answers may well surprise you, annoy you and upset you all at the same time. The good news is you can start to turn these situations around whenever you like. I recommend starting as soon as possible.

If you have educated people to behave or think a certain way with you then the answer is to educate them to behave or think in a way which works better for you. Only you can make the choice to do this and commit to seeing it through.

In almost all modern societies we generally feel we can expect certain rights. For example, I personally believe, in my personal life, I have the right express my feelings, opinions, values and needs and have them heard. In my working life I believe I have the right to make reasonable requests and refuse unreasonable ones. I believe I have lots of other rights as well; too many to usefully list here. The rights you believe you have or deserve to have will vary with you as an individual and vary with your current situation.

If you accept and embrace these rights there is a caveat. All rights come with responsibilities. It is a simple relationship. If you believe you have a right to expect something from someone else you also have a responsibility to reciprocate and provide the same right to them. For example, if I believe I have the right to say no to others I also have a responsibility to allow others to say no to me. If I believe I do not have to justify my choices to others then I have a responsibility not to expect or require others to justify their choices to me. If I believe I have the right to change my mind I cannot complain if other people change theirs because it is their right also. I am sure you get the idea. Like I said, a simple relationship.

As mentioned earlier, assertive people tend to take an "I win you win" approach to life and in their interactions with other people. If you take your rights seriously and you accept and live up to the accompanying responsibilities, you will be behaving with an "I win you win" attitude in your dealings with others. You are well on your way to having an assertive influencing style. What about the other three types? Well, passive people tend to cede their own rights whilst allowing others to have theirs; the "I lose you win" approach. Aggressive people tend to assume all their rights and more whilst not living up to their responsibilities by denying the rights of others; the "I win you lose" approach. Passive-aggressive types end up honouring neither part of the equation. They end up adopting the "I lose you lose" approach.

Your choice of language and the way you deliver your assertive messages are vitally important in your pursuit of greater assertiveness.

You need to use positive language delivered with conviction. Do not ever apologise or start with weak phrases such as: "I do not want to be a nuisance but..." Or "Sorry to seem negative but..." To this I say, no, no, no! Make your statements in the assertive language of someone who is in control of their facts and emotions and who knows what they want. Practice your responses and delivery with a trusted friend and get them to whole-heartedly play the role of aggressive or demanding boss. This can be fun as well as useful.

Here then is a basic yet solid framework for constructing useful assertive statements. I suggest you practice creating assertive statements and try delivering them when you get the chance. This is one occasion when I would recommend committing some or all of the statements you create to memory; this way you will be ready to respond assertively when someone tries to catch you on the hop. Here is the formula with an example to follow:

Step 1: Clarify and paraphrase the situation to show you understand it and the other person's concerns.

Step 2: Deliberately use the word "but" as this negates your previous statement ready for the assertive part.

Step 3: Clearly state how you feel about the situation. Note the other person or situation cannot make you feel anything so stick to the facts as you perceive them and remain objective.

Step 4:   State what you want to happen next or what you are going to do next.

Step 5:   Check for agreement with the other person.

Your body language is at least as important as the words you use. Do not stand there wringing your hands and staring at the floor whilst mumbling through your statement and shuffling your feet; this will not help your cause. Your facial expressions and physiology need to support and reinforce your message so you need to be fully congruent when delivering your brilliantly constructed assertive response. Maintain a neutral yet steady and determined facial expression and take a rooted stance which conveys confidence and poise. Keep your hands quite still unless you want to use them to enhance a point. Make good eye contact and keep your voice calm, steady and evenly paced.

You may have to go round the doors a few times if people try different approaches to get you to comply. Stick to your plan unless the new offer works out well for you.

Here is an example to show the structure of a workable refusal response to a manager request for Diane, an employee, to come in on a Saturday for overtime. Her response is clear and assertive.

Manager: "Hey Diane, I need you to come in to work this Saturday because we've had a last minute rush order. I'll pay you time and a half. What do you say?"

Diane: "Look Steve, I appreciate there's been a last minute rush order but I can't come in on Saturday. I do feel a bit annoyed and unfairly pressured right now. I've made it very clear to everyone all week that I'm going to the fun fair with the children this weekend. I've worked three out of the last four Saturdays so I suggest you ask one of the other technicians to work this Saturday. I trust you understand and respect my stance on this occasion?"

Now, I would like to demonstrate another useful variation of the above technique which utilises the concept of a "straw man" or third party as a way to assertively deflect the undesirable request. Do you remember Steve, the guy who kept filling the photocopier for Reg? Here is a very useful example of how Steve could respond assertively next time Reg rocks up to ask him to sort out the machine.

Reg: "I see the photocopier is out of ink again. Fill it up for me and send an email when it's done as I have some important printing to do. OK?"

Steve: "I realise having no ink is a problem for you and I'd love to help you out but my line manager has given me a ton of work and a tight deadline. He'll be very annoyed if I get distracted in any way. Of course, if you'd like to go and see my line manager Dave and tell him you want me to drop this work to fill the photocopier machine he might be able to re-prioritise my workload. Until then I'm afraid my hands are tied."

The caveat here of course is Steve discussing the approach in advance with his line manager Dave so he will not be surprised if someone does ask. It also demonstrates to Dave that Steve is keen to keep focused on his priorities. It is extremely unlikely Reg would ever consider speaking to Dave about such a trivial task anyway. In reality Reg will not care about Steve or his workload any more than usual; he might be a bit annoyed after the exchange but only because he has not had his problem dealt with and he will have to do a bit more work himself. He will simply go and find someone else to ask. One or two repeats of the same assertive approach will re-educate Reg not to even bother asking Steve to fill the machine in the future. Great result for Steve!

Here are a number of useful and practical language techniques to use in conjunction with and in addition to the framework ideas given above.

The broken record technique involves calmly repeating what you want over and over again. It is helpful to use clear statements such as, "I understand your point but I want..." or "I hear what you are saying but I would like..." By using repetition you maintain your position and can resist any manipulative comments, irrelevant or distracting tangents or argumentative emotional bait which the other person might use.

The statements used above employ another useful technique; acknowledge and respond. You can acknowledge there may be some truth in what the other person says or believes but at the same time the broken record technique allows you to remain strong, non-defensive and undeterred.

It is entirely possible the other person has something valid to say. You can look to establish a workable compromise as a practical solution to any situation involving genuine conflict. You can often feel under personal attack in any conflict situation so once you can this is not the case you can begin to negotiate a compromise everyone is prepared to accept. However, make sure you never lose sight of what you really want in an effort to restore harmony.

Sometimes any sort of criticism is hard to take. However, practising and using the technique called negative assertion helps you handle both hostile and constructive criticism. The idea is by agreeing with and accepting some of what is actually valid in the criticism you show you are listening closely and self-aware. By the way, doing this does not mean you will feel diminished in any way. On the contrary, offering small genuine concessions like this is a great assertive technique for taking the tension out of a stressful situation and gaining control of and occupying the moral high ground.

The idea of negative enquiry is closely linked. The idea is you proactively prompt the other person to provide criticism. This may feel counter-intuitive but it helps you use the information provided (if constructive) or to expose it for what it actually is (if manipulative or hostile). This also gives the other person an opportunity to express honest negative feelings and leads to a general improvement in communication. It can diffuse a tense situation. Use questions throughout, without defending, attacking or explaining.

To illustrate the above concepts, here is an example conversation showing all the techniques in action:

Gary: "Hey Jane, I need you to help me finish my financial projections tonight so we can finish the new contract by tomorrow afternoon."

Jane: "Gary, I understand we need to finish the new contract but it's not due until next week. I've not had a chance to see my daughter before her bed time this week and it's just not on. I'm going home to relax with my family so I'm afraid I can't help you tonight. OK?"

Gary: "Seriously? I thought we're supposed to be a team. You know I'd help you if the situation was reversed."

Jane: "I've worked late all week to complete my assigned tasks. I understand the contract is important but tonight my family comes first so once again the answer is no, I can't help you tonight."

Gary: "Look Jane this is important. If we get the contract finished early we'll all benefit. Just one more big push. What do you say?"

Jane: "I say no Gary. How many more times? I'm aware of the benefits but the contract is still not due until next week. I've promised my daughter I'll be there for her and I will be there. How can I make this any clearer?"

Gary: "Some colleague you're turning out to be. I've heard several other team members saying you're becoming less and less willing to stay late and help out in these situations. What gives?"

Jane: "Thanks for the newsflash and in all honesty it might actually be true but only to a certain extent. I'm less and less willing to give up my time now my family is growing. I am sticking to my guns though and I'm not staying on late tonight. I'm really working hard and making sure I have completed all my assigned work on this project. Look Gary, there's obviously more to all of this. Be honest with me here, what do you think the real issues are?"

Gary: "Look, Steve is keen for the team to make a good impression with head office. He mentioned finishing it early would be a great way to do that. I think the whole team is being looked at in a poor light this year. We simply are not hitting deadlines. You are a key player and if you refuse to help out I don't know where we'll be. You do realise by not helping this time you're making the rest of the team look bad, don't you? You're a part of the team too you know."

Jane: "Thank you, I really do appreciate your honesty Gary. Look, whilst Steve hasn't actually said anything to me about this, I can see why you'd think these things and I can also accept it might well be true; Steve is seeing an imbalance in the team and so are head office. All

287

that aside, the financial projections were assigned to you and the other team members are leaving things late as well. What I can't accept is unfair and undeserved pressure on me to give up my personal and family time to cover an imbalance in other people's results."

Gary: "So you still won't help then?"

Jane: "No I won't because I promised my daughter. What I will propose is this. We all have strengths and skills and on paper we should be a high performing team. First thing tomorrow let's all get together and thrash this out. We may need to look at how we plan projects and assign workload for next time. Maybe we can all start to finish on time more often? How does that sound?"

Gary: "Actually that sounds good. I think Steve's a bit out of his depth and he needs some help and a wake-up call. If we all get together and act in concert, we might turn it around by year end. I'll send the meeting request right now. Nice idea Jane, thanks. Before you go can I just apologise if I pushed too hard earlier, I've been a bit stressed. I would rather be home with my own family if the truth be told so when I saw you going, well, you know. Anyway, sorry. Have a great evening and we'll chat tomorrow."

Jane: "No worries. I'll see you and the others tomorrow."

In this hypothetical scenario Jane was very assertive throughout despite Gary taking a few cheap shots. She stuck to her guns and kept her composure. Because she worked hard to keep the conversation neutral and objective they actually went far deeper into the issue than might otherwise have been the case and also developed a good idea.

Let us look at some more specific strategies for dealing assertively with the other types.

The openly aggressive type gives many people the greatest cause for concern. When someone attacks you physically or verbally it can easily trigger our fight or flight response. It scares us. When this happens we lose objectivity and think with far less clarity and logic than we normally would.

Being aggressive in response to their aggression leads you nowhere except into hostile pointless confrontation. Being passive makes their life easy and yours hard. Not the best way to go. You could be passive-aggressive and get them back slyly later but do you really want to be that person? I hope not. Keep the moral high ground; assertiveness is definitely the way to go.

Think like The Scouts and always be prepared. Being prepared allows you to more quickly recover from any fight or flight response you may have. Bullies often use aggression as a defence through offence tactic; they dominate through bluster, intimidation, force and reputation. Know all your facts, do your research and provide clear evidence to support or defend your position. It will give you the edge you need. Often you will know the sort of person you are going to have to deal with in advance so you will have the time to fully prepare. When you are able to make a firm case and stand your ground the bully will generally give up and move on to easier prey. They may even respect you for your approach. Word of your tough stance with aggressive people will spread and dramatically improve your reputation as someone who is organised, firm and not easily bullied.

The use of effective questioning technique to expose flaws and inconsistencies in other people's arguments is also a great way to combat an aggressive approach. Good questions will allow you to take the initiative and take the steam out of the other person's boiler. Particularly effective questions are open, deep, constructive, incisive and probing; these expose poor logic, poor preparation, poor consideration and a lack of consultation on their part. Here are some suitable example questions: "What is your evidence for this claim?" "How exactly have you arrived at this conclusion?" "Who have you consulted with about this?" "How will you prove the effectiveness of your proposed solution and are there any better alternatives?"

Stick to your position doggedly and do not allow the other person to dodge or ignore your question or questions. A great method is to use the broken record technique until they answer it or concede the point. They are trying to wear you down by force so combat this with steely determination.

There is a lovely children's short story which has always stuck in my mind. It concerns the North Wind and the Sun. The North Wind was always boasting about being more powerful than the Sun. The Sun eventually got tired of this boastful wind's prattling and one fine autumn day he proposed they settle it by seeing which of them could make a certain man of their choosing take his hat off first. The North Wind immediately declared this would be an easy victory for him. The chosen man left his home wearing his favourite old hat; an eminently suitable hat for the crisp and clear weather. As soon as the man set off the North Wind started to blow hard. The man was surprised but buttoned up his coat, pulled his hat tighter onto his head, hunkered over and strode on despite the wind. North Wind's intention was to blow the hat right off the man's head so he blew ever more fiercely. The more he blew the tighter the man pulled his hat down over his ears. North Wind blew as hard as ever he could but the man took some strong string out of his coat pocket and tied his old hat to his head with it making it tighter than ever; the man refused to risk losing his favourite hat just because it was windy. The North Wind finally gave up and grudgingly told the Sun he could try now. The man was surprised when the wind died so suddenly so he removed the string and resumed walking along his route. The Sun now began to beam. The man noticed this and smiled. The air grew warmer still and the man took off his coat. The Sun shone even more brightly and the man loosened his tie. The temperature rose and rose until finally the man had to take off his hat. The Sun had won the contest and the North Wind finally ceased his boasting. The North Wind was aggressive and the Sun was assertive.

This story always brings a smile to my face and reminds me there are many kinds of power; not all of them have to be noisy and forceful.

Always approach interpersonal situations by attempting to anticipate how the other person or people involved will likely behave. In my experience it is well worth while taking some time to prepare and role-play your own useful responses to certain scenarios you think could unfold. You could also arrange for other key people to support and defend you. Being well prepared will always increase your self-confidence and enable you to be maximally assertive and confident.

If you are excessively passive then consider, identify and use your personal strengths rather than your perceived weaknesses. Have faith in your skills. Bullies and dominant aggressive types have their methods and passive or non-assertive types have theirs. Even if you are non-assertive right now, you may well already be extremely strong in such skill areas as following process, attention to detail, dependability and reliability, getting the job done, checking and monitoring, communication, interpretation and understanding as well as collaboration with others. When used against them, all these strong capabilities and any others you may have, can reduce a once dominant bully, who often has no proper justification anyway, to an impotent ranting clown. So find your strengths and use them to defend and support your position. The biggest hissy-fit or red-faced tantrum in the world is no match for a well organised, logical, provable and solid defence presented with conviction and self-belief.

If you find yourself dealing with a passive-aggressive type in my experience the key is to shine a metaphorical bright light onto both them and their activity. They will naturally try to remain in the shadows and do their dirty work in secret. They will not like being made visible to you and others. Their petty and mean behaviours, once revealed, are not pretty and will stop quite quickly once other people see them for what they really are. Do not try to play them at their own game as it never ends well and they are better at it than you anyway. Do not get angry with them because you will lose this battle too. Remaining passive plays right into their hands so there is only one realistic approach left; assertiveness.

Always confront them assertively and right out in the open, preferably with other people you trust around you. They often like to show how clever they are by trying to show others up in public situations. This is the time to assertively confront them and make them explain exactly what the mean. It takes courage but it is mightily effective. As previously recommended, have all your facts to hand and challenge them with probing questions. Keep challenging them assertively to make them justify their behaviour. They invariably will not be able to and will back down. They will probably try and get back at you in some subtle or underhanded way so be prepared for this. If they do it again repeat the process. They will soon see you as too powerful an adversary and move on.

As a general comment on passive-aggressive behaviour, if you have such a person in your business, team or life you might want to give a lot of consideration to getting rid of them entirely. They are a toxic influence and creators of massive negativity in any situation. Do not let them ply their nasty trade near you if you or the people close to you if you can possibly avoid it.

Dealing with overly passive people can be a problem even for assertive people. Passive people essentially invite others to take advantage of them. Obviously, if you are a bully or a manipulative sort this can work out well for you. If you are overly passive as well then generally nothing ever gets done but at least there is a relaxed atmosphere. If you are an assertive type you may find the passive style very annoying. You have to resist the urge to shake them and shout, "Get a grip!" Maybe that last one is just me?

The best way I know to deal assertively with passive types is to be assertive for them. Rather than take advantage, even by default, it is best to simply not allow them to be passive. Managing passive types requires a slightly unusual and counter-intuitive strategy. You need to take control out of their hands in order to get the best from them; take away their options to give you both better outcomes. Unfortunately, if you allow them to choose from several options they will choose passively and usually to their own detriment so assign them fair tasks or duties. Only instruct them to do reasonable tasks for you. You need to become in effect a benign dictator. Set reasonable deadlines and always set clear instructions for them to come to you immediately anyone tries to interfere with the tasks you have set. This sort of instruction prevents more aggressive types trying to take advantage again. It sounds like you have to treat them like children but trust me, if you want great results from passive people, this really works. You never know, change their environmental system they might start to become more assertive themselves.

I will finish this section by re-stating (broken record) the fact that assertiveness is a state of mind. All the techniques presented above have to be approached with this assertive mindset, as well as using assertive language and physiology, to be effective. This can all take practice. You will feel uncomfortable and, as when learning any new skill, you will make some mistakes. Stick to it and before you know it you will have assertiveness right there in your emotional resilience toolkit and it is a powerful tool to have at your disposal.

You are not alone

As the title of this section says, you are not alone. Being emotionally resilient does not mean being emotionally closed off or isolated. Far from it. This part is all about the systems you are a part of and the systems you can affect and be affected by. Independence is a wonderful thing and I would encourage everyone to aim and work towards becoming more independent and self-reliant but there is a wider world full of other people and, like it or not, you have to interact closely with at least some of them. Interacting successfully in a general sense has been covered in the last two sections; emotional intelligence and assertiveness. This particular section is about helping others when they need it and also about reaching out to people you trust to get help when you need it. I have been fortunate, over the years, to have met and been helped by a number of truly inspirational people. I have tried likewise to help as many people as I could within the limit of my capabilities at different stages in my life.

I mentioned in the stones and ripples section you cannot change anyone else; only they can make changes. I want to really hammer this point home. You can help them change if they ask for help but only they can make personal change happen and stick. Keep this idea firmly in your mind whenever you offer to help or respond to a request for help. You are meant to be helping someone and not doing it for them.

Helping others is a nice thing to do; for them and you. It is tempting to try and help others pro-actively, especially when you are developing your own skills and learning new things. I am the first to admit I have done the very same thing myself and suffered the rebukes and resistance from people who did not want my help. I learnt not to do it the hard way. Now I wait until people ask me for help and I also now do it professionally; people pay me to help them in various ways. This is a very effective way of working because when someone has some skin in the game, i.e. they have invested some money and time, they tend to value the help and input far more. You might want to bear this fact in mind moving forward because even when people do ask you for help, and you put your heart and soul into giving them the help and suggesting potential options or solutions, they may well ignore it all and do their own thing. If this happens, and it does frequently, it can be a dispiriting experience for you. The problem is, whilst you believe your help is just what is required and is the acme of common sense and utility, the other person has the final say about what they consider best for them. It is all too easy to get overly flattered by the request for help but be aware some people like to ask everyone they know for an opinion or help and may consider your input has no more value than anyone else's. I therefore strongly recommend you take a dispassionate and neutral view of it all and protect your own self-esteem and gumption levels. Offer the help, information and guidance as requested but temper your enthusiasm and belief in it by assuming it will not actually be taken on board by the other person. You will then be pleasantly surprised when it does get listened to and possibly acted upon. Helping others so you feel good is not the real goal here; this is ego-centric helping. Helping others so they can grow and develop is the real goal; feeling good yourself is a bonus.

Because you are this far in, and assuming you have had a go at and practised using many if not all of the new tools in your toolbox, you are at the stage in your emotional resilience improvement journey where you have access to a wide range of strategies, techniques, ideas and mental states which will allow you to accept, deal with and bounce back from most of the things life can throw at you. This also means you are more than capable of helping others deal with their problems if asked to do so. It can be an exciting prospect but it also comes with some important responsibilities.

Usually, when someone asks for your help, they do it because they trust you in some way. You have to ensure trust is maintained. If they trust you not to tell particular people about it then do not tell those people about it. The person asking for help may be feeling vulnerable so you have to respect this.

You have to be sure you understand what help is being asked for and stick to the request. Tempting as it might be, do not try and force the full range of your skills and ideas onto them; just give them the help they requested in the way they requested it and leave it there.

For example, imagine someone in your office has observed the new and effective ways you can now assertively handle the office bully; they now want help to achieve the same results. There are now a number of ways you could help them. To list just three: You could simply give them some language patterns to use next time or you could explain your own emotional resilience journey and point them toward the sources of help and guidance you discovered or you could take them under your wing and guide them as if you were their personal guru. Which one of the three might be the best solution? You might straight away think it is obvious given what I have just said but here is the strange thing, all three could be the best solution depending on what the other person really wants. Remember, it is not up to you to decide what is best for them. Ask some probing and incisive questions and then give help to the best of your ability based on the answers. They might already be confident and would simply like to try out the cool language patterns they heard you use. This would make option one favourite. They may wish to gain the same level of confidence and emotional resilience you now have and own it for themselves. The second option is favourite for this. They may be having real problems at work due to a bully and would really benefit from some hands-on assistance and personal coaching, at least for a while. This would make option three viable with option two applicable later if they wanted to take a longer journey on their own. Life is complicated and there are no absolutely right or wrong answers in life, there are only choices and taking personal responsibility for those choices.

Another responsibility, and it is a big one, is being ready and willing to say no to someone who is asking for help. This can be hard to do as we all generally like to help other people. The thing is, if you are not the best person to help them you might actually be doing them a huge disservice by agreeing to help them in the first place. The best thing to do would be to explain you appreciate being asked but they would be better served by seeking more expert advice and assistance. You may be far too busy or burdened with your own problems to be of any real use to them at the time of asking. There could be any number of reasons why you need to say no; both personal and professional. Have you ever felt emotionally blackmailed into doing something? It is not pleasant and you rarely perform at your best or with the best attitude under those circumstances. Ideally, the way you could be of maximum help to them would be to say no then assist them in finding an alternative option and, better yet, introduce them to the better person or organisation. Saying no is sometimes far better than saying yes.

Helping others, especially if it is not something you are used to, can be hard work emotionally. It can be hard to know what to do for the best without digging deeper and not everyone is skilled at or even comfortable with this type of questioning. As I mentioned above, it can also be hard to say no to a request for help. You will also discover what good and bad requests look like and how they affect your response and your answers. All these useful insights allow you to confidently approach others with clear achievable outcomes in mind and a reasonable idea about some of the internal conflicts they might be experiencing when being asked to help. Always allow the other person the option of saying no to you. Never try to force or coerce anyone into helping you and never use emotional blackmail as a way to get what you want; you will have become the bully pursuing the "I win you lose" strategy.

Many people have told me they get extremely nervous and uncomfortable when asking others for help. They do not want to be an annoying burden to anyone else or appear overly needy. I can empathise with this as I have experienced many of the same feelings in the past. I have given this particular question a lot of thought in recent years and, after analysing how I have most successfully provided help myself over the years, I am happy to offer some practical guidance.

The key to it all is to make helping you as easy as possible for the other person. The natural question of course is how exactly do you do this? Here are six useful suggestions you can use when approaching someone else for help:

The first suggestion is to work hard learning as much as you can about the topic yourself before asking anyone else for help. This might seem obvious but I have seen far too many people treat another person as simply an easy shortcut to getting what they want. Either deliberately or unknowingly, they take advantage of someone else's good nature to get information and assistance without trying to make any progress themselves. There are many negative outcomes from this approach. Because the person asking knows so little about the subject the questions they ask are often too simple or too broad. The person helping will likely get frustrated when the answers they give are not understood fully or even valued at all in some cases; it quickly becomes a waste of their valuable time and energy. When it becomes obvious the person asking has made no effort themselves the helper will withdraw their support and will probably refuse to help again in the future. If someone does this a little too often, word will spread and they will find their source of helpful experts will dry up. The secret for you is to learn and experiment yourself first; remember to give yourself permission to make some mistakes and learn from any feedback. When you do get stuck you will have more specific questions to ask and more importantly you will have a better chance of understanding and using the answers you are given. People will enjoy helping you and will likely continue to do so.

The second suggestion is closely related to the one above; make the help request specific, focused and achievable. Many times already we have looked at breaking down large complex situations and events into smaller and more manageable chunks. This prevents overwhelm.

You can also overwhelm someone else by making too big a demand on them with your request for help. Creating overwhelm will increase your chances of getting a no. Getting a yes under overwhelm conditions will still result in a less than ideal outcome for both of you. The important thing for you then is to ask for a very specific and focused form of help and one the person you are asking also has a good chance of being able to provide. This will mean you will likely ask for help less often and you will be able to more easily relate the answers to the knowledge and skills you already have. Even if they are willing to help, if the person you have asked will struggle if they do not have the skillset or knowledge you need, you will be placing them in an awkward and potentially embarrassing position. Do your research and ensure they can actually help you with your specific issue before you even think about asking them.

The third suggestion is for you to ensure the other person knows exactly why you have asked them and no-one else for the specific help you seek. Everyone likes to feel special and valued so letting someone know you value what they do or know and would like to learn specifically from them is a powerful influencing technique. It is of course a form of flattery and there is quite a bit of ego massaging going on but it also demonstrates your focus, informed intent, discernment and emotional intelligence. There is nothing really wrong with greasing the wheels now and again. The one key consideration on this point is to not ask anyone else the same specific question. This shows respect to no-one as it implies lack of trust in the value and ability of your sources; word will get around and help will dry up before you know it.

Suggestion four involves always allowing the other person room to say no gracefully and without pressure. No-one likes to feel pressured into doing anything they do not want to. Some people find it difficult to say no to anything so I urge you to clearly allow them the option to do so. State it explicitly. You have sought them out for a specific reason but you can also clearly let them know an alternative source recommended by them is more than acceptable. Imagine yourself in their shoes. It is good to have the option of saying no even if you still intend to say yes? It shows respect for the feelings of others.

This next suggestion may appear obvious but is often forgotten about. Do not overload one person; try instead to spread the requests thoughtfully and logically. When you do find a valuable source of assistance it is tempting to try and get all your answers and support from that one source. Try and avoid this as it really is not fair to them. They may be reluctant to help you again in the future so think carefully about your approach. How would you feel if someone dumped all their problems onto you in one big heap? At the very least, spread the requests out over time and structure them so they follow logically and build one on the other. The answer to the first question may well lead to you being able to solve some or all of the other issues yourself. Make your requests count and always respect the valuable time and energy of the person you are asking.

The final suggestion I will offer is to make full use of any and all opportunities you do get. There is nothing worse than trying to help someone by providing information or showing them how to achieve something only to find them back again asking the exact same questions again and again. Seriously, if you do this you will be thought of as a time wasting pain in the backside. The way to ensure you only ask once is to keep a record of all the information and guidance you get offered. Take lots of notes, take screen shots or even, with full permission of course, video or audio record the session for later analysis. Once again, if you respect your mentor and truly value the assistance you are getting you will clearly demonstrate this by taking appropriate and copious notes. If you do come back later it will be for the clarification of or expansion of a specific point or two; not the whole thing. Ask for any explanations you need then and there. If you do not fully understand something, then say so. The worst thing of all is to pretend you have got it and then go and ask someone else the exact same question. Take a checklist of specific information or instructions which you want to cover or get in the session and make sure you get it. Send this list to the other person in advance. This serves to give them a chance to prepare more fully and you may well get more comprehensive and enthusiastic support this way.

If someone else asked you to help how would you like it to go? With this thought in mind, make the helping experience as easy as you possibly can for the other person. You will find people will be more than happy to help you.

Here is an example of some approach language and statements which will give you an idea about incorporating these six suggestions into your future requests for assistance:

"Hi Ray. It's good to meet you at last and thanks for agreeing to chat with me today. I know you're busy so I'll cut right to the chase. I'm not sure if you're aware of it or not but I've been instructed by my line manager to write and produce an introductory guide to the TX43 Production Database for new employees. Even though I'm an end user of the system I've had to do a load of reading, research and good old-fashioned hard work to get my head around how it really does what it does and also how to translate the knowledge into something genuinely useful for the new starters. I've completed all the work which I'm confident on and it's about ninety-five percent there. Unfortunately, I've hit a couple of technical brick walls which I can't crack on my own. I've come to you for some pointers because there is no-one on this site who knows more about the TX43 system than you. Right now I need some guidance on how to best explain the data link between the production and packaging schedules. As you know these are generated by the ProPackSched module and there are two or three specific error codes that seem to have no documentation associated with them. I have several other specific questions in other areas but my aim is to complete each section as I go so I don't become a nuisance. Given the amount of project work you are involved in, if you feel you're going to be too busy to help me please tell me now and I'll completely understand. I'm more than happy to work with anyone else you might recommend for these follow-up questions. If you are happy to help do you mind if I take some detailed notes and screen shots as we go?"

I would like to think Ray would be receptive as a result of this approach. You have put in all the hard work yourself and you are being very specific with your questions. You state exactly why you are asking Ray for help and you have given him a no strings attached exit option if he requires it. You have adopted the strategy of "I win you win" and it is delivered very logically and assertively as a bonus. Try some or all of these suggestions every time you need to ask for help in the future and see if they make a difference to your success rate.

We all sometimes forget we are part of a much system bigger than anything else we have specifically discussed - life. Ultimately, life for us humans is a team sport; we are not naturally solitary creatures. Helping others and reaching out for help is natural for us and it is the right thing for us to do. Remember and strive to always try to enjoy life and enjoy life with others; make the most of it whenever and wherever you can.

Case study - Butter fingers

Here is a brief and cleaned-up version of a true story from my long distant youth which taught me some very valuable life lessons and a way of thinking which has helped me greatly in a number of subsequent career phases. I felt bad at the time but then so many really valuable lessons tend to happen like that.

Back in the early eighties I was a proud member of the Territorial Army or TA. It gave me pretty much everything I needed as a healthy young man: Money, beer, weaponry and explosives.

This story concerns explosives.

It was the chilly morning after the night before and some beer had been consumed. Now when I say some beer, it was actually a lot of beer. Come to think of it, when I say a lot of beer, I actually meant far too much beer. Well, I am sure you get the idea even though I am a bit hazy about the details.

We were all on an explosives demonstration event somewhere on a South Wales mountain and I had a hangover.

Two expert regular military engineers were there to teach us about the explosives. These guys were the real deal; they blew things up for a living. As far as I was concerned, this was really cool and today we were going to get a go.

The first talk was about safety. Boring! I wanted explosions not safety. Straight away I was given fifty press-ups to do. I must have broken some rule or other so down I went and managed around twenty arm-wobbling repetitions before landing on my face; to be fair my massive hangover might have contributed somewhat to this pathetic effort.

They started talking about safety again and I started to shuffle about to keep warm. This upset them again for some reason. Something about not paying enough attention to the safety briefing. I was sent away to run round the field ten times with a metal bar held out in front of me – ironically it occurred to me that my punishment for not listening to the safety briefing was causing me to miss the safety briefing.

I got half way round the second lap, threw up and all but passed out on my hands and knees. My arms felt like jelly by now. I still felt slightly queasy when I got back into line.

Then an armoured box was carefully brought out of the back of a truck and the long awaited explosive was finally revealed in all its glory. Was that it? It looked disappointingly like a few small lumps of pale blue modelling clay. It was then explained that just one of the small lumps could completely destroy a ten tonne truck. Things were looking up.

"Hey you! Catch!" One of the regular soldiers had thrown a lump of the explosive at me. At that moment my whole world had gone into slow motion; like a movie. I could hear people around me yelling and running away. There was gravel and dust flying everywhere. Someone was screaming just like a little girl and I realised it was me. I made a valiant attempt at a catch but my arms felt like someone else's. I managed to grasp it briefly but it felt almost alive and my tired fingers could not get a proper hold of it. I made a last feeble attempt at juggling then it happened. I dropped it. My world was still in slow motion and I knew the second the blue lump hit the ground my world would end, literally. I took the only reasonable action available to me at that point; I curled up on the ground and whimpered.

Right then was when I started to hear it - the unmistakable sound of the regular military personnel laughing fit to bust a lung. My so called teammates had now returned from wherever they had run off to and they were laughing at me too. On the plus side I was still alive but somehow, right there amid the laughter and shame, it did not seem to be enough.

Here is the thing. Those guys had withheld one vitally important bit of information from all of us. The pale blue modelling clay was indeed plastic explosive but a small impact such as hitting the ground would never have set the stuff off; it would take an explosive detonator to do that.

I was the butt of the jokes for a good while afterward; people kept yelling catch and throwing things at me. Eventually, someone else made a massive fool of themselves and the attention moved on.

I had, however, learnt several extremely valuable lessons that day. Unfortunately avoiding the perils of drinking too much was not one of them; I never learnt to avoid that for a good many years.

I realised, later on, I had been set up by the two regular soldiers; right from the start.

This was probably a skit they did each and every time with a TA audience. It was not personal; I was simply the first one who did anything remotely punishable. I gave them the opportunity for some fun and they took it. The press-ups and the arms out running were guaranteed to turn my arms to jelly; the hangover was a bonus. They knew there was no way I could have caught the lump of plastic explosive. If it was not me it would have been someone else.

There was a happy ending of sorts. I think they took pity on me; I got to press the button and explosively cut a small steel girder in half. Happy days.

They unwittingly did me a real favour that day because I instantly developed full-blown paranoia at least where jokes at my expense were concerned. In many social situations for quite a while after I was deeply suspicious of everyone and everything. I admit, on reflection, this does not appear to be much of a favour but the experience proved extremely valuable to me. I quickly learnt to turn it into a more healthy and useful form of social paranoia. I became highly attuned to matters of cause and effect, system interaction and consequences. I became a keen student of human nature, especially the analysis of social motives and language patterns.

From that point on I wanted to know everything about everyone I came into contact with. My patience levels grew, my attention to detail improved and I learnt to identify and focus on the important issues in any situation. It got me through ten years of the construction industry and fifteen years of the chemical industry with very few successful practical jokes at my expense. Both are dangerous industries and I am still here and in one piece.

Developing a healthy and properly directed paranoia has proved to be a very good thing.

Onward and upward

I started all this thinking it would be a relatively short volume and, as you have steadfastly read this far, you might well be wishing it had been shorter. I hope it is only as long as it properly needs to be. I initially day-dreamed, brain-stormed and mind-mapped. I analysed, strategised and produced my logical outline. I began to write and as I wrote and immersed myself more and more in the subject matter, it started to take on a life of its own; books can be like that. Emotional resilience is a deep, wonderful and hugely interconnected subject. As I said earlier, this is not an attempt to capture everything about emotional resilience; simply a practical guide to developing and improving it. I have tried hard to stick to this ethos but I found as I wrote that everything connects and links to everything else. The connections, sometimes obvious and sometimes subtle, created a wonderful and ever expanding web. I hope you take your studies and interest further. I will be hugely pleased if I have encouraged you.

There is one key thing for you to remember as you go on with your self-development and growth. All of the practical ideas, tools, techniques, processes, approaches and attitudes provided herein actually work. They have been developed, tried, tested and applied in the real world with real people. They will continue to work well and they will work well for you. The only caveat is, this stuff only works if you try it out and use it. This volume is not meant for theoretical entertainment or amusement. It is meant to be a hands-on, or brains-on, toolkit. Reading about carpentry will not build you a cabinet. Designing, planning, wood, tools, glue, hard work and patience will build you a cabinet. Always take things one step at a time. Pick a strategy or technique and try it out; if you like it then keep using it. Not everything in here will work for you because you are a unique individual. Get things that do work for you "in the muscle" through repetition and fine-tuning. Rome, as they say, was not built in a day.

Developing and maintaining your emotional resilience and confidence is an ongoing process which requires constant thought and application of effort. The results can be life-changing.

I encourage all my clients to develop a standout personal growth ethic and become a lifelong learner. I would encourage you to do the same. You bought this guide after all so you know how important these habits can be and what a difference they can make to your life. I have spent a great deal, in both time and money, on my self-improvement over the last decade or so and I wish I would have started sooner. I read numerous non-fiction and business books every year; some good some bad. I watch and listen to as many courses as I can; again some good and some bad. I am always hungry for new knowledge and the practical skills to apply it. I am a seeker and the more I learn the more I want to learn. Sometimes, the more I learn the less I feel I know anything at all; when this happens I need to summon up and draw on all my resilience and gumption levels. It can be hard but I keep going. I look deep and I find a way.

I hear many people saying they simply do not have any time to do these things. I hear them say if they did not have to work or look after kids or a million other excuses they would get that dream goal started and finished and they would seek that personal El Dorado. Well, here is a surprising little time calculation for you:

If you committed just thirty minutes per day every day of the year for self-improvement or learning it would add up to over one hundred and eighty hours per year. This is equivalent to over twenty two working days or around a full working month. What could you do with a working month all to yourself? You could get through a lot of self-improvement or other educational material in this time. If you travel extensively on business, you could use some of this time to listen to quality audio based materials. You could perhaps complete at least one high-quality home study course. You could learn a new language. You could even write the novel you have always dreamed of yet never started because you, "Just do not have the time." Newsflash! If you wrote at an easily achievable pace of only one hundred and sixty five words every day you could complete a first draft in excess of sixty thousand words. This paragraph alone contains well over three hundred words and it did not take too long to write and edit. What could you do to free up an average of just thirty minutes a day? Could you find even more time? Be honest with yourself here and analyse where you are wasting your valuable time right now? Are you letting time vampires steal this valuable time from you? What do you want to learn or achieve which you believe you do not have the time for right now? I challenge you to find some time, and commit to using this time, for personal growth; what you achieve as a result might well surprise you.

We have covered the concept of success and failure right back near the beginning. It is at the beginning because it is incredibly important. If you try new things then rest assured you will fail at some point. If you never fail, you are either the luckiest or most able person in recorded history or you are not stretching yourself enough with challenging new situations. Take baby-steps by all means but keep stretching and growing your comfort zone. Keep on experimenting and trying out new skills and techniques. If you fail frequently this is a good thing. The feedback you get will allow you to get better and better and nearer and nearer to you goal. Choose your success and failure criteria carefully. Do not let others set the criteria for you unless there is no other option. Here is another challenge for you. Aim to try something new each day. Start off by doing it for a week, then a month and then a year. For example, you could change your daily travel routine, sing karaoke, try a new hobby or sport, talk to someone you have never met before, visit a shop you would never normally go into, try some new food or drink, wear clashing colours or dye your hair. Go ahead and try something new and see if you begin to enjoy the process. What can you discover about yourself?

Always back yourself to win and be your own loudest

cheerleader. Cheerleaders at sporting events are there to liven up the team supporters and get them engaged. Having vocal and visible support is a great lift for any team so why not become your own cheerleader and get the same lift? There is a saying in the sales industry about the first sale always being to yourself. This means you have to believe in the product enough to buy it yourself. If you will not buy it yourself, why would anyone else buy it? Have faith and belief in your ability to plan and execute winning strategies. Have confidence in your own confidence and skill to deal with whatever situations and events occur in your life. Always back yourself to win and give yourself maximum support by ensuring your internal voice is your cheerleader. Have your internal voice constantly spouting positive and encouraging language which enhances your self-esteem and self-belief. Refer back to times when you have succeeded at something rather than failed. Make your internal feedback constructive and fair. Use your external voice well and use the positive language of success which will attract other positive people to you. Keep your physiology upbeat and choose the mental attitude which is most appropriate and useful for you at the time. Monitor your mind and environment for negativity and either snuff it out or avoid it completely.

You have come a long way on your journey toward improved emotional resilience. You have discovered and hopefully experimented with many new techniques and ideas so start to pass it forward whenever you can. Always be ready and prepared to help others when they ask it of you. Remember, what goes around, comes around. Life tends to give you back more of what you put out there so make sure you put out the right things.

Do not take it all too seriously

I will share another key point here. It is not actually a secret but the number of people I meet who seem genuinely unaware of its power makes it feel as if it genuinely might be a secret. The secret is laughter. Laughter is a powerful expression of emotion. It is often said that laughter is the best medicine. It can indeed be incredibly liberating and cathartic during times of intense stress. It can relax us and those around us and it can bring us back into balance when we are taking ourselves a little, or a lot, too seriously. The importance of our internal self-talk has been referenced time and again so laughing at ourselves must be done in a way which benefits rather than undermines us.

For example, I will often go upstairs in our house and forget why I am up there. I only remember why I went up once I come back down again. The reason I forget is simply because I am distracted by the many competing thoughts racing round in my mind. I will often laugh quietly at myself in my confusion and jokingly put it down to a senior moment. This is fine and serves to keep me focused for a while in order to avoid the same thing happening too often. It also stops me getting annoyed or worried about the situation; many people do it and I am in fact getting older. There would be a real problem however if I was laughing in a jeering and spiteful manner at my own absentmindedness. It would imply I am worth less as a person due to the memory lapse. It would not be healthy to laugh at myself in this way and it would not be healthy for you either.

The ability to laugh at ourselves comes more easily with maturity. It is a sign we can comfortably forgive ourselves for the small mistakes we all make; a wonderful diffuser of tension when used appropriately.

Learning to laugh readily, openly and freely both at ourselves and with others is indeed one of the best ways of becoming more emotionally resilient and more emotionally intelligent; it is a fabulous mental and physiological tool for your toolkit.

I love this quote from philosopher Ludwig Wittgenstein:

"If people never did silly things nothing intelligent would ever get done."

Another superb way to become more emotionally resilient is to regain your wonder and awe at the world around you and the people and things in it. Reconnecting with your childlike (not childish) sense of wonder about everything around you, and your relationship with those things, is a delightful and life-enhancing habit to develop.

I deliberately used the word childlike rather than childish because children think differently to adults. Adults can and do behave like children and in childish ways. If we are honest we have all behaved childishly at some point in our adult lives; it cannot just be me again can it? I recommend keeping carefree fun in your life whenever possible but this is not what I am referring to here.

Young children have little in the way of mental baggage. They crave reference experiences and are constantly searching for them. Everything they see is new and they look at these new things with few judgements and wide-eyed wonder. Everything is interesting to them. They want to examine everything and are happy to experiment with whatever they find or see. We as adults would do well to reconnect with this wonderful mental state.

I challenge you to try it. Give the following exercise a go, at least once a day, and see how you get on. If you do it often enough it will become a re-awakened habit. You will wonder where and when you ever forgot to do it or felt the need not to do it anymore.

Start with a safe natural item like a flower or a nut or perhaps a leaf or twig. If you have a garden of your own it is a bonus; if not, go to a park or someone else's garden. When you have a short uninterrupted period of quiet time available, find somewhere to relax comfortably and simply look at the object you selected. Imagine you are wearing a set of magical invisible child view goggles if it helps. Start by looking at the overall shape of the item. Then look at the colours it displays. Look more closely and see if other colours or shades become apparent. If you have access to a magnifying glass then use it to examine it in even more detail. Is it the same on all its surfaces? What shapes does it contain or form? Now touch the object to feel the textures of its surface. How heavy is it? Is it smooth or rough? Hard or soft? Can you make a sound with it? Unless you know exactly what it is and where it has been, I recommend you give the old taste and smell tests a miss; I do not want any of my readers inadvertently poisoned. How does the item make you feel? Does it remind you of any other experiences or even other people? What could it be made of? How does it hold itself together? Why is it coloured? If you have children of your own this style of questioning will all be very familiar.

Ask as many questions as you can think of; or indeed want to. Ponder the answers and let your mind wander down as many avenues as it likes whilst you are doing this. Maybe just look, admire and enjoy the many beautiful aspects of something so apparently simple as a flower or a leaf. What else could you look at and see with new eyes? I challenge you to look at the world afresh whenever you can.

Despite all the apparent doom and gloom there really is a lot to enjoy, a lot to laugh about and a lot to feel good about in this world. There is a lot to look forward to if you take the time you need to fully consider the matter. Take the time. Look for and celebrate the good things in your life whenever and wherever you can.

Final thoughts

That is it for now. You have arrived at the end. It has been a fascinating journey and I have had a truly fabulous time writing this one. I am pleased you remained steadfastly by my side to this point. Before you carry on with your own journey, I would like to take my leave with some thoughts which always help me maximise my emotional resilience and maximise my time by filling it with the people and activities I love and value most.

Here is a saying I love and it is one which I repeat often:

"Do not count your days, make your days count."

Resolve from this point forward to treat every day as if it were your last. Please do not imagine you are dying or anything equally horrible but do ask yourself the following questions:

If this was my last day on Earth how would I like it to go?

When I am gone, how would I like to be remembered?

Am I doing everything I can right now to ensure my days count?

So live, love and laugh as much as you can and your confidence and emotional resilience will grow.

Your days will definitely start to count.

I wish you well on your onward journey and it has been my great pleasure to share some time with you.

About the Author

Hello there, I am Andy Pope.

I hope you have enjoyed your journey toward increased emotional resilience.

I am aware that many people prefer to invest in a more personal and tailored experience when working to improve their emotional well-being and interpersonal skills. With this in mind I am happy to work with committed clients on a one to one basis. Please visit and contact me on the website address given below to start the ball rolling.

I am also well aware that many organisations would benefit from, and are indeed actively seeking, more emotionally resilient teams, staff and employees. I have created a companion program called The Resilient Professional Program to provide just such an outcome. This modular and tailorable offering would be of particular benefit to business organisations, third sector and charity groups, the educational sector and schools as well as the healthcare sector to name just a few. If you feel an investment in this dynamic and effective program would be of real benefit to you or your organisation, please visit the website given below for more details on the options and outcomes available then contact me to work out the best solution for you.

http://www.theresilientprofessional.com

I look forward to talking with you soon.

Virtual appendix

In order to keep this guide as up to date and current as I can for you, I have decided to create a virtual appendix.

This virtual appendix will comprise a number of pages on my main website which will only be available to you and my other wonderful readers.

The appendix will contain updates, additional articles, new case studies, related videos and anything else which might be of interest or help you on your quest for improved emotional resilience. No sign-ups required and no BS guaranteed. This appendix is exclusively for you and your personal development.

The web address for this virtual appendix is:

http://www.theresilientprofessional.com/trpvirtualappendix.html

I would love for you to provide some feedback on the pages and you can do this via my site contact page or even connect with me on social media if social media is your thing.

Enjoy.

You might also be interested in my previous book

Business Networking for the Bewildered

Available in print and eBook form from **Cambria Books**

ISBN: 978-0-9574894-5-5

CPSIA information can be obtained at www.ICGtesting.com
Printed in the USA
BVOW06s1005150216

436759BV00022B/301/P

9 780993 356797